Rosas / Anne Teresa De Keersmaeker

La Renaissance du Livre
Michel De Paepe Éditeur

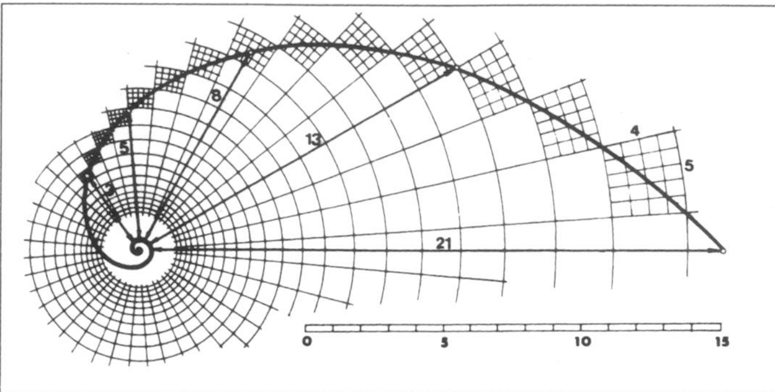

Abb. 3-7 Die Spiralen einer Muschel deuten an, wie der Goldene Schnitt auf Wachstum hinweist (aus F. Cramer und W. Kaempfer: »Die Natur der Schönheit«, Frankfurt 1992).

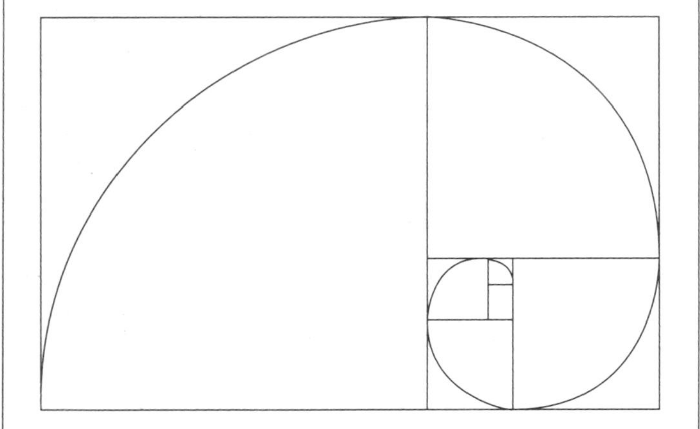

Abb. 3-8 Wenn man ein Goldenes Rechteck zeichnet (siehe Abb. 3-1), dann kann man es in ein Quadrat und ein zweites (kleineres und anders orientiertes) Goldenes Rechteck aufteilen. Mit ihm läßt sich der Prozeß wiederholen, der ad infinitum fortsetzbar ist. Es ist nun möglich, in diese Anordnung von kleiner werdenden Quadraten und Goldenen Rechtecken eine Spirale einzuzeichnen – als Folge von Viertelkreisen in den entstehenden Quadraten –, die sich auf den Punkt zu bewegt, in dem sich die Diagonalen aller Goldenen Rechtecke treffen (schneiden) würden. Die Spirale besitzt die Eigenschaft, die man als Selbstähnlichkeit bezeichnet, das heißt, man kann einen Teil von ihr nehmen und wird es dem Ganzen ähnlich finden. Darin steckt erneut die Idee der Zeugung, und so ist es kein Wunder, wenn sich Spiralen häufig in der Natur finden (siehe Abb. 3-7 und 3-10). Die Selbstähnlichkeit führt zudem zur Schönheit.

TRIGRAMS / UPPER ▶ / LOWER ▼	Ch'ien	Chên	K'an	Kên	K'un	Sun	Li	Tui
Ch'ien	1	34	5	26	11	9	14	43
Chên	25	51	3	27	24	42	21	17
K'an	6	40	29	4	7	59	64	47
Kên	33	62	39	52	15	53	56	31
K'un	12	16	8	23	2	20	35	45
Sun	44	32	48	18	46	57	50	28
Li	13	55	63	22	36	37	30	49
Tui	10	54	60	41	19	61	38	58

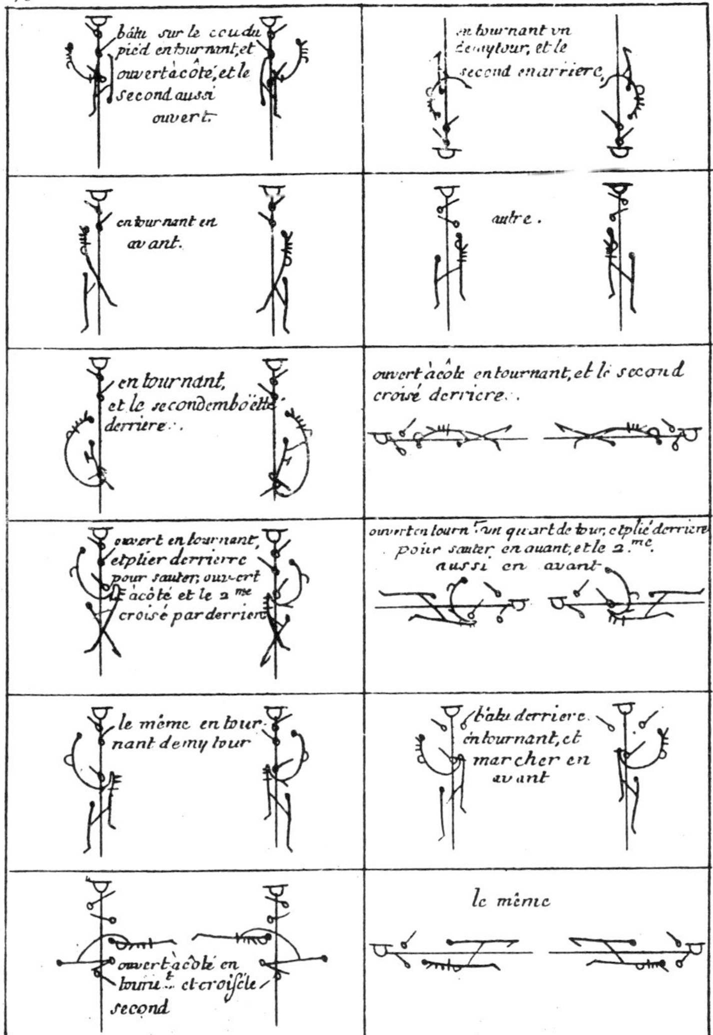

78
Table des Contre-temps.
le même
autre.

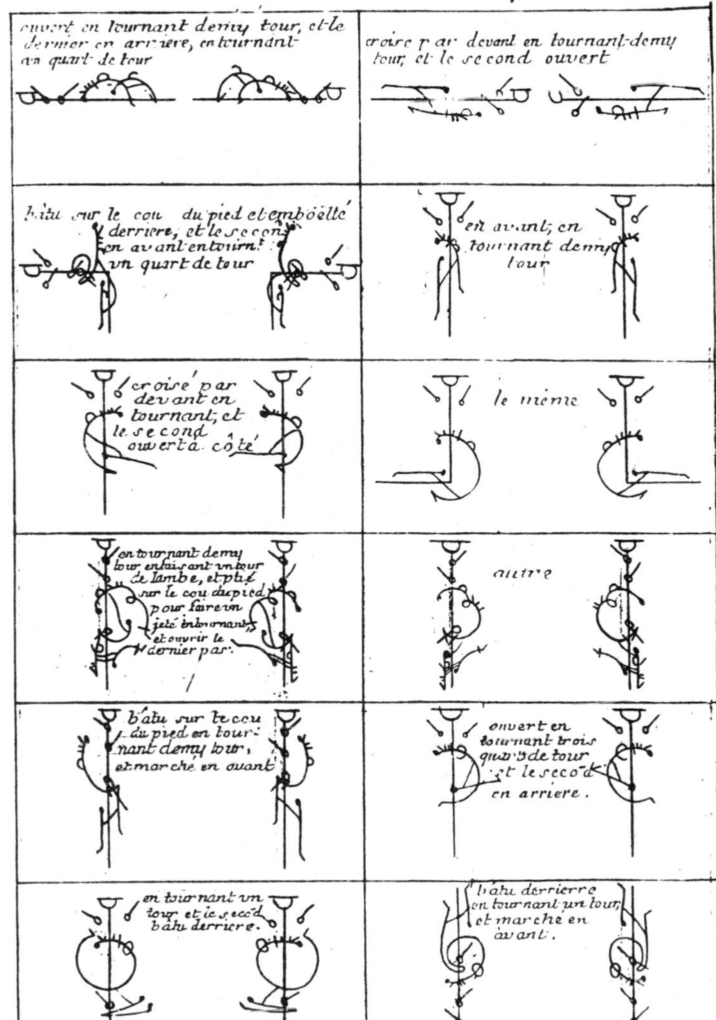

Table des Contre-temps.
79
le même
autre

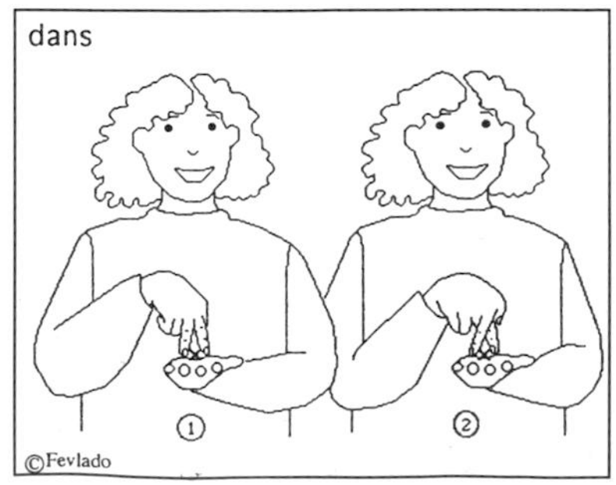

dans
©Fevlado

danser
©Fevlado

muziek
©Fevlado

CENTRA

Winter

University of Notre Dame Campus

Summer

These two pictures, taken a few months apart, show a slalom traced in perfectly free way, and —after the snow had melted—the engineered path, designed with a transit, and straight. It would be good practice for designers to let the lanes be made naturally for at least a year before deciding on the final design, which should be directly inspired by the signatures of man's motions across the landscape. The result would be of simple and natural beauty: it would eliminate fences and mangy corners.

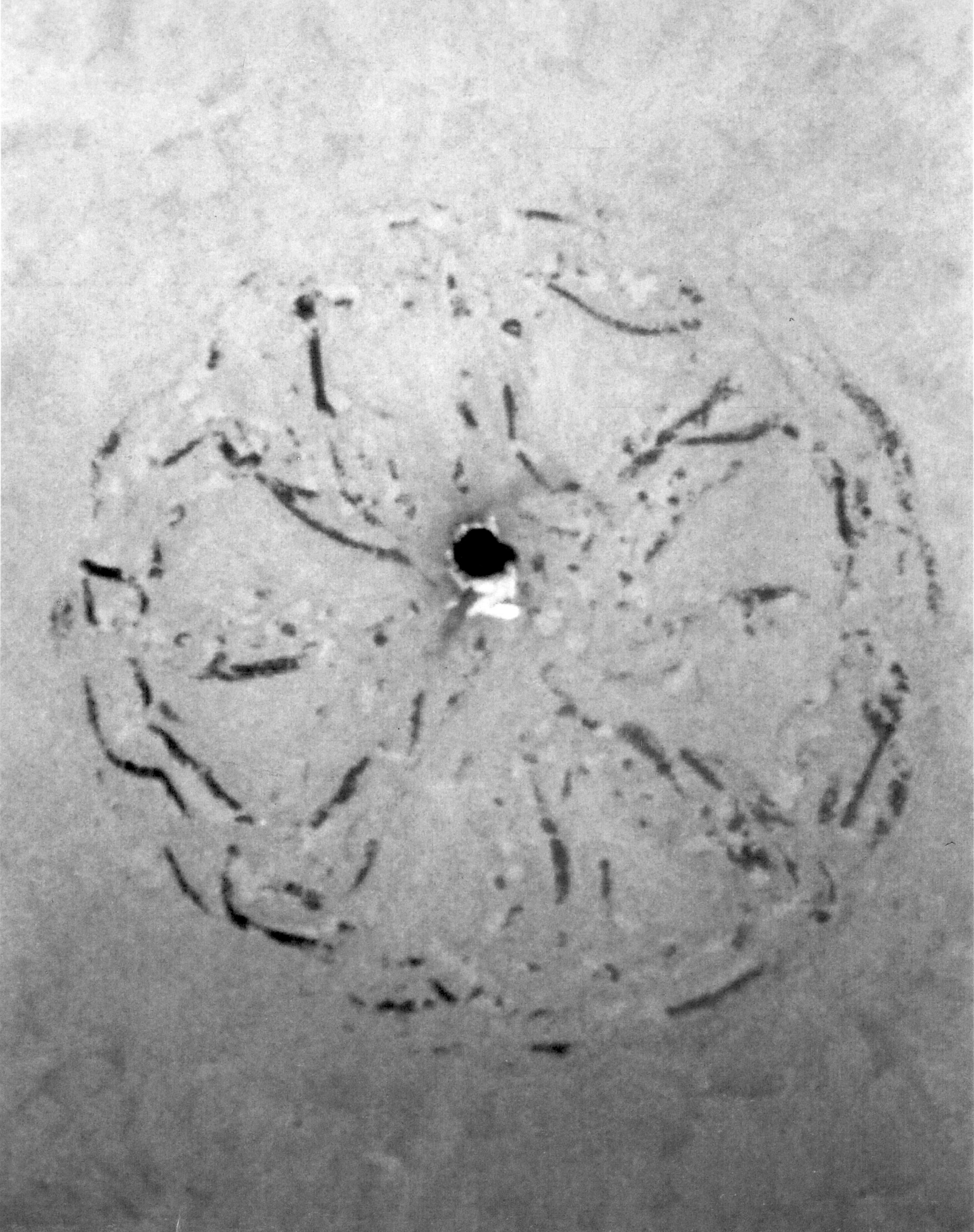

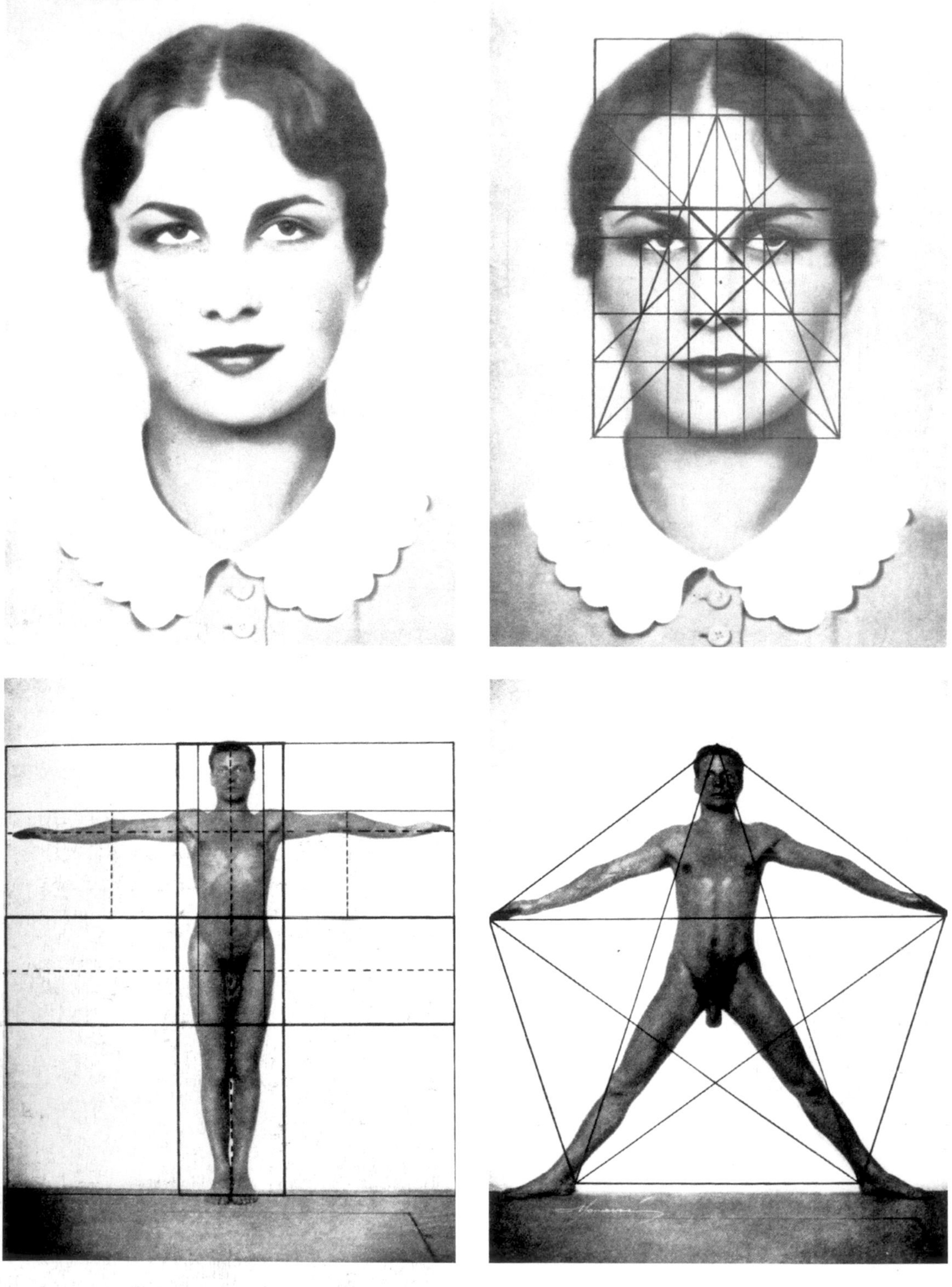

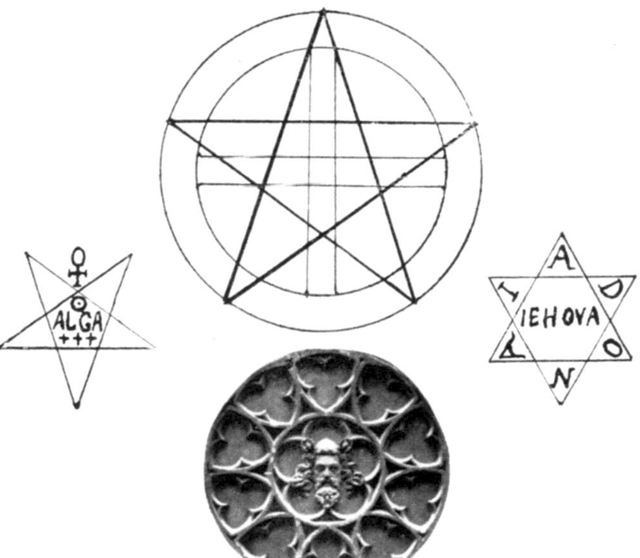
ALGA
IEHOVA

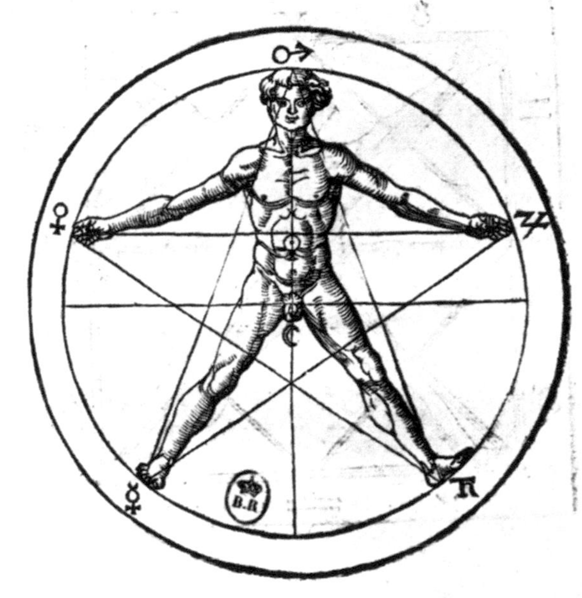
B.R

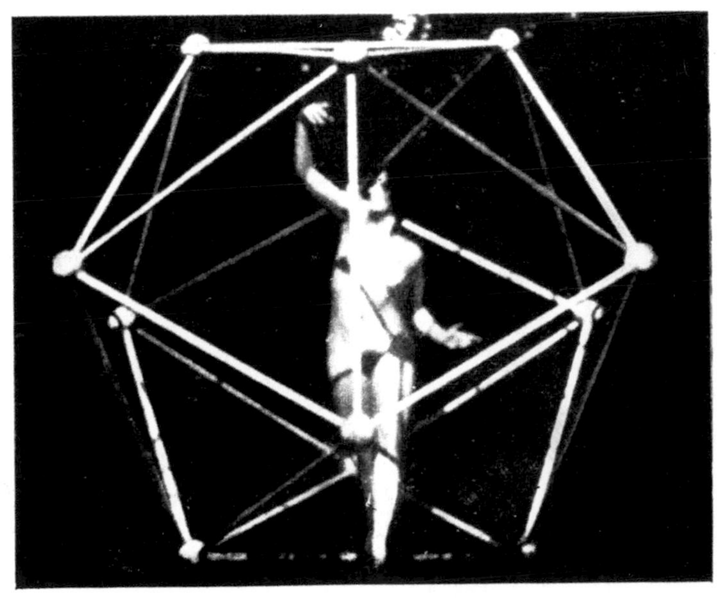

Museo Nal. de Antropología. México.
Indio Triste. Cultura Mexica.

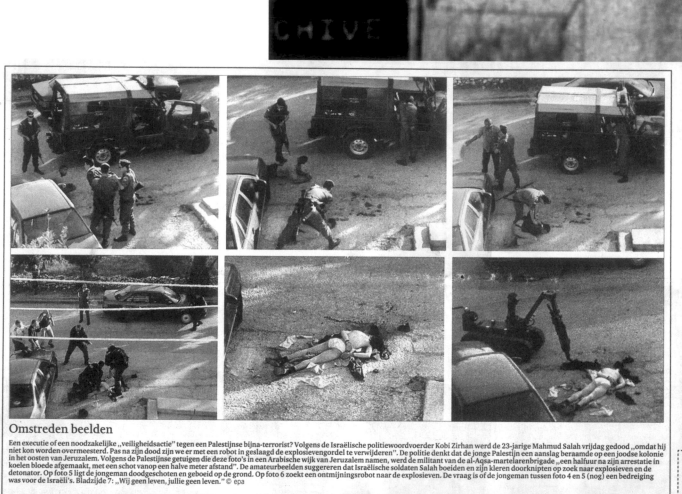

Omstreden beelden

Een executie of een noodzakelijke „veiligheidsactie" tegen een Palestijnse bijna-terrorist? Volgens de Israëlische politiewoordvoerder Kobi Zirhan werd de 23-jarige Mahmud Salah vrijdag gedood „omdat hij niet kon worden overmeesterd. Pas na zijn dood zijn we er met een robot in geslaagd de explosievengordel te verwijderen". De politie denkt dat de jonge Palestijn een aanslag beraamde op een joodse kolonie in het oosten van Jeruzalem. Volgens de Palestijnse getuigen die deze foto's in een Arabische wijk van Jeruzalem namen, werd de militant van de al-Aqsa-martelarenbrigade „een halfuur na zijn arrestatie in koelen bloede afgemaakt, met een schot vanop een halve meter afstand". De amateurbeelden suggereren dat Israëlische soldaten Salah boeiden en zijn kleren doorknipten op zoek naar explosieven en de detonator. Op foto 5 ligt de jongeman doodgeschoten en geboeid op de grond. Op foto 6 zoekt een ontmijningsrobot naar de explosieven. De vraag is of de jongeman tussen foto 4 en 5 (nog) een bedreiging was voor de Israëli's. Bladzijde 7: „Wij geen leven, jullie geen leven." © epa

Actieplan tegen

Michel wil EU-missie naar Bagdad sturen

Content

I/Trying to Capture the Structure of Fire
20 Years of Rosas

Marianne Van Kerkhoven

Fire is in rest
while changing
Fire is changing
while in rest.

Heraclitus, 5th century BCE

I. An *oeuvre* spanning 20 years is not easy to summarize, certainly not one as unique as that of Anne Teresa De Keersmaeker. It has become so rich and multifaceted that it is difficult to accentuate certain aspects without losing sight of other equally important ones. Moreover, ideas and material initiated in one project are further developed in the next so that the whole body of work forms one creative stream within whose flow it is impossible to isolate crucial choreographic moments or even one's own 'favourites'. How could one possibly choose between the poignant desolateness of *Elena's aria*, the compelling theatricality of *Ottone Ottone*, the mad energy of *Stella*, the compositional genius of the *Grosse Fuge*, the choreographic purity of *Toccata*, the fascinating interplay of dance, music and text in *I said I* or *In real time*, the incessant flow of changing structures of movement in *Rain*, or the architectural gem *Small hands (out of the lie of no)*, about which Peter Verhelst metaphorically wrote that it is like 'a blush that works its way across the skin of a girl in a room who tries to understand her own bewildered body'? And to think that this is only a random sample. Nevertheless, here is an attempt to describe a few aspects in words.

(...), we that don't know our feeling's shape,
but only that which forms it from the outside.
Who's not sat tense before his own heart's curtain?
Up it would go: the scenery was Parting.
Easy to understand. The well-known garden,
swaying a little. Then appeared the dancer.

Rainer Maria Rilke, *The Duino Elegies*

II. Like an embryo, the early work of great artists often contains all of the seeds of what will emerge in, and stem from, later work. Performances such as *Fase* (1982) or *Rosas danst Rosas* (1983) are full of glimpses of what is to come. One of these is the creed already formulated very early by Anne Teresa De Keersmaeker that structure and emotion engage one another like the two halves of the same shell, bound to each other for life. Structure is not only rational and 'premeditated'; emotion does not only convey meaning; both simultaneously contain each other's characteristics. De Keersmaeker is in search of both the emotional richness of structures and of the structure of emotion.

Anne Teresa De Keersmaeker's work largely rests upon this triangle: emotion - structure - body. In his *Esquisse d'une théorie des émotions* Sartre wrote that emotion 'is the behaviour of a body in a specific state: (...) emotion appears when the body that is upset manifests a specific form of behaviour. (...) *in order to believe* in the magical behaviour, one must be upset. To obtain a clear view of the emotional process proceeding from consciousness, we must remember the dual character of the body, which on the one hand is an object in the world and on the other hand is immediately experienced consciousness. Then we are able to understand its essence: emotion is a phenomenon that persuades.'

In very early interviews, Anne Teresa De Keersmaeker refers to her desire to move people, a desire for which the moments when her body is 'upset' play an essential role. She calls working or choreographing in this state 'the haggling between structures and what your body is able to do.' These are pronouncements that are still valid with respect to her present work. Another constant is the great level of reserve in expressing emotion, a fear of saying things too explicitly. It is precisely through this that her work derives much of its power. Someone who doesn't communicate in a direct way must seek out subtler, more complex means to express feelings.

The waves of the sea, the little ripples on the shore, the sweeping curve of the sanding bay between the headlands, the outline of the hills, the shape of the clouds, all these are so many riddles of form, so many problems of morphology...

D'Arcy Thompson, *On Growth and Form*

III. Although textual elements quickly make their appearance in her work and, in recent years, have been very prominent, the interplay of movement, dance and music remains a more important mainstay, a more comprehensive area of research where risk was, and still is, confronted. Who would dare as she did already so young, to bring into being a musical and a choreographic composition *at the same time – Rosas danst Rosas* in 1983 – a collaborative venture with Thierry De Mey? This initiative grew out of the choreographer's and composer's joint conviction that both disciplines are inextricably linked with each other. Thierry De Mey calls the detachment of music and dance 'a danger for the coming generations', a loss of the faculty 'of communication by which music and dance are able to mutually enrich each other. (...) In fact the relationship between music and dance is something that we are barely able to define, it remains poetical.'

Although less evident in her work, Anne Teresa De Keersmaeker certainly possesses an interest in working with song and opera (see the danced opera *Ottone Ottone*, the work with the singers in *Mozart/Concert Arias* and her operatic direction of Bartók's *Duke Bluebeard's Castle*). Twenty years of Rosas also marks 10 years of Rosas in residency at the Théâtre Royal de la Monnaie, Bernard Foccroulle's invitation to the company to become part of this great opera house, surely demonstrated a conviction – that an interaction between dance and opera of a very different nature than the former subordination of ballet to opera was possible. The creation of a new music theatre requires a different relationship between the various disciplines. Foccroulle is on the same wavelength as Pierre Audi who said in this regard: 'Perhaps dance could play an important role in this future music theatre. Perhaps one of the fundamental creators should be a choreographer who has this permanent concern about the body and space. The singer is a dancer who needs to be made aware of his or her body.'

In a similar way the cohabitation of Rosas and Ictus in the same premises is much more than the solution to a housing problem: it is the basis of their mutual fertilisation; modern dance and modern music together find fertile soil.

The history of art is a history of prophecies. It can only be written from the point of view of the direct, existent present; because each time contains its own new and uninheritable possibility to explain prophecies, which contain art from an earlier time related to it.

Walter Benjamin, *The Work of Art in the Age of Mechanical Reproduction*

IV. Anne Teresa De Keersmaeker's interest for musical composition extends way beyond the realm of modern 'classical' music; her interest includes the entire history of music, in which Bartók *(Bartók/aantekeningen, Mikrokosmos, Rosa, Duke Bluebeard's Castle)* seemingly occupies a key position, functioning as an interchange between 'old' and 'new'. Through him she journeyed far back into the musical past – to Mozart, Bach, Monteverdi... And from Reich, De Mey, and others. she traced an organic link with tradition. There has never been anything resembling opposition to tradition in her work, more a process of slowly, deliberately and patiently getting acquainted. All in good time.

Anne Teresa De Keersmaeker has always dealt with dance tradition in the same way: in the early years she sought her own personal dance language, one that belonged to her own body. At the time, she usually danced in her own pieces. Gradually she developed an interest for the classical idiom, filtering it through her own personality. In *Toccata* (1993) this new language became very clear; it was no accident that this was the first production in a long time (since *Bartók/aantekeningen*, 1986) in which she danced herself. These 'traditional lines' can still be felt in later pieces such as *Woud, With/For/By, The Lisbon Piece*...; Parallel to this, in *Just before*, a completely new group of performers appeared, totally disrupting the movement vocabulary developed during previous works. A new 'chaos' came to fertilise the hitherto 'structured' field. In *Quartett* and in *In real time* actors began to dance, as did, a bit later, the musicians in *April me*.

All aspects of the world of music and dance - from Monteverdi to techno, from old court dances to breakdance - are seemingly able to enrich Anne Teresa De Keersmaeker's continuously evolving artistic sphere. She possesses a strong desire to patiently investigate and unravel everything, to never remain still, to push research processes steadily forward. Not systematically, but simply because one step naturally leads on to the next. The work is never finished. Paul Valéry: 'That which is finished, is not created.' At the end of each project, routes always remain open that lead to new, unknown territories. Building blocks from the one work are brought to the next. As in nature, one thing comes from another. Gradually the whole of man's artistic history is incorporated. With unerring attentiveness, an inventory of life itself is charted. Life, not only in its earthly material dimensions, but also its world of ideas and the interior motives of the human person: 'I am beginning to view dance more and more – in the most physical and spiritual sense – as a bridge between heaven and earth. The glory of the person as a link between the spiritual and the material, as a place where the two approach each other.'

... do I separate myself from the centre in movement that is continually freer? or are my movements more and more bound to a centre, until it finally absorbs me completely? (...). At stake in the question is nothing less than life or death.

Paul Klee, *Kunst-Lehre. Die Geschichte von der Spirale*

V. Spirals, the Golden Section, Fibonacci Numbers... these are the forms, structures and principles prevalent in nature that fascinate Anne Teresa De Keersmaeker and that she, time and again, will integrate into her choreography. Perhaps she will discover what 'growth' is, what 'becoming' means – in other words, the secret of life. How does an embryo grow? How does a seashell take form? How does a tree grow branches? How does a coral reef become what it is? How is a crystal made? As if she wants to discover the incomprehensible structure of fire and flames. Her awareness of the repetition and the continuous change present in life dominates all of her productions. And so it is natural that someone who is so interested in 'being' and 'growth' founded a school, P.A.R.T.S., and thus concerns herself with *forming* those who will come after her.

I came into the world.
I became.
I was begotten.
I originated.
I grew.
(...)
I moved.
I moved parts of my body.
I move my body.

Peter Handke, *Self-Accusation*

VI. 'We understand how the objects (of nature) are put together', wrote Paul Valéry,' which is why they interest us and hold our attention; but we do not understand how they were made and that is why they intrigue us. Though we ourselves are created or formed by imperceptible growth, we are unable to create in this way.' Thus, we are obliged to appeal to structures, principles that we recognize as present in the world that we then abstract to gain workable instruments. This is also the path travelled by Anne Teresa De Keersmaeker, in which she tries to approach, as closely as possible, the basic principles of time and space and the changeability of life.

'*Creating:*' Valéry continues, 'is nothing more than re-creating by thinking.' However, this re-creating in no way implies that in there is a desire to imitate reality in Anne Teresa De Keersmaeker's work. It is more concerned with the creation of another world that has everything to do with the existing one, yet which differs, which is completely '*art-ificial*'. Susan Sontag called 'doubling' 'the most fundamental principle of the work of art - of form itself.' In Anne Teresa De Keersmaeker's oeuvre, the doubling of the body of which Sartre spoke (object in the world and immediately experienced consciousness) is an answer to this doubling of the world; and of course, this consciousness is double.
Consciousness always contains a perception from without, the creation of an 'other', by which one looks and the other is seen. *I said I.* Interiority and exteriority as one. Consciousness is always consciousness of an 'other', which can also be its own 'I'.

Meurteuil: No, sir, do not retreat from your tender offer. I'm buying. I'm definitely buying. There'll be no feelings involved. Why should I hate you, I didn't love you in the first place. Let's rub our hides together. Ah, slave trade of the bodies. The torture of living and not being God. Having a conscience and yet no power over the elements.

Heiner Müller, *Quartett*

VII. Both abstract works, the ones about which one cannot immediately say 'what it is about', and more theatrical pieces, in which text often is also used, make up the oeuvre of Anne Teresa De Keersmaeker. If one adds up all of these, a world- view, a vision of reality emerges that can be clearly described. We have touched upon the 'being' aspect of life, but with regard to earthly matters, 'the stuff of the person', across the board Anne Teresa De Keersmaeker primarily emphasises that which takes place between man and woman. Often this basic relationship is placed in a social, politically coloured context *(Verkommenes Ufer/ Medeamaterial/ Landschaft mit Argonauten, Ottone Ottone, Quartett).* The couples that populate her world (Marat/ Charlotte Corday, Jason/ Medea, Nero/ Poppea, Bluebeard/ Judith, Valmont/ Meurteuil and also He/ She from *In real time..*) often have problematic relationships.

Nevertheless there are also productions in which the warm, soft side of a relation gains the upper hand – in the harmony, melancholy and even romanticism of *Woud* or the lightness of *Drumming,* for example. In *Mozart/ Concert Arias* one can even detect joy in love, although this is moderated and relativised by the 'absurd' nature of the behaviour of the men and women and boys and girls towards each other.

Within the chosen themes, there seems to be an organic path following the curve of life. And although death – including violent death – is certainly present, it never plays a leading part. De Keersmaeker's world is essentially concerned with what 'the living do to each other.' Unlike many artists, she does not opt for an obvious connection between love and death. Only once is this link explicitly made – in the poem *Amor constante más allá de la muerte* in the production of the same name. The production is more abstract than theatrical; yet even then, death appears like a phoenix that rises from the ashes. In all respects, the work of Anne Teresa De Keersmaeker embraces the theme of life 'becoming', and reaches out for the intangible essence of fire.

It could close my eyes, the very last
shadow that my daylight brings to an end;
Is for my soul no less than a godsend,
the long-awaited moment when adrift it's cast.

But it won't leave behind, there on the vast
shore, the memories of each lover and each friend:
My flame can swim that gulf from end to end,
and stand proud and unbowed unto the last.

Soul by no less than a God imprisoned,
veins that stoked their fires, calm or rough,
marrows whose glorious flames have risen:

its body will abandon, its care's enough;
they will be ashes, but they'll have a reason;
dust they will be, but dust that's still in love.

F. Quevedo, *Love Enduring Beyond Death / Amor constante más allá de la muerte*

II/Anne Teresa De Keersmaeker

I. A Two-Piece Philosophy

'The taoistic way of thinking based on the dichotomy between yin and yang is both intellectually and intuitively a guiding principle for me. There is one: the unity. Then two: the antithesis or complementarity, the basic fact of opening or closing, two powers such as day and night, man and woman, construction and deconstruction. Then comes three: heaven and earth, for example, with mankind as the link between them. After three there are infinite possibilities. It is a very practical and eminently manageable philosophy in a material way. It seems to point to oversimplification, but in fact it allows the greatest possible complexity. Moreover, this philosophy is linked to the notion of movement. Everything changes constantly into its opposite; as long as there is life, there is transition from one thing to another; when there is only one thing, it dies.'

'Things are different, but they carry each other, such as structure and emotion. That sounds like a cliché, but I feel it in my very fibre. Structure and emotion differ from each other, but I have never been able to regard them as independent. In fact, this entire philosophy of dichotomy is something that I have felt from the beginning and which has developed over the years (partly thanks to the lessons of Fernand Schirren). Taoistic philosophy has ultimately given me confirmation. Emotions have always been a major guiding principle in what I do, but, on the other hand, there is always a kind of longing for abstract beauty, for unrelenting, independent order.'

II. Control and Letting Go

'Emotion is an intangible something which goes its own way. In the past, I was very much preoccupied with the order that I wanted to impose on things; now I have a much greater trust that things will all work out by themselves. If you just keep going, things do come to the surface. In the working processes, I feel that if you dare to let something go at a certain time, clarity begins to unfold. A lot of that 'desire to be in control' has to do with ego, fear, and the desire for recognition. Wanting to be loved, the fear of not being loved: that's what pushes you to take control of things. Being capable of letting things take their course: maybe you can only do that when you have had some experience of life. If you have had a few good knocks, after a while your fear lessens. Then you think: just let it come. I experience this kind of 'contradictory trust' as one of the pleasant things of becoming older, especially as it does not take away any energy. You have to keep it up, with all things. You can intervene, but you have to be concerned about things, look after them and give them love and energy. And if it still does not come, then there is certainly a reason for it.'

III. Children and Work

'I used to be much more one track minded in my commitment to work. Now everything is planned three or four years in advance and I work on various projects simultaneously. It is already a kind of meditation exercise to say, for example: now, from 4 to 6, I will rehearse and after that I will peel potatoes. I then also try to be really engaged with those potatoes: that's a challenge. Maybe it's because of the arrival of children. In the past, I only had my work, but now I also want to be there for them. You learn to focus on what is happening 'at the moment'. Time is becoming something very precious: I find it very difficult if it is treated lightly. I want to get the maximum out of the minimum. I still want to enjoy dancing myself, but the greatest challenge is combining children with creative art. That's also part of my greedy side. I can now put things in perspective and focus more clearly on what I know now to be important. I also notice at work that other women who have children become much softer. If you think about what we used to argue over! Now we're are happy if we can get something done efficiently in two hours, for example. We know that there are other things in life to get up about. Even if we still aim to remain rigorous in work.'

IV. Improvisation and Composition

'You have to know what you can do with composition and what you can do with improvisation. With composition, you are largely preoccupied with strategy, organisation of time and space, and the distance between past to the future. You know: that is where I have been and that is where I am going. In improvisation, you combine your energies with other people's. Time is then the moment, the here and now. You work on a kind of instant composition. You have to find those things which ensure that crystals can always be shaped in changing ways, but you do not know yourself how that will happen; there are thousands of possible combinations. You continue to look on in amazement from one moment to the next, as generous and open to the possibilities as you can be. You let things come, even though they can go completely wrong. This said, in improvisation there are patterns you can learn: you can guide people's energy along the right paths. You are on the borderline between total freedom and guided freedom. Setting certain limits in time and space gives both more focus and more freedom. What is also very beautiful in improvisation are those *secret programmes* which someone can bring with them. Improvising together means sharing a pact. That creates unity. Nevertheless, you continue to be amazed about what people do with those secrets.'

V. Together and Alone

'In recent years, I have been very preoccupied by group dynamics. They're crucial for a dance company: you have to create together; you work for a long time with the same people; people's egos are constantly challenged. For me, psychology is also energy. I find leading people difficult. I still have a lot to learn. How do you impart 'life' to a company? I don't think that I'm a natural leader. I have had to learn that there are a lot of things best left undone. This has a lot to do with your own fears. Here, too, you must find serenity and clarity and be able to pass it on. It's a duet of loneliness and togetherness. You work together with them, but you also have to learn to be alone. Artistically, I have found that difficult: the feeling that on the one hand others can help you, yet on the other there's a risk of you losing yourself. In fact, it's about a movement of pushing open and then afterwards recoiling to recover all your strength. In the successive productions you see the same movement: there are productions in which things are consolidated that, in previous projects, you've tried out in an almost explosive manner.'

VI. Simplicity and Complexity

'It demands patience to make people look at certain things. The public has expanded and it is a challenge to continue making productions within the spectrum of Rosas' work, productions that can appeal to a broad public without you having to make artistic compromises. Sometimes there are people present who have never seen a dance production: I am very pleased about that. Working for a broad public is more important than ever before, when you think of the competition from sources like television and the resultant impoverishment. At the same time, I am absolutely committed to making productions that ask the audience to 'work' harder. With the public nowadays you certainly feel a dangerous vacillation: people like to see simple things; nothing must be too complicated. This desire for simplicity is in part healthy, but it is also dangerous. I do not want to dismiss it too quickly as laziness. I want to take it into account, but some things are simply more complex, more difficult, and require more time and thought. Diversity in the productions is important. There is now a logic of alternation in the repertoire: on the one hand, I want to carry on with one thing with a minimum of means, but on the other hand I want to make things which are more kaleidoscopic, more baroque, and more complex in their construction.'

VII. Nature and Music

'I am amazed and fascinated by natural shapes and processes, the most compelling of which are spirals. I sometimes try to escape from this, but they seem to be so *basic* that they have a particular intrinsic value so that you have to refer to them. A spiral is such an essential shape; you do not have thousands of them. The universe is said to be one large spiral which swells, the various currents in the ocean are all spirals on top of each other, the DNA structure, the hair on your head, yin and yang: a spiral which opens and one which closes, two directions plus the notion of acceleration and deceleration.'
'Alongside nature as a source of inspiration, music is a, or perhaps the, source of beauty and comfort for me. All kinds of music. I draw a lot from all levels – its vital when I'm fathoming time and space for example – but, and perhaps it sounds simplistic, even when I am sad, music does me good. With nature I have a similar feeling: the mountains, the forest... have become more important over the years. There are so many nice things said about people via music; even in folk music: the way in which communities use it to give expression to their ups and downs. Dance and music are of vital importance in the world as it now is. They can bring together smaller and larger groups of people and speak about our humanity in a non-materialistic way.'

VIII. Love and Death

'I have the feeling that death is a part of nature for me; as a child, I was often confronted with death; and therefore saw it as something 'normal'. Although a number of people close to me have died, I still feel very distant in relation to my own death. I have never had an experience that has made me realise what it would mean for me to die. Maybe I push it all away in fear. What I fear terribly is the death of one of my children. That is the hardest thing that I can imagine.'
'I find it difficult to define love or to speak about it. There has always been a great desire for love, to be loved, to love. It is as if the relationships between men and women in the work run strangely parallel to the world and humanity outside, acting as a source of energy and fierceness. Sometimes I feel that I no longer want any of that man-woman stuff in the work. Maybe that will also change with age, wisdom will come, that erotic energy or explosiveness will be transformed into something else. Maybe into serenity or whatever. Now it is too much of a main spring, a kind of fire.'

III

I desire in every way-life, the ability to live, and then all is well ; then we don't need to ask ourselves whether it is beautiful or ugly. The feeling that that which has been created contains life stands above all that and is the only criterium for art.

Georg Büchner, *Lenz*

1. Time

Between heaven and earth there is a world of people. A lot has changed there in twenty years.
Fumiyo Ikeda, who had already helped to make *Rosas danst Rosas* in 1983, says of the starting period of Rosas: 'I used to feel that I had to defend Anne Teresa's work most passionately. Even when I was unsure, I went on the offensive. It was fighting, fighting, and fighting. I no longer have that feeling. Not because Anne Teresa's own artistic position is more certain or because the group structure is now more stable; no, the more I dance, the less I have the feeling that I have to defend something. I think that I now take more pleasure in dancing, but that does not mean that I no longer accept responsibility.'
Cynthia Loemij, who, in 1992 when *Rosas danst Rosas* was incorporated into the group's repertoire, rehearsed one of the roles, adds: 'I feel that *Rosas danst Rosas* belongs to the eighties. The aggression that emanated from it is no longer so prevalent; in the Netherlands, even the eighties were rather lukewarm. That production had something revolutionary, almost political, something pleasantly feministic as well: those four women who stood on the stage very timidly, yet without fear. Although dancing *Rosas danst Rosas* all those years has been a major experience for me, I nonetheless wonder if the essence that the production had when it was created has been, or is being, lost.'

Is the distance that separates Rosas' work of the beginning of the eighties from that of the present period simply to be explained by the difference between the 'rowdy' approach of a passionate young choreographer at that time and that of a mature artist refined by her experience in life? Or is there more to it? The development in Anne Teresa De Keersmaeker's work runs parallel with the steady development of Flanders into a politically autonomous power supported by the current economic prosperity. The generation of artists from the eighties was perhaps the first to be able to rid itself of the previous decades' latent feeling of Flemish cultural inferiority. They were able to profit from that privileged moment where the belligerence of a formerly suppressed culture coincided with a new self-assuredness in the ability to be able to throw off that suppression. Art, at that moment, could forget the obligation 'to serve the Flemish cause' and could devote itself with complete freedom to its artistic ends and this within an international context.
The political aspect, the time of social awareness has not, twenty years later, disappeared from the work of Rosas. Even if the microcosm of the man-woman relationship is still the systematic connecting theme in the *oeuvre*, productions such as *I said I* or *In real time* link the spectrum of human relationships to social behaviour and, one presumes, underlying 'political' events over which the individual has only partial control. The disappearance of the communist world, the militant arrangement of the Islamic world, globalisation at all levels, the growing gulf in wealth between north and south, the increasing impact of computerisation and the media, the multiculturalism of society, the various armed conflicts (some of which are very close by, such as in former Yugoslavia) etc. have transformed the world into an ever more rapidly changing, complex universe in which the individual seems to be losing his or her grip. It is a world in which Flanders and its specific problems are a minute fragment. Nowadays, the context of the work is the entire world; it forces its way in through every chink of the rehearsal room and imposes its unpredictability, its uncontrollable nature on the work demanding it to be more complex and to ask more and different questions.

We shall not cease from exploration
And the end of all our exploring
Will be to arrive where we started
And know the place for the first time.

T.S. Eliot, *Four Quartets*

II. The Dancer/The Work

Between the start of the eighties and now, Rosas as a group has developed from a small creative nucleus to a moderately large dancing company, in residence in (but independent of) a large opera house, built on a firm organisational structure, co-habiting with a school and a music ensemble whose work is synonymous with the creation of contemporary music. What are the consequences of this for the work and for the dancers whom we can call (or is it irreverent?) the choreographer's most important *material*?

Cynthia Loemij says: 'In such a large group, a lot of things have to be 'regulated'. Certainly if you also work with live music, you need a strong hand, someone who can make decisions quickly. Even having a discussion with a lot of people at the table is difficult: there is always someone who takes the lead and brings order. That sort of role distribution within the unit is necessary.'
Fumiyo Ikeda says: 'When I returned to the company in 1997 after a few years absence, everything was organised ten times better. Now when we start to make something, Anne Teresa comes along with material and a structure and puts it on the table. She says: 'I have already searched for that and now we will search further.' In the past, we usually started from a small base: a movement, a picture, a book... She probably still does that now, but she has already passed that stage when she meets with us. I have some fine memories of the period in which the four or five of us, all girls, worked together. We were able to produce a lot then, with regard to both the movement and the structure. But if you want to do that with thirteen dancers, you need a secretary. Everyone wants to do their own thing and there is no end to it. When we work in small groups, on a duet or something like that, we once again have more space. With thirteen together you have to keep quiet and listen. Otherwise, everything is too slow.'
Cynthia Loemij says: 'When you work in a small group with Anne Teresa, you feel like a fellow creative artist; in a larger formation you are more like a performer, even though you change your material and apply things. Anne Teresa makes the basic material; when she elicits it from the other perople, there is less cohesion. There has to be a mutual germ which gives her a connection. When I have doubts, I talk to her and I think she appreciates that. I find it hard to talk to her when we are in a group. When we are together it is nicer, more peaceful, and we can talk in Dutch: then I can express my doubts more subtly.'
Fumiyo Ikeda: '*Ottone Ottone* was the first experience of a large group and with men present. That was a shock: suddenly, 'control' of the company was necessary; we had never known anything like that. The working process itself was very difficult, but the production was fantastic. In the last five years we have again had a very good group, but with each change in our line up we have to search again for the right balance.'

A little group has become a larger group; if the earlier work could perhaps be called 'more collective', it has now developed towards a more traditional hierarchy. The dividing line between the dancers as fellow creative artists or the dancers as performers remains an open field. These dancers do not operate like the young members of a ballet company. They carry the entire production and not only via their own roles; they possess both information and responsibility in relation to the whole. They are thinking dancers who make decisions independently at any time both during the working process and during the performance.

The transition from a small to large company also changes the working methods. The *work in progress* quality is perhaps less tangible at the beginning of the creative process, although adjustments continue to be made even after the première. Organisation of the work is necessary; everything is now predetermined. Should everything be quite so prearranged? When one works in the even larger organisation such as the opera house, like for Bartók's *Duke Bluebeard's Castle*, for example, where everything has to be rehearsed very quickly and with a double cast, a premeditated structure is inevitable and there is little space left over to 'search together', little time for that waste which is so vital in art. What you really gain in working with a lot of people is an enormous expansion of the compositional possibilities; the potential diversity and complexity of working with a large group make an exterior eye, someone who sits and oversees the whole, who can play, build, and break off from that position and structure something else indispensable, essential.

Clarity appears in such strange ways;
one is never prepared for it.

Rainer Maria Rilke, *Die Aufzeihnungen des Malte Laurids Brigge*

III. Movement/Questions

How do you keep this work so open and flexible? How do you ensure that 'movement' is still guaranteed?
Time alters everything – giving importance within the work to the ever changing political environment is one way. 'Politics' quite often make a direct entrance or even a very indirect one via the text. Both Cynthia Loemij and Fumiyo Ikeda refer to working with texts as something exciting, where there is still a lot to discover, something that gives the dancers more freedom in time and space, something that requires a working procedure in which, inevitably, more discussion follows. Fumiyo Ikeda says: 'In a text, you can suddenly stop; in the dance pieces, as they run in unison, you must conform to an agreed architecture.' Are words more chaotic, vaguer, less precise than choreographic structures?

The dialogue with the dancers is, of course, the principal means of keeping the material fluid in order to keep things moving. The fact that the dance group occasionally changes its composition opens up another difficult but undoubtedly fruitful search for a new unity. But there is also the relationship with those other 'strangers': the live musicians or the actors who bring another discipline to the work in every sense of the word. Whenever they also start to dance, there is a kind of unpredictable behaviour which is typical of their 'amateur' status.
And then, there is working with improvisation (perhaps initiated by the musicians?). In relation to the 'fixed elements' such as reaching

back for building blocks from previous productions or the spiral structures (of which Fumiyo Ikeda says: 'These are the soldiers who protect the castle'; and Cynthia Loemij says: 'In recent years, we have run out and worked out so many spirals that it is now almost second nature to us.') today the border where the structure ceases and freedom begins is being explored. A growing field where longer and deeper excavations will be made in order to give freedom an added value.

And then, of course, there is the basic philosophy of Anne Teresa De Keersmaeker herself: 'As long as there is life, there is transition from the one to the other; when there is only thing, it dies.'
A constant question of the 'second element', the 'third element', from the 'other'. An eastern and a western wisdom: did Hegel not write that 'everything becomes pregnant from its opposite'? A wisdom derived from nature where multiple dichotomies go over into each other, lift each other up, come back to life again, where the old one is supported by the new and vice versa, where the 'other' is not always contradictory or complementary, but also equal and can be anywhere at the same time or where the 'other' is not (yet), and must be searched for...

gone: the only thing which was permanent for him until then, the only thing that could always be repeated and which has existed for years in the repetition in ever different ways, but, without leaving this path, revealed forgotten insight. (...) And another clause: that he, going his own way, had had the future image, always walking in twos. Future? Let us finish with questions.

Peter Handke, *Once more for Thucydides*

Trajectory 1980-2002

Asch 1980

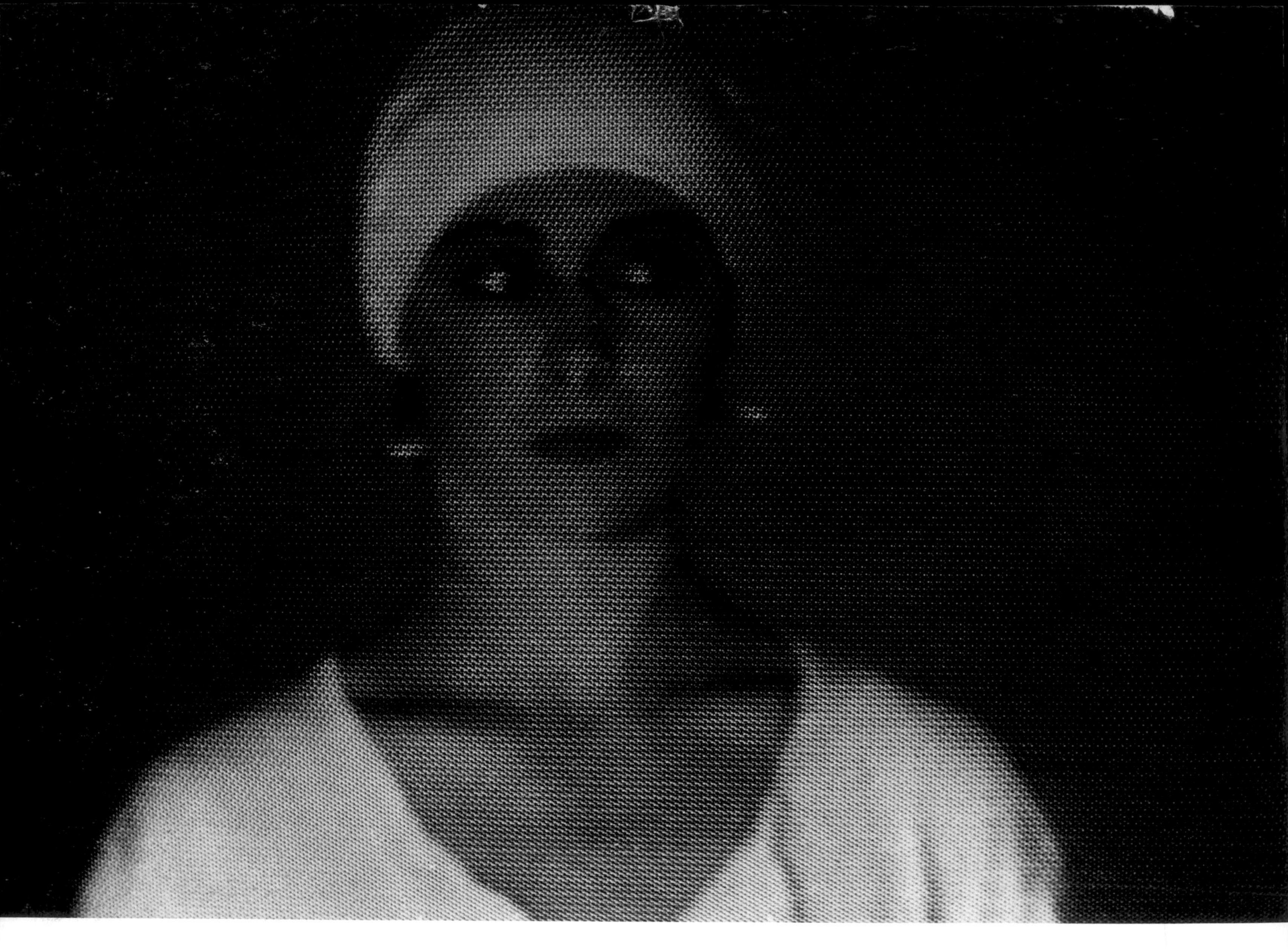

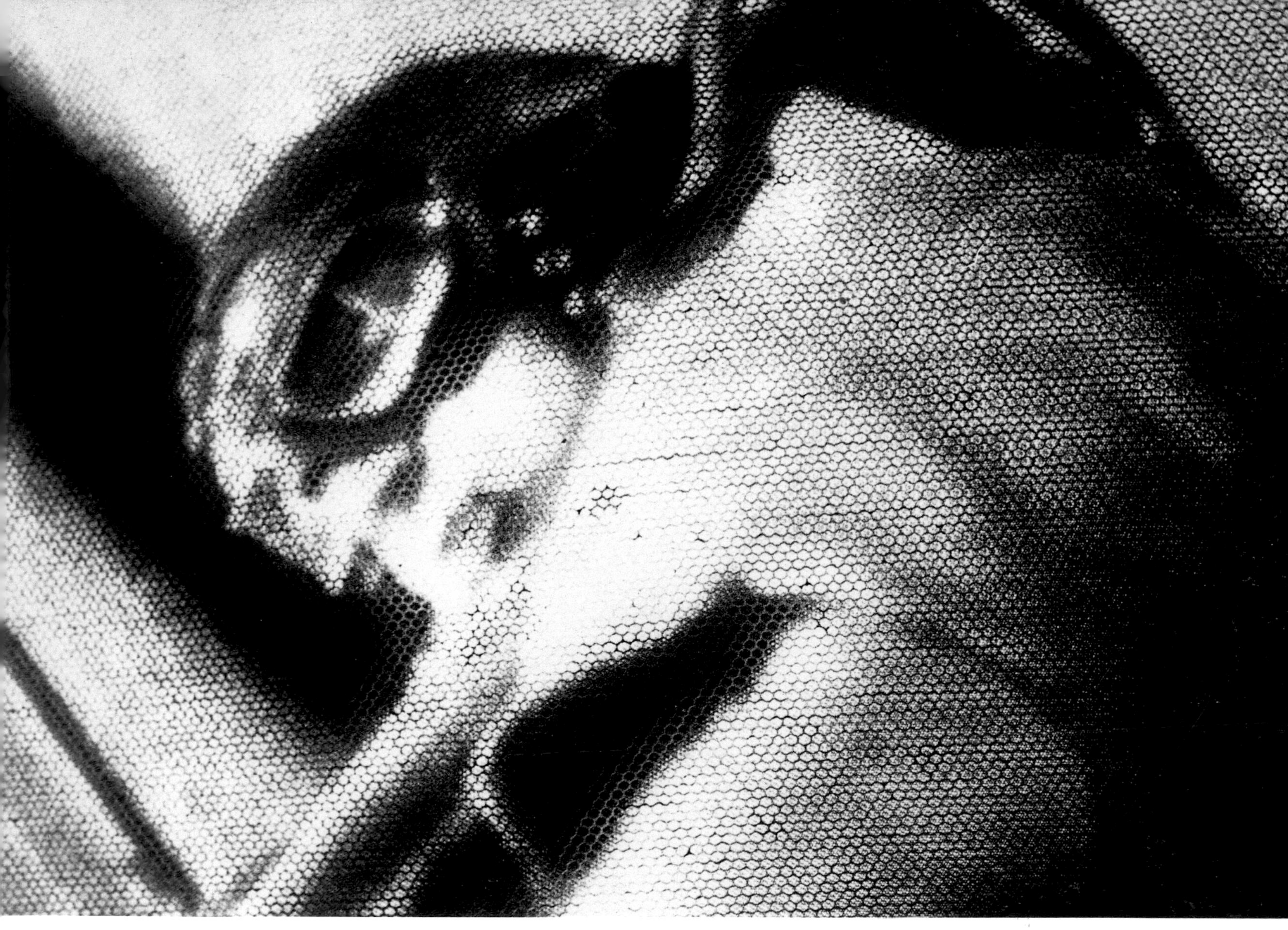

She was our youngest cousin then. She was sent on holiday to us; the three big boys. Every day one of us, usually myself, had to play Prince Charming and marry her, and every day we lived happily ever after. Not for very long however, because we all knew that she would one day marry (the) Prince Philip.

Later on, when the world changed from hippy to punk, our little cousin was always talking French because she was a student at Béjart's. The whole family was invited to attend her first ballet composition. There were lumps and neon lights in the old industrial spaces of the Nieuwe Workshop.

When it was all over, my mother said that she had seen that little princess in action once again, the same movements, the same storytelling with a prince as the victim and a set and everything. Little did she know that this was a completely new contemporary dance language which was ready to conquer the cultural universe.

Gorik Lindemans

Fase, four movements to the music of Steve Reich 1982

In 1981 or '82 I received a letter from a young Belgian choreographer and dancer asking if it was all right for three musicians in my ensemble to perform *Piano Phase*, *Violin Phase* and *Clapping Music* live for her new choreography, which would also include the tape piece *Come Out*. I replied that it would be fine. It didn't strike me at the time, but her name was Anne Teresa De Keersmaeker. She was to become one of the most important choreographers in the world. It was not until 1998 that I finally saw *Fase*, the hour long masterpiece she was working on then. I had never seen such a revelatory choreography done to my music. She knew precisely what my early pieces were about.

The performers to date have always been De Keersmaeker and Michèle Anne de Mey. The carefully detailed use of lighting right at the start in *Piano Phase* creates overlapping shadows that accentuate the repetitive motions that slowly move in and out of phase. The second section, *Come Out*, is done on a darkened stage with two small hanging lamps directly over the dancer's heads while they sit on stools. It suggests a police station. The movements, all done while sitting, serve to intensify the feelings of interrogation, brutality, anger, and sexuality which are all implicit in the tape. Implicit but never understood or mentioned by music critics until de Keersmaeker captured both the technique and the audible theater in *Come Out*. The third dance, to *Violin Phase*, is de Keersmaeker's solo. Again she not only captures the formal aspect of the piece but, during the extended resulting melodies near the end, goes to the heart of its underlying lyricism. The final section, done as a kind of *vaudeville step* unison duet to *Clapping Music*, is a light touch at the end, yet when the two dancers work their way from upstage left to downstage right, directly under the two *police lamps* still in place, the whole piece snaps together.

Steve Reich

Blekerijdreef

Rosas danst Rosas 1983

Half an hour in silence, stretched out on the floor, from very slow to very fast.
Eighteen minutes on chairs and a mechanical cadence.
Twenty minutes standing with solos with hand clapping and clarinet.
Twenty minutes standing together. Clarinet, sax, and piano.
Five minutes summary in silence.
Exit.

A robust Italian girl. Big green eyes, jet black hair, large mouth, low voice.
A soft, jocular face which unexpectedly burst open into wild laughter. A chic gypsy.
A bright Flemish girl. Sharp in her movements. As a knife.
Surprised, as though she didn't really know what she was doing, but of course she knew.
Sweat on her upper lip. Feet on the floor.
A little Japanese girl. Ready to explode. Severe, straight wrinkle between her closed eyes.
Pain and anger. And then she laughs it all off. It was only for fun. She loves dancing so much.
A big Wallonian girl. A face of nobility. Straight nose. Laughing eyes. A mouth of, well,
it's not so bad. A strong body, but always unsteady. She likes to topple, but prefers to float.
That was it.

Josse De Pauw

I first discovered the work of Anne Teresa de Keersmaeker and Rosas in 1983. I had no preconceptions, as I myself knew almost nothing about dance. The discovery had a name: *Rosas danst Rosas*, actually a brilliant title, both programmatic and tautological. The experience of seeing the performance was unforgettable. I was totally fascinated by the repetitiveness of the movements (annoying for much of the audience, riveting for me). The uniformity of the performers and their superhuman precision gave me a sense of euphoria which no dance had ever given me before and indeed, which I have never felt again since. My perception of the piece was first and foremost, sensual: as a spectator, I was literally swept along by the energy of the dance, enthralled by the choreographic systems. The dance appealed to me personally and 'nervously'; by that, I mean that what happened on the stage was transferred directly to my nervous system. After the performance, I couldn't even think of a single argument to defend the piece to my friends who hadn't enjoyed it at all! A year later, I saw *Elena's aria*, which, in my opinion, stretched the limits of dance to an even greater extent than *Rosas danst Rosas* had done.

In 1993, all excited, I entered the theatre where *Rosas danst Rosas* was being restaged. The cast was different, the choreography was identical and me, I was no longer the same person. Ten years had gone by, and I knew somewhat more about dance... This time my view was completely different, reflexive let's call it. The choreographic ideas of the piece touched me both because of their simplicity and their extreme sophistication. The piece is structured in four parts, based on simple positions: lying, sitting, standing and standing whilst taking up space. These sections are a fairly precise summary of the human body's possibilities! Onto this pared down scheme, other, much more complex, challenging elements are grafted. As the piece progresses, the merciless choreography gradually erodes the dancers' infallibility. Not that their movements become less precise, but ... a phenomenon which I still cannot explain occurs...I had the impression that each of the four dancers were, little by little, revealing themselves; as if their deepest, most intimate part was imperceptibly taking over their faces, and as if this new state was altering their movements, creating minute differences between them. We the spectators discovered that a difference in the movements, however small, has enormous effect on their meaning. However, the most gripping thing was that there was no will emanating from the dancers themselves: they were not aware of what they themselves were offering: ... Indeed, it would have been horrible if it had been the case: what we want to show of ourselves is definitely not ourselves, only a few great oriental sages are capable of that. Each of the dancers broke free from the uniform group of which they had previously been a part in order to appear again on their own, unique, incredible – strangers even to themselves. That impression that you know them better than they know themselves felt almost embarrassing, indecent. But what would art be if it did not offer us such experiences, if it did not give us the impression of seeing something which we should not be allowed to see?
The supernatural dancers had become human beings. In this way, Anne Teresa de Keersmaeker shows us, brilliantly, that dance can be just as an effective a means as science for fathoming human nature.
I hope that Rosas will continue to dance Rosas over and over again...

Jérôme Bel

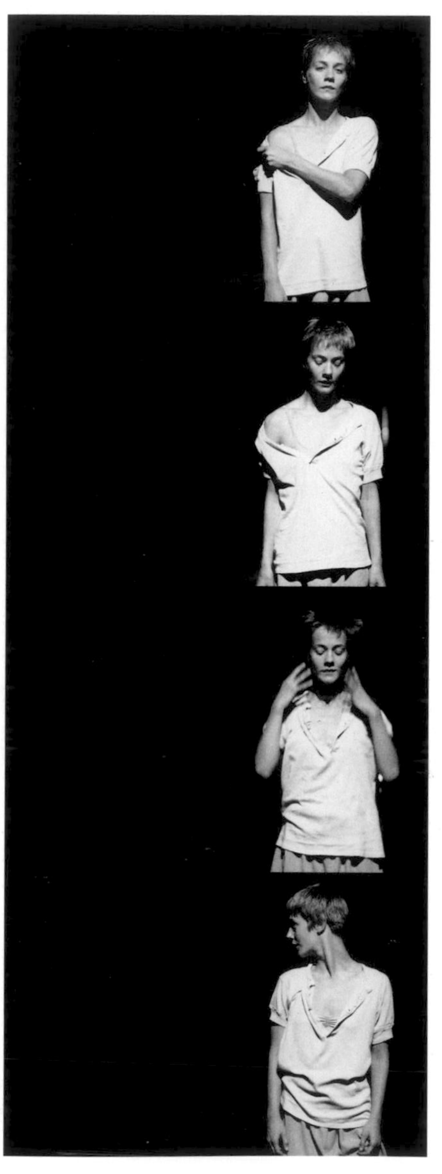

Elena's aria 1984

Five Women - 'so lonely'

I.
Do not forget that it was 1984, the year that George Orwell chose for his utopian novel about totalitarianism. The Eastern Block still existed, but here in the West we had already given up hope of a just society. In those days, 'Post-modern' was still a significant term which suited the confusion of a transitional period. We danced to the music of Prince, just like the emerging yuppies who were to make stock market capitalism acceptable. We were hesitantly extricating ourselves from the ruins of a nineteenth-century utopia, and in the meantime they (the yuppies) were making the right investments. Only art could save our incandescent faces. We dabbled in contemporary dance, we were not yet ready to acknowledge the unexpected turn which world history had taken. The economic substructure had proven us wrong, so we turned our attention to the superstructure. Art as a Great Truth against social inequality which would no longer be corrected: now I hear the 'pfff...' of a punctured bicycle tyre.

II.
Do not forget that the performance you saw at the Stadsschouwburg in Leuven in November 1984 annoyed you intensely. You wanted to leave the auditorium, get away from all that female distress which you as a man had nothing to do with. You thought that art was there for you, you could not have imagined then that your body could be claimed by it. You had not yet grasped the fact that something could happen to you in a theatre which you would not be able to understand until a long time afterwards. Art was supposed to grasp your convictions immediately, not sometime in an indeterminable future. Years later, you preserve the residue, actually no more than a few images that *Elena's aria* left behind in your memory. You had seen so much more in the meantime, but that did not matter. You had been convinced by the echo of the memory of a performance which you had wanted to forget. It would not be the first time, yet you still always make this mistake. You talk enthusiastically after a performance, whilst you know perfectly well that only the silence of your body can give you an answer the day after tomorrow or next year. You are just too impatient every time.

III.
Do not forget your forgetfulness. You recognised the chairs, the white chalk circle, the slow music, the dress cautiously held up from the hips, the images of the collapsing buildings, the voice of Castro, the silent gestures during the coda. You were surprised at the many unisons, you had forgotten that the dancers regularly perused each other over the row of chairs at the back of the stage. You once again enjoyed the preciousness of the gesture, the mixture of puerility and femininity, the hesitations of the text. But the video recording cannot recapture the performance for you.

IV.

Do not forget your powerlessness. In 1992 you wrote: 'The performance has a well established keynote which is related entirely to a single word: powerlessness. Female powerlessness towards the absent beloved; human powerlessness towards the human world and towards injustice and oppression; powerlessness of the 'stage writer' towards the absurdity called a stage... – all these various forms of powerlessness are symbolised in the fleeting moments of physical weakness. (...) As the performance progresses, there is more dance. However, the keynote of powerlessness, physical inability or incapacity, continues to sound. (...) The expressed powerlessness relates first and foremost to the powerlessness of expressing, the inability to find a suitable dance language for emotions.' You want nothing more to do with this writer. Not that you now write so much better, on the contrary. It is just that you have discovered in the meantime that art is not about hidden meanings.

V.

'Elena is a girl with a past without a future.'

Rudi Laermans

DEMOLITION

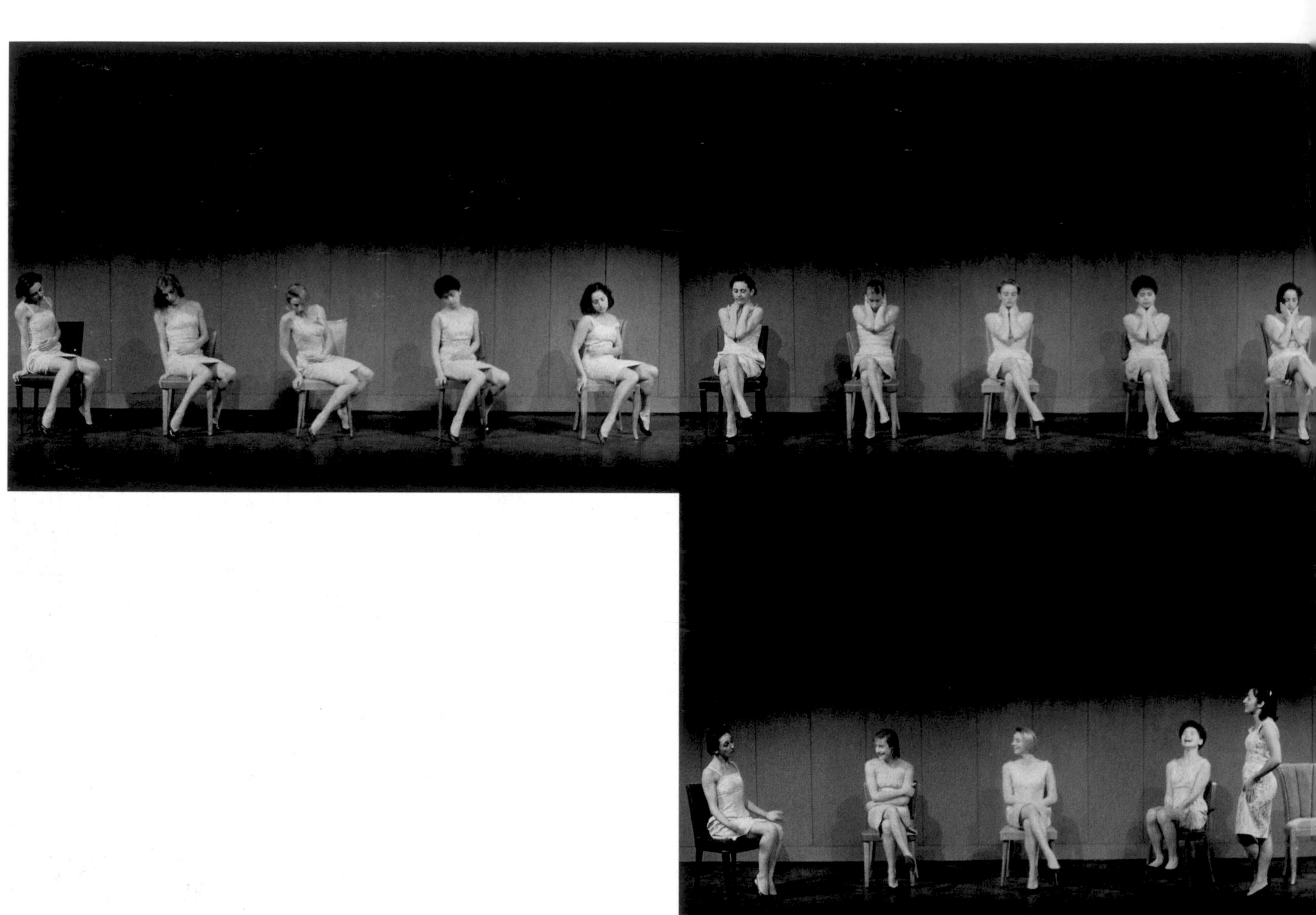

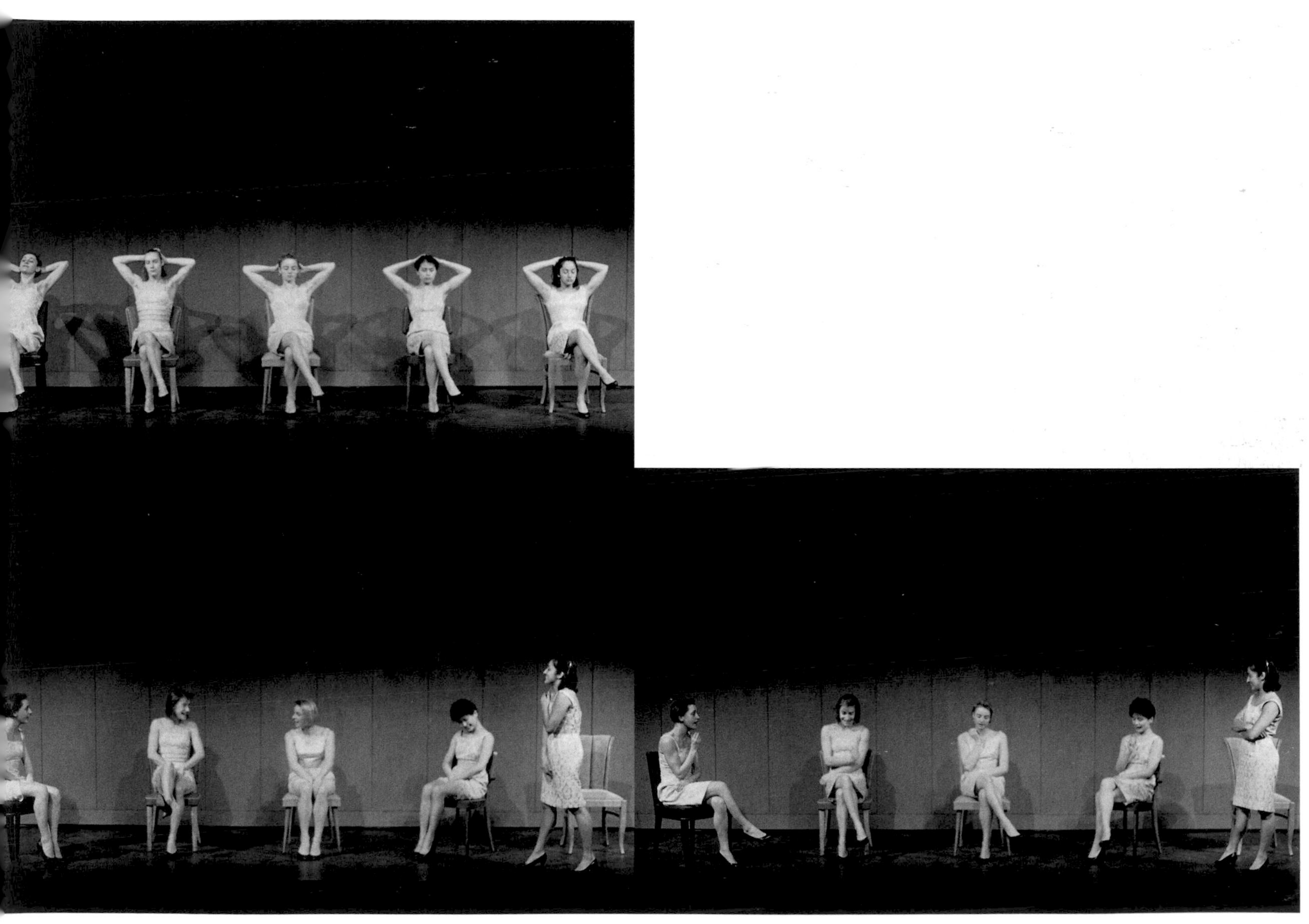

Aria's Echo

What remains after seeing a dance performance? We the audience submit to the operations of the artists, and leave the theatre when it is over, hardly knowing if the operation was a success or not. I am remembering *Elena's aria* performed by Rosas in a Klapstuk festival.

What remains for me is the effect of movement phrasing. There is not much else to appeal to the senses. The stage is open and empty except for a line of chairs. A number of women are dressed in little black dresses, little black pumps. The phrases they dance are intricate chains of turns, rises, collapses. The phrases are long, and we see that they repeat. They are done in unisons, and the unison has the effect of robotics, as though each dancer is programmed to dance exactly like the others.

However there are emotional overtones in the phrases; if one dancer were to hit these tight little moments in the phrase by herself, the effect would be of an expression. This becomes weird in the unison context. Apparently private matters are shared so that even emotional nuance seems collective. These are telling moments, but we don't have the references to understand. The dancing is energetic, full bodied, and the odor of discipline is almost stronger than any other impression. Yet each time the emotional cusp of a phrase is danced, whomever we are focused upon gives us something personal, something like a sob in a story.

This is the Chorus. The collective, the crowd or the mob represented by a select number of elegant women who treat their chic negligently, whose considerable energy does not soar but swirls and whips, whose faces are too naked for their clothes, emotionally wrong for the apparently social occasion they seem to be dressed for. Within the constraints of their phrase, their chair, their dress, they seem to ache completely, and their faces are those of women who have just wept while, multitasking, they execute their movement flawlessly.

There is only one man present. Caruso sings from far offstage. Perhaps from a nearby apartment, another theatre, another time. The voice creates a series of strange fractions; distance / proximity. Sound / dance. Man / women. Then / now. Dead / live. There is much to attend to, but we seem not to move. The effect is relentless, and the phrases are the irreducible matter of the event. Each woman has been dealt the same hand, and each plays it the same way.

The operation is over, and I leave the theatre. I don't know whether it was a success. I do know I am changed. This is what I like best, a question to gnaw on, as long as memory persists. How can something be so precise yet not be more specific? How can we not know why these women dance, or why they dance as they do? They have been insistent and intense, but I cannot understand. I feel like a man. The limitations of this state are almost knowable, in the aftermath.

Steve Paxton

Bartók/aantekeningen[1986]

Notes on Bartók: searching for the notes on a production which I saw in the Centre for Amateur Arts in Anderlecht sixteen years ago. More than the performance itself, I remember the deep impression it made upon me: the slightly drunken, euphoric feeling with which we all stepped back outside into the winter evening in Brussels. Something had changed. A few days later, I asked the editor of *Etcetera* if I could write about the performance.

Between that evening and now Wolfgang Kolb made a film using images of the dance sequences to Bartók's fourth string quartet set in the decor of the Boekentoren in Ghent. It was a revelatory vision of Anne Teresa De Keersmaeker's choreography as seen through the lens of a silent camera. You could feel the filmmaker's fascination for the music and the dance, how they complemented, propelled, and commented on each other. And also, inevitably, his eye for detail, for dissonance, for the individual.

Since recently reading a text about the life and work of Bela Bartók I have been more aware of the intentional contradictions in his music. Bartók lived through the rise of Nazism and saw with horror his home city of Budapest gradually became filled with hate and prejudice. In 1936, when Goebbels opened his exhibition of 'degenerate art', which included work by Stravinsky and Schönberg, Bartók sided openly with the artists. He wrote a letter to the government stating that his name and music should also be included in the exhibition. That is exactly what took place and in 1940, he was obliged to flee to the United States.

My old *Etcetera* article arrives by fax. From behind the accompanying photo of the playful, dancing girls in black frocks and laced boots the memory of the performance resurges. I see the metal ventilation screens which surround the stage, the grey walls with the white film screens via which the world forces its way into the space. I see the stuffed deer. I hear Fumyio Ikeda wrestling once again with a monologue from Peter Weiss' *Marat/Sade*, in which Charlotte Corday expresses her horror over the revolution's brutality. Fumyio's difficulty with French is in contrast with the firm, abrupt hand gestures.

I am reading an annotation from years ago: 'Suddenly, there is a military song, the dancers, all in line, automatically take over the rhythm. For a moment, it seems that the ghost of Corday has surfaced, but one of the four, stamping their feet just like the little Oskar with his tin box, begins to mischievously disrupt the monotonous, military rhythm of the music.' And I can imagine how the makers of *Bartók/aantekeningen* must also have had that euphoric feeling when they got to know Bartók, both the man and his music.

Mark Deputter

Verkommenes Ufer/ Medeamaterial/ Landschaft mit Argonauten 1987

FROMMS
ACT

I still remember it well. Two rather bewildered people listening to my passionate outburst. It was after the performance in the dressing room. I wanted them to realise that they had something very beautiful in their hands.

I was preparing for *Wittgenstein Incorporated* with Johan Leysen. I did not know Kitty Kortès Lynch. A few years later, I was to work with her on *Kopnaad*. They did not believe that it had been a good performance. But I really enthused. For I know that phenomenon, that tragic feeling, that the actors who are at the origin of everything, have no idea themselves of their own performance. For them the whole thing will always be invisible, the performance never even existed. They learn about the performance through the eyes of the spectators who, even whilst watching, see the performance going up in the smoke of a vague recollection. Theatre: the art of remembering, is the barometer, the measure by which a performance will survive.

I think that I can still remember it well: Kitty's violet suit, the dancing along the wall, the turning around the wall, the unsure searching for support, the abrupt stops; Johan's deep voice, his calmness; André Verbist, Anne Teresa's parents' gardener, slowly peeling potatoes in a long black dress with open shoulders, long black hair blowing in the breeze generated by the wind machine; Kitty and Johan's German; Herman Sorgeloos' set, all those 25 by 40 centimetre hardboard plates lying strewn on the floor with the fluorescent lighting hidden from the spectators in the floor, a lantern that the players operated themselves, the bench against the wall (too low to sit on) where the three of them sat right next to each other, each at a different height. I still remember how organically the dance and the text ran over into each other, how that evocative, expressive text by Heiner Müller was measured by the stylisation of the dance, (but perhaps, stylisation is not the right word) by the controlled, succinct use of the dance.

We know that Medea cut her brother to pieces in order to hinder her pursuers, her family. In this way she freed Jason, the Golden Fleece, and herself in the flight from Colchis. A deed of love and betrayal. A deed for the future and the past.

Anne Teresa lets André Verbist (the nurse) cut potatoes into slices. To put it more precisely: he makes chips out of them. Kitty Kortès Lynch (Medea) asks André. 'How long have you been living in the ruins of your body, with the ghosts of your youth, nurse?' Meanwhile, Johan Leysen (Jason), a few metres to the right, constantly tosses a potato in his hands, playing, it seems, with the food called love. Until that moment in the performance we had especially seen Kitty's long legs (her opportunities, for in Müller's world between the thighs of a woman, there is hope even in death) and the worn out soles of men's feet, the symbol of their uprooted unrest.

'You owe me a brother,' calls Kitty to Johan.

'I gave you two sons for a brother', replies Johan.

But the debt is not paid quite so easily.

Kitty wants Johan to give her two more sons first.

She who betrayed her family is now being deceived herself. She who refuses to live in the ruins of her body with the ghosts of her youth, she who gave up her brother and the Golden Fleece to her love can now do nothing but offer her love and her sons to his betrayal, to her hate.

And then the agitated dancing begins, the vain attempts to dance and escape the ruins of her body and the ghosts of her past, to erase a future which is no longer a future. It will all be to no avail, just as her attempts to cut out a path through the jungle of her life have failed and will continue to fail. The jungle will grow back behind her for sure, hardly a trace will be left, but the memories remain, and the memories will only be strengthened because in attempting to dance them away she is actually engraving them on her body. And the body forgets with even more difficulty than the head. It is not a bad thing. It's a distinctive feature.

These were my thoughts, I remember, when I saw this beautiful performance which, sadly, has not often been played.

Jan Ritsema

Mikrokosmos/ Monument/ Quatuor N°4 1987

Ottone Ottone[1988]

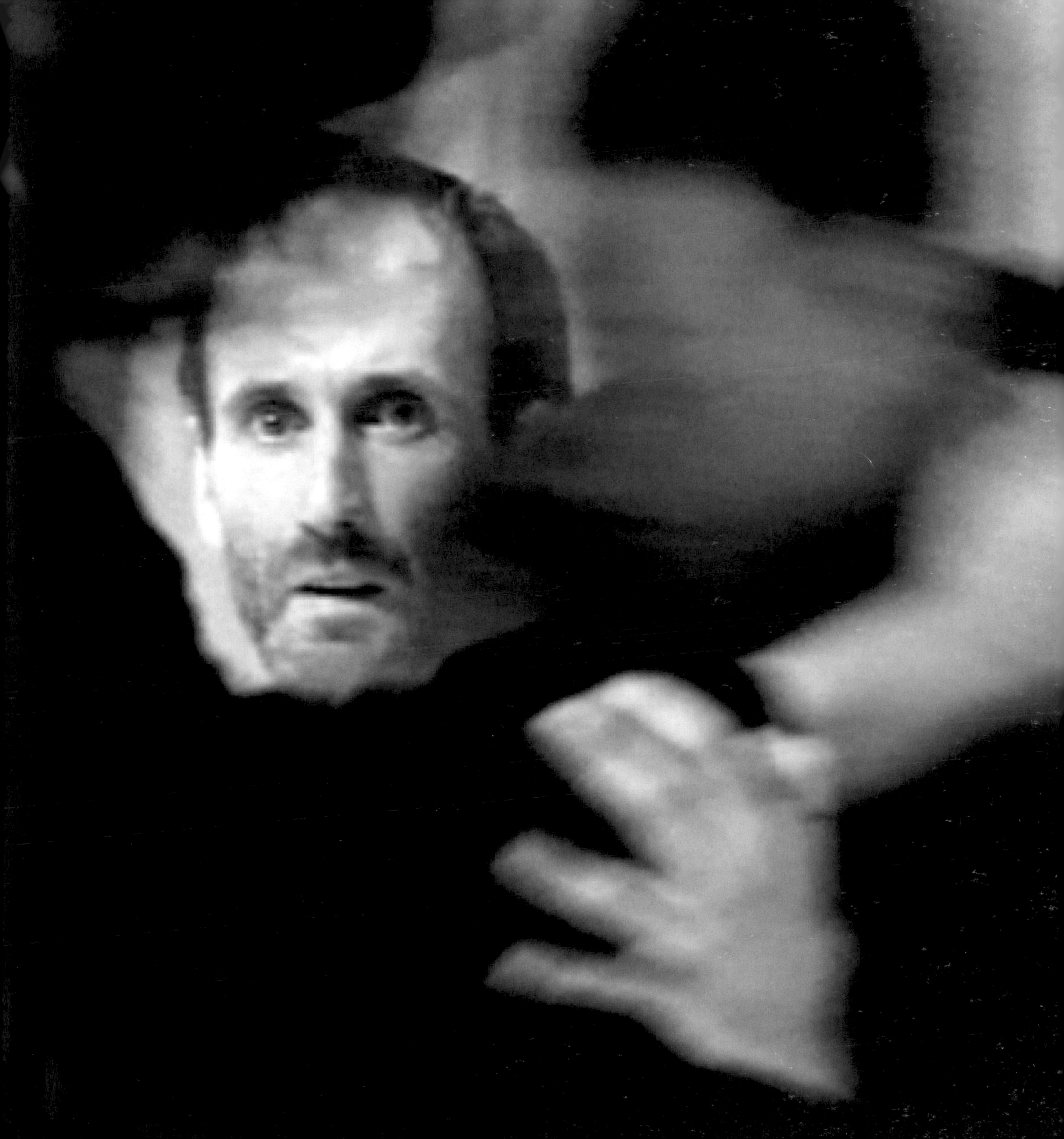

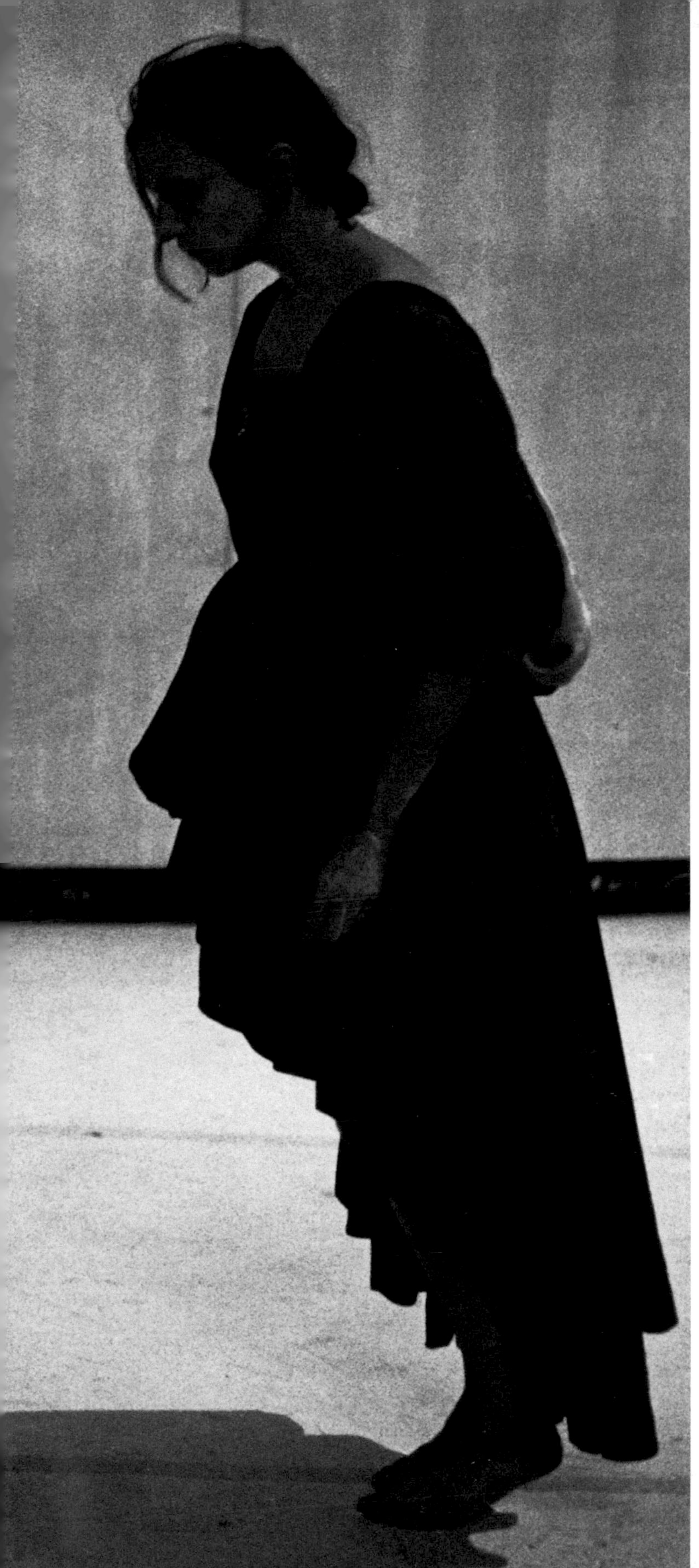

When a Bucket Full of Feeling Overflows

If I have to put a colour to it *Ottone Ottone* is blue.

Forgive me, but it has been fourteen years since I saw the show and I only saw it once. Yet since then, the occurrence has made its home in my head and is leading its own life there. I saw it in the Bijloke in Ghent. In a space which resembled a building site at the time. There were quite a number of eminent people and important guests whom we did not see again after the break.

I think the performance started with Vincente Saez standing at the front on the stage. He just stood there. That was a fine start! And then... no, a reconstruction would be pointless. What everyone was talking about at that time was that 'she' (Anne Teresa) on this occasion, had worked with men. With men?! It must have been a terrible struggle. At any rate, we witnessed slices and fragments of scenes of terrible, exuberant, and intimate struggles. With Monteverdi providing musical accompaniment. The faint sounds were played over and over again on a tape recorder on wheels pushed too and fro by an angelic figure.

Ottone Ottone worked on me like a corkscrew that slowly but surely turned my emotions around. I saw sounds, images, and people piled up next to, and on top of, each other in a jumbled fashion. There were poignant scenes between the men and the women. Combined with the baroque music: it was a strange marriage, yet it worked. Those who know Monteverdi's *L'Incoronazione di Poppea* will perhaps have recognised fragments of the story. Those, like myself, who sat there in unabashed ignorance could only surrender themselves to the experience. The heart, the brain, and the imagination were all working overtime. It was one of those performances which I hoped would never come to an end.

In 1989 a video clip by Walter Verdin appeared: *Monoloog van Fumiyo Ikeda op het einde van Ottone Ottone*. For me, this is still one of the best dance video clips ever made, if not the best one.

Because of Klapstuk nr. 10, I asked Anne Teresa if she could perform *Ottone Ottone* once more. She gave a long and deep sigh! I felt at once that this was an impossible demand. I might have guessed. Anyway, maybe it would not have been a good idea. Some things should just be left in peace.

Alain Platel

Stella 1990

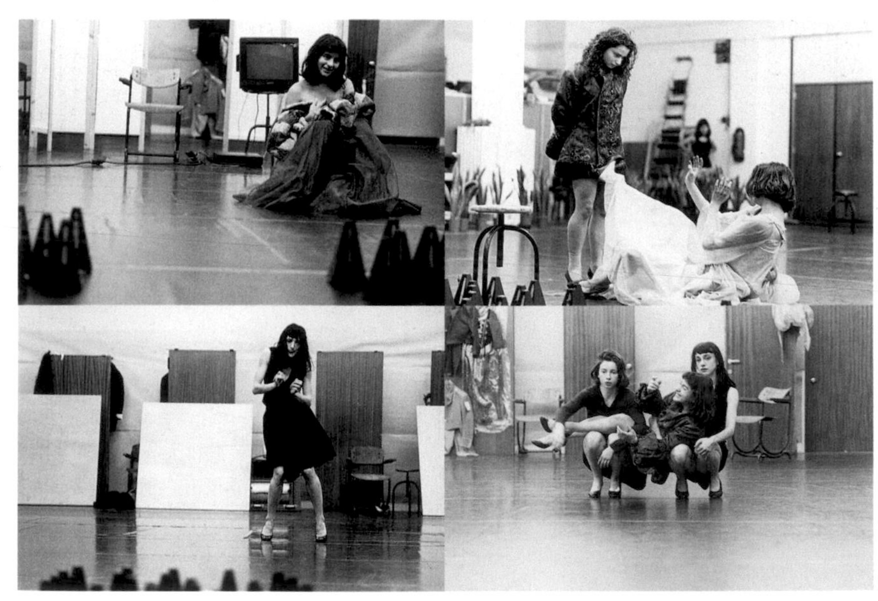

Remembered Stella

I was startled by the explosion, gripped by what seemed like wonderful untidiness. By the laughing and the talking in fragments and the running and the ducking and the falling and the yelling. By the lines they traced on the stage like chaotic uncontainable scribble. By their all alone-ness. By their watching of each other. By their watching of me. By the sudden thundering choruses of all of them together. By that energy that had me move in my seat. Clattering footsteps. I knew there were patterns of course, repetitions, shapes and structures but back then (and even now) I was hardly trained to read them. That didn_t matter. Humour, energy, passion, anger. That reminded me of the world.

It says in my notes that I saw *Stella in* 1990. I can't remember 1990. But by the slow mathematics of this morning I can be certain that I was childless. And with some effort I can calculate that we had probably just made the theatre piece called *Marina & Lee*. That seems like another world, a long long time ago, a lot of blood flowed under the bridge.

I am writing in England. It is inevitably raining. I remember the woman who took the text of Blanche Dubois from *A Streetcar Named Desire*. The way her eyes came straight to us then shifted away. These flickering movements. Brittle hands and arms. I didn't know the text (still don't) but that didn't matter. There was a line like 'I don't know how to turn the trick...' I did not know. But that's no matter.

I was shocked about what happened to the neat, and angular world I'd seen in *Rosas danst Rosas*. I'd loved that. And someone seemed to have set off a bomb inside that world. And the world was changed. A rent in its fabric. Ruined, imperfect. But I loved this new place. A dirty, funny, painful place.

I remember potted plants, tall ones. Fluorescent light. Bare wood. And the sound of metronomes. Like rain. Tiny. Gentle. Monotonous. A lot of waiting. Time passing. One of the dancers seated near the front of the stage (?). The relation between noise and music made manifest as the 100 metronomes ticked down. People leaving in the audience. Gentle movements continuing deep in the space of the stage. A woman moving. Self-absorbed. It's unclear the closer I look at it (the memory). But the taste is sharp; touch vivid. I can feel it, still moving against my skin. I can feel that time moving in me and against me, its friction, its texture, touch vivid. Waiting for those metronomes to stop. But of course they never will.

I ask Seth (the youngest of the children that did not exist in 1990) about a character in a story he has invented. Where is the character? He answers quickly, matter-of-fact, he says 'In my memory.' But how did the character get into his memory? He says 'Oh. I opened my mouth and he sneaked in.'

Sometime in the year called 1990 something sneaked into me. A bright-lit space in which five women waited, played, danced, trembled, yelled, laughed and stretched time.

Tim Etchells

Achterland 1990

Achterland. I have seen this piece twice, one time being in Montréal (I think). I vividly remember one specific, symbolic moment: a quintet of girls in the spotlights at the front of the stage. In discovering the film, I was not only able to see the piece again, but also revive my memory of it. After all, one of the characteristics of a performance by Anne Teresa is that they remain in the memory for a long time; half indelible image, half hazy dream. When I looked at the videotape there seemed to me to be two cuts in conversation with each other: my reconstructed memories and the actual film (remarkable). Let's talk about the film. In her work, Anne Teresa combines various styles of writing, sets them against each other and gives them a voice: choreographic writing, musical writing, and cinematographic writing. The film carries her stamp. It doubles the choreography, intensifies it even (the dance and its doppelganger). It was recorded in black and white, which enables a stronger appreciation of relief and light – of the texture of the skin in the light. In short, of the entire substance of the dance material – its very grain.

The stage is deep. At the front, two rows of lit squares on the floor lengthen the space. Shared space, heterogeneous and complex: light-shadow, far-near. Same thing with the musicians: the violinist in the foreground, the piano all the way at the back. The violinist's physical presence is very tangible. The pianist is translucent. A musical dialogue: Eugène Isaÿe's finesse and Ligeti's structures. In fact the piece starts with Johann Sebastian Bach. A dancer enters the stage: irruption-interruption. The first small conflict: musician vs. dancer. Subtle connections are revealed through close-ups: signals, relations, and mutual expectations that you would not always notice during the actual performance. Here are the men. They cross the space, try to hold on to the floor. They can't find support. Next comes the women's scene. They have the keys to the space. The space becomes rhythm. Here the Rosas company's strong link with theatre becomes apparent. Not in the narrative, no words need to be said. Building up what Edward Bond called 'accidental time' requires rhythmic work and very strong accents. The space and floor as percussion. Pedestals for the female dancer-statues, female dancer-instruments: they tick, scratch, make music with hands and feet. And then, that recurring motif throughout the piece – the loud fall – momentum brusquely arrested. The floor as the orchestra to bodies leaning away from their axis. Hectic madness, moments without tone, sudden blankness. Then, Anne Teresa's writing is at its most articulate, in the moments between the passages that are loaded with tempestuous energy and the almost stationary, breathless intervals. The composition's general rhythm – contrasts in the intensity of detail and tempi.

The rhythm is also tension; pauses between the tension. Men-women. Two communities. They do not really confront each other. The conflict that theatre is based on remains latent, suspended. This is perhaps precisely the work of dance vis à vis theatre: to wipe out the too obvious, ostentatious contours of tragedy; to express emotional metaphor through bodies. Keeping tension as pure drama. There are signs on the body too – heels for the girls. I have read somewhere that a 'De Keersmaeker dance' is a leg dance. That is true. There are many legs in *Achterland*; lots of legwork. They even used them for walking (a few times). The heels excite, are worshipped as fetishes. The balance is disturbed. A boy tries to do the same: he also wears shoes, large, ugly, unlaced shoes; small smiles play on his feminine lips. You can see he's not succeeding because the others' faces speak: smile, communicate, and express emotion. It is the intimate condensement of presence that exceeds the acting. This piece breathes the feminine as a way of driving the world, as a way of transforming the earth. The whole ground in a heartbeat.

Laurence Louppe

Rosa 1992

Erts 1992

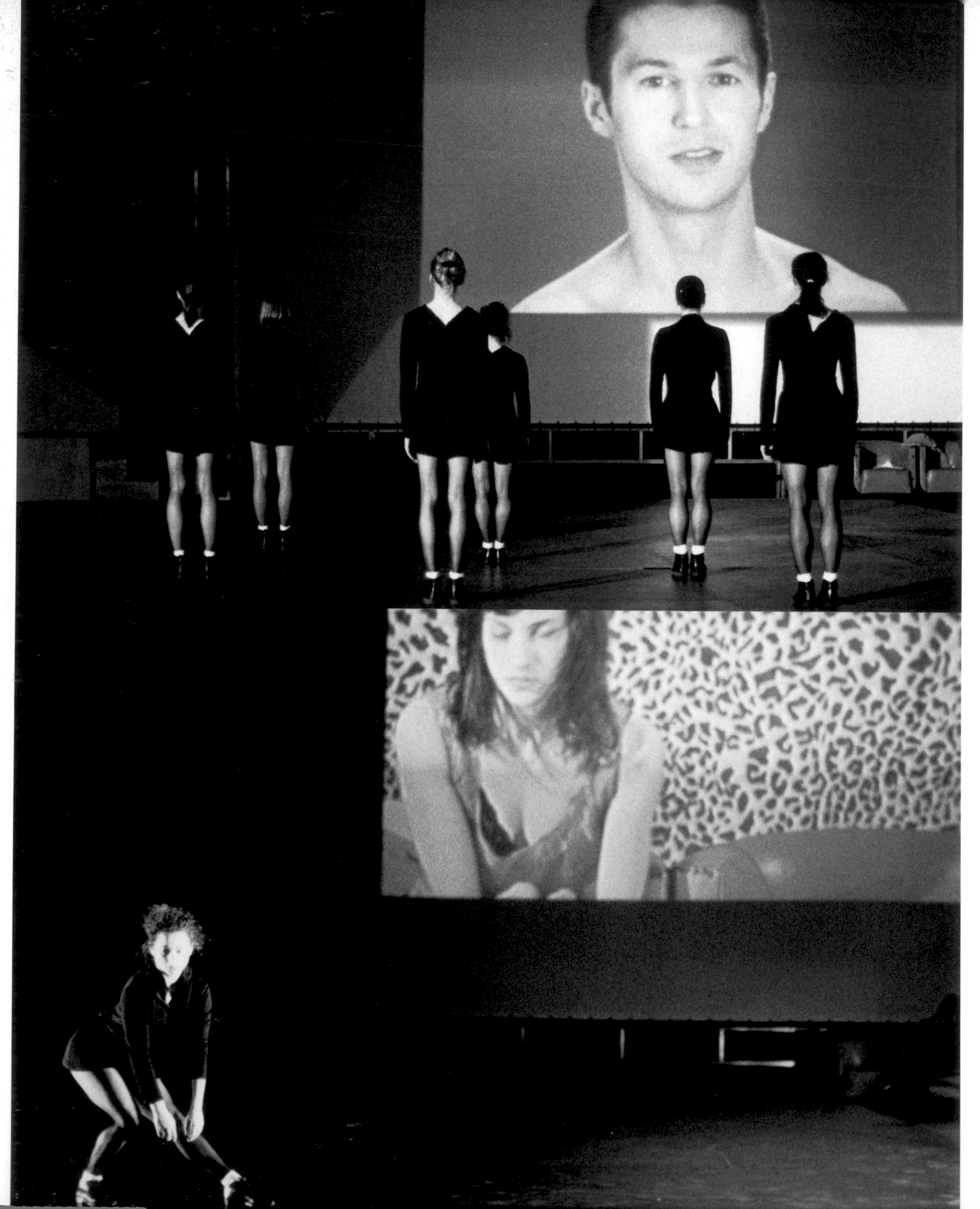

Mozart/Concert Arias, un moto di gioia[1992]

One morning, a young man was on the way from the town of his residence to the town where he hoped to earn his living, when he saw a strange flock of birds. They were numerous and of all different sorts and sizes. They leapt and fluttered back and forth forming a most enchanting circle in the sky. They whistled and chirruped, and moved in an incredible fashion.

The young man hid himself in the shadows of some large trees and, without disturbing it, observed the magnificent merry-go-round. The birds continued to fly by tracing graceful shapes the air. There were so many that he could barely see that in the middle, amongst the colour of the feathers, the flapping of the wings, the jostling of the bodies, the shadows and the lights, there was the most charming girl that he had ever seen.

The young man, fascinated by the spectacle which was unfolding before his eyes and by the glimpse of the young lady, leapt for joy, joined the group, and accompanied the pretty young girl in her tender dance. She was wonderfully beautiful, sprightly, and pure. Her dancing radiated such loveliness that his heart began to beat passionately for her; his head began to spin and he fell into a swoon.

When he came round, the beautiful girl was beside him. She was holding his hand and was giving him fresh water to drink from her lips. The birds had disappeared and had flown back to the forests and meadows where they continue, to this day, to fly and sing in celebration of the joy of united lovers. Since then, if the young man turns his head slightly, softly closes his eyes and sighs, he sees a carefree, colourful, chattering flock encircle the face of his beloved.

Laurent Busine

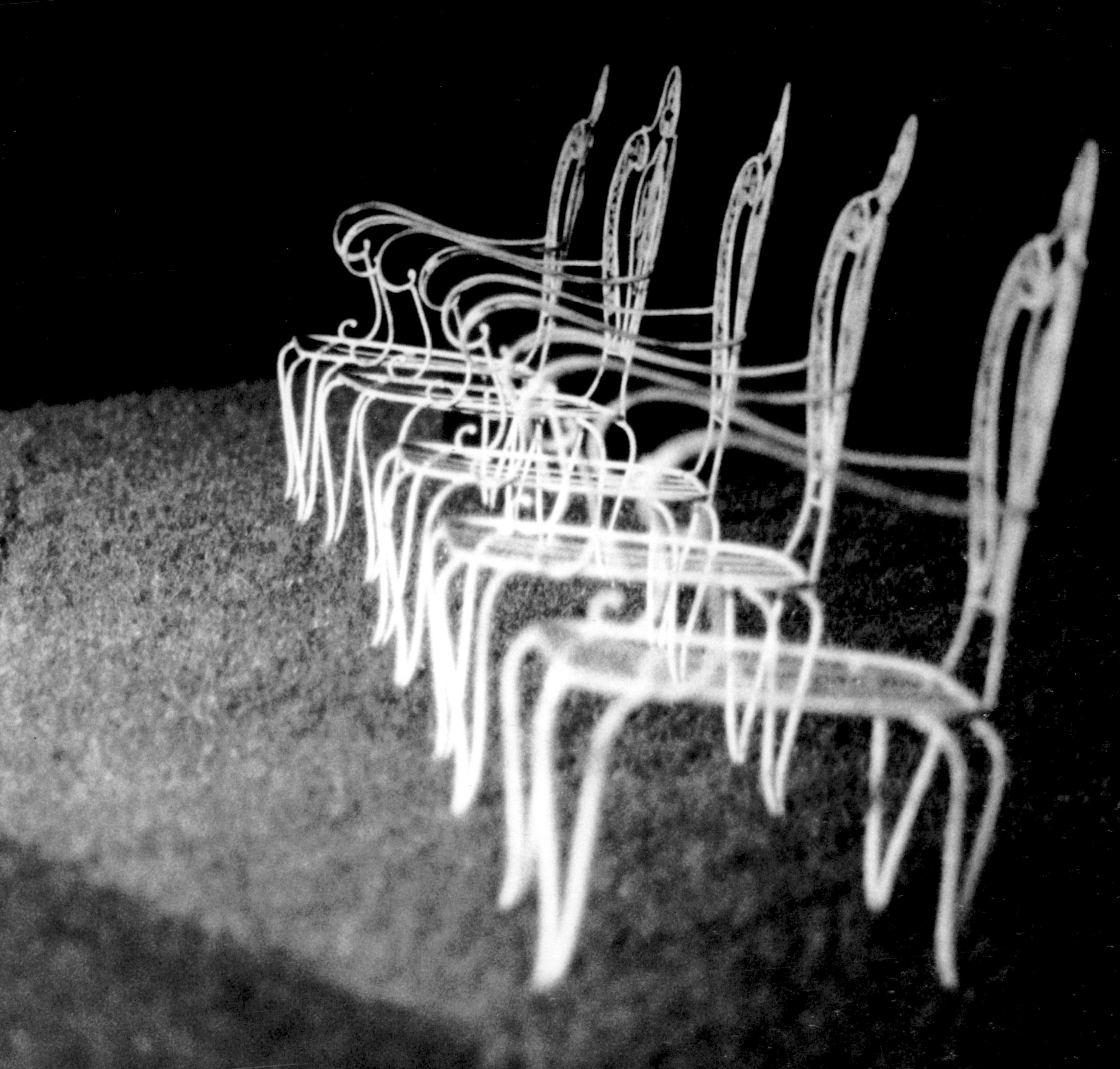

Toccata 1993

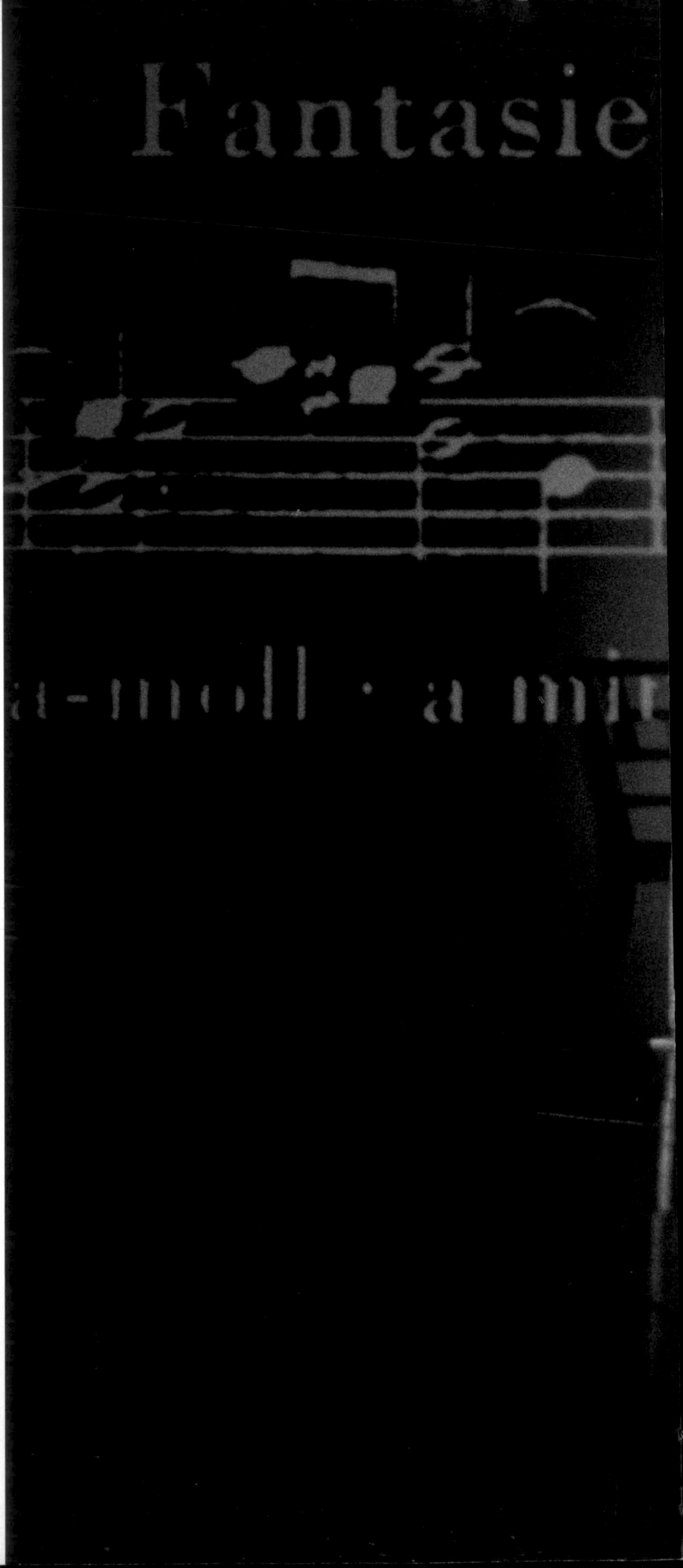

Fantasie

a-moll · a mi

nd Fuge

la mineur

ata nach der Violinsonate
ré mineur

Fuge

Kinok 1994

Amor constante más allá de la muerte 1994

A stage that exceeds its own boundaries, contorting itself in pursuit of not only more space, but, more particularly, of a different shape. What takes place upon it runs off in all directions: *Amor Constante más allá de la muerte* was pure excess that night in Montréal, at the Festival Nouvelle Danse, 1994. It was deeply infused with the baroque style of Quevedo, upon whose poem the piece was based.

Thierry De Mey wrote the music, which seemed to form a new partnership with the dancing, less the bellicosity of *Rosas danst Rosas*. It rather called to mind the precise, mathematical planning that precedes an attack, a calculated strategy for action – so much so that the music required constant motion, the dance occupying one area of the stage after another. Could this be a trick of the memory that transforms everything, especially something that happened 8 years before?

The complexity of the paths and spirals of the first dance left the spectator breathless. Johanne Saunier's precision. Marion Ballester dancing the percussion segment at the back of the stage. The surprise of Osman Kassen Khelili speaking Portuguese. The poem in sign language. The strong influence of classical language without the burden of the spatial and temporal codes that usually accompany it.

Dance generating music and vice-versa in a ceaseless exchange of plots and rhythms. A rain of spirals in ascending and descending movements, both inward and outward, until reaching the point where it is not beauty that is in evidence, but rather the intelligence behind what is being viewed. A knockout to the senses, which the rigorous counterpoint had already set on edge.

A way of talking about love that made the talk more important, the love dissolving among layers and layers of events and meanings. The movements were the response to specific sounds, as if each body were dancing to a different instrument, all the while remaining personal, even as they assumed musical personalities. A strange combination of submission and independence.

It was impossible not to recall Prigogine's words about the alliance between nature and art after seeing *Amor constante*. To my surprise, during the interview the next day at FIND, Anne Teresa responded that yes, she did know Prigogine, had met him even, when both received the title of Doctor Honoris Causa the previous week.

The spirals of nature are interwoven indeed.

Helena Katz

Woud, three movements to the music of Berg, Schönberg and Wagner 1996

Verklärte Anne Teresa

Mum had a habit of reminding the children that 'the floor is to be walked on. You can lie down in your bed, at night.' Children who lay on the floor in front of a radio with pictures could be found in American films. Sometimes they lay on their stomachs in what appeared to be their 'own rooms.' Did their mothers allow such things?
Mum herself had a mother who had been given lessons in *maintien* (deportment and etiquette) at a girls' boarding school. That was at the end of a previous century. Without having had any education, mum tried to honour the tradition: *maintaining le maintien*. And so, grandma, who had Dutch blood, actually did nothing else than preserve the motto *Je maintiendrai* (I shall maintain).

In 1934 when a ballerina simply collapsed and fell on the floor at the end of Balanchine's wonderful ballet *Serenade*, is was a shock. Balanchine explains: 'As the dancers were leaving the stage during a rehearsal, one of the girls slipped and fell on the floor. She began to cry.' She fell on the floor and cried! That was a faux pas in the world of classical dance. The ballet world collapsed for a brief second. For that matter, the great choreographer claimed that in his work it was the music which was danced on, not the floor. The music was the floor and you never fall on music. Such discord must not happen twice.

In modern dance (and also in modern theatrical production), flops, falls, drops, and crawls are accepted as a matter of course. Great passion, despair, helplessness, attacks of rage or epileptic fits, the code cries: fall! crawl! lie down! As if the ground no longer supports, but cushions.

One usually only lies horizontally when asleep at night, and so what a delight it is that in Anne Teresa de Keersmaeker's version of *Verklärte Nacht* she simply has the dancers moving vertically across the floor. That night of Schönberg's is then considered to be 'verklärt'. *La nuit transfigurée – Transfigured night*. For it is a night which – 'einen beseligten, glücklichen Ausdruck erhält' – 'gives you a happy and blessed expression.' That was the beautiful definition of 'verklärt' in my Duden dictionary.

Eric de Kuyper

Three solos for Vincent Dunoyer 1997

Just before 1997

Anne Teresa de Keersmaeker traverses performance art's most difficult terrain: the boundary between movement and language, dance and ideas, choreography and drama. Prima facie, there is no reason why movement should not be an expressive vehicle of the whole human spirit. Yet in practice, it has assiduously segregated itself from integral experience, preferring formalism and reflexive kinesthetics. The medium of words (the ether I breathe as a philosopher, social scientist and playwright) can be as hostile to movement as choreography can be hostile to words. For while both words and movement seek meaning, words constitute an architecture of conceptual abstraction, whereas movement is grounded in the concrete specifics of the human body.

In her inspired *Just before*, de Keersmaeker reminds us again of how challenging the choreographer's quest for meaning can be, and how powerfully touching it is when it succeeds in pushing across the conventional borders of dance. Set to ten pieces by John Cage, Steve Reich, Debussy and others, *Just before* explores human experience through the clash of memory and *reality* – though we know that reality is never more than memory agreed upon. The dancers puzzle out in sharp movements and truncated text remembered (invented?) stories from a past that may or may not be their own.

For the audience, the puzzle is compounded: for we have to fathom both the stories that unfold and the relationship between what the dancers say and how their bodies interpret the narrative. We are twice removed from their recollections though we are also liberated from *the truth* of the past, since it is not our own that is at stake. The result is our engagement in a process without terminus – a merging of neat words, pulsing music and specific movement that creates a picture not of certainty but of the indeterminate, which, of course, is life itself.

In a fragmented era of specialization, where the political is as far from the aesthetic as the ideational is from the kinetic, Anne Teresa takes on the indeterminateness of life whole and uses it to bring together what others prefer to sunder. This is what is often taken to be the sign of the prophet: but Anne Teresa is in fact more of what the Greeks called a seer – one who sees whole what others see in pieces and whose access to meaning is mistaken for prophecy.

Benjamin R. Barber

Duke Bluebeard's Castle 1998

Drumming 1998

Perfect World

In Vienna I saw the first showing of *Drumming* and it was a shock. Rarely has a performance been so gentle, like a caress that makes you quiver. A world of saffron in which men and women move in harmony. I remember a lady dancer being carried by men like a goddess. And Cynthia, like a butterfly fluttering through the light, a group dance which was so slow, as if the dancers were weightless. In *Drumming*, the music, the costumes, the style, and the choreography blend together into a single work of art. Or even more: into a world in which people treat each other gently, with attention, oriental, full of sunshine. Quite different to the stress, fights, and unfulfilled desires in that other favourite performance of mine: *Ottone Ottone*. And fifty minutes later, when the final saffron thread had covered up the final piece of black floor, I could only think of that other masterpiece, by Lou Reed: *Perfect World*.

Ivo van Hove

Quartett 1999

Three Years of Silence

I saw *Quartett* in Porto in the summer of '99. As any actor, when I see a performance by fellow actors and friends, I always have one thought in the back of my mind: 'At the end, I'll have to say something about it to them.' When I go to the movies, I have the right not to have an opinion. I like that. When I see a theatre or dance performance, even if I don't know any of the artists involved, a strange cloud of responsibility hangs over my head and pushes me to develop an opinion. I relate this feeling to my catholic family. So... I don't like this feeling, although I normally obey it. Anyway, I sat down in this big old Portuguese theatre to see Cynthia Loemij and Frank Vercruyssen, interested in the 'free performing' vs. the 'strictness of choreography', the actor and the dancer, word and movement making love and war on stage, and all that bullshit! There was also the movie *Liaisons Dangereuses*, with Glenn Close and John Malkovich, which left a powerful impression. I didn´t know the original text by Choderlos de Laclos nor the beautiful Heiner Müller text about to be performed. This made me feel ignorant. So, I sat down on my chair with all this in my head. *Quartett* was, before it started, already too important in my life.

However, after the first minutes of the performance, I understood the stupid smallness of my previous thoughts. I think this always happens when you see a masterpiece. When you watch beauty, you always realize how small and irrelevant most things and thoughts are. The violent sound and the violent silence, the intense talking and moving of Loemij and Vercruyssen, the way truth was striking the audience, of which I was a part, that's what I carry with me from that night in Porto three years ago. During the whole performance, I forgot everything that before occupied my mind and was able to watch, just watch a dancer and an actor, two people looking for redemption. I was not blown away by the power of illusion. What struck me was the truth in it. The way both of the performers accepted each other's body and voice, using each other's feelings and choices, to really, I mean really as in reality, to really save themselves. Not only to survive a devastated world, but to be happy in it. Not the devasted world of the French Revolution of Laclos' time or the World War of Müller's time, but the devasted world of '99, that summer night in Portugal.

Something I won't forget: the moment Cynthia speaks. I thought, 'that's perfection, she can even speak.' I don't mean this as a joke. I was actually in love with her voice. It was not the fact that she could produce sound that surprised me. It was the fact that she spoke with her body and also really spoke with words. This simple fact made me fall in love several times during *Quartett*. Something else I won't forget: the moment Frank danced. He not only moved, but he danced. This magical absurd moment he danced, I was in love again. And something I definitely won't forget: there's this moment during *Quartett*, I don't know when, but I remember a moment they touched each other. They were dancing and Frank's fingernail touched Cynthia's dress just before she danced away from him. That moment I was truly touched.

That's what I remember from *Quartett*: a man and a woman pretending to lie, but really trying to overcome the borders of dancing and acting in order to save themselves and their precious truth from the ruins of a fucked up world. At the end, I stood up applauding, as if that could help them. Each clap was an attempt to participate in their beauty. Walking out the theatre, I realised I had nothing to say about this performance. Nothing at all. Writing this text now, I talk about *Quartett* for the first time and I feel like applauding again. Again trying to be part of that beauty by breaking my 3 years of silence.

Tiago Rodrigues

For 1999

I said I 1999

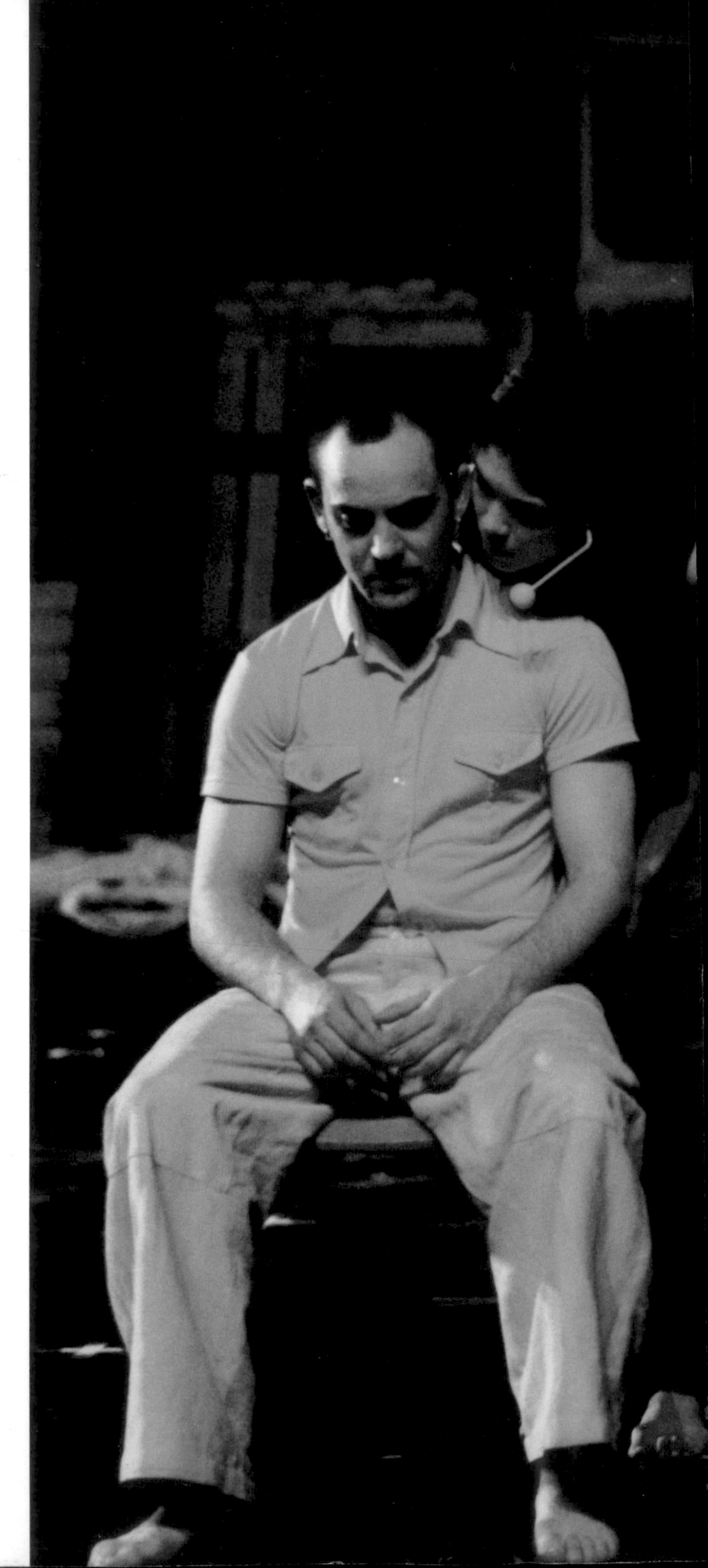

27 IV XCIX
/ SAID /

Some years ago, I saw *I said I* in Kaaitheater in Brussels.

I remember that I found Handke's text fantastic: a stirring litany of I-sentences; how the text was initially split up between the various dancers who casually directed their words to each other or the audience. And how the text became more compelling, how an awareness developed, how rules were accepted and rejected, and how a place on the stage, in the world, was sought for.

I remember during the performance a constant process of constructing and destructing, in the dances, in the manipulation of the decor, in the meticulous piling up of household goods which were then later put down in another place in an other order; the changes of clothing...

I remember how someone looked for comfort and shelter under a blanket, and how life suddenly seemed to drag.

I remember how Iris spoke the final text at the end, alone in the middle of the stage. There was a roar of laughter when she imitated the safety instructions given by air- hostesses, and how I fell in love with her as she was standing there.

I remember how I said I went further than stories or images of reality, and how it offered an insight into the world, the grammar of life and the beauty of abstraction.

I remember how I kissed Anne Teresa after the performance; she had lipstick on.

Sigrid Vinks

In real time[2000]

Time. We feel.

Linear Time of a clock that hangs on the wall counting every second of the passing performance.
Cyclic Time as the last daylight falls through the windows of the Rosas Performance Space before the spots take over.
Time taking shape through silence, words, music. *In real time* molds these into space and thus picks up the thread that spins through Anne Teresa's oeuvre: giving time a physical, emotional, esthetic reality.

Real. It is.

The fragmentary use of text, acting and dance evokes the paradox of making art, especially performing art: we have to construct something real although we know that any construction must be artificial.
Or speaking with Picasso: 'Nous savons tous que l'art n'est pas la vérité. L'art est un mensonge qui nous fait comprendre la vérité.' (We all know that art isn't truth. Art is a lie that helps us understand truth.)

Vérité, truth, is a delicate term in art as anywhere else. Its condition is personal experience, and art is fundamentally based on everyone's personal experience. In real time we can experience the passage of the present moment.
When a man is continuously speaking on his mobile phone, when a musical phrase of Aka Moon fills the space like a torrent on which the dance evolves, when a man almost melts with the floor in a relentless flow of movement, when a wild conversation bursts out at the long dinner table... This passage of moments, like fragments of a puzzle evolving in time, is our only indication of truth.

In.

In real time is a step on an artistic path that surprises with questions and contradictions rather than answers – that experiences fusion of elements and ongoing transformation rather than stale truth.
It is a work about the pulsation of the present; its many moves, its many melodies, its many words that lead us from the present moment's chaos into structure and sense and back into the same fundamental disarray, leaving us with experience, an open door *In real time*.

Arco Renz

Rain 2001

Downpour in the Concert Hall in Bruges

Converging projections which suddenly fall. This is the image that lodges in your mind. That is all you have afterwards for you are powerless to stop the tide, this dance is far too vast. It is swept away along with the music of Reich.

But there are other features which remain in your memory, namely how these dancers take up their places, how they make a spiral entry into the space and join up as a group to then move away again. Running in a circle, winding together, concentrically hand in hand, only to break open into rectangular and diagonal shapes.

We can't forget how this *rain* dance filled the space, how the architecture was taken and melded with a contrasting space of dance. You have understood, the only possible reaction is to blissfully sink down and disappear in the audience, forever incognito. Jan Versweyveld's cylindrical theatre set penetrates the Bruges Concert Hall's auditorium connecting them in a singularly empathic way. And thus an exciting ambivalence arises between the dance's territory and the space in which dancers and public are united to share a joint adventure.

But there are also the individuals in the dance whose faces steal briefly away from the group picture. The female dancer who effortlessly catches the male dancer in mid air: the line, which starts at the finger tips and runs along the forearm, circles around the upper arm, stretches over the shoulder and widens, only to narrow again, contracting small enough to snuggle somewhere behind the ear. And there it stays.

The physical phenomenon of dancing which takes place in the heart of a building made of rigid stone whose geometrical outline has itself, been inspired by a body. A constructed body flanking the city. This is why the auditorium is endowed with shape that resembles a pair of hands cupped over the mouth like a kind of human loudspeaker. A spatial modulation that creates an architectonic area in which the human movement heightens the tension.

You have to think of Leonardo de Vinci's Vitruvius Man whose finger tips and toes touch the circular and square configurations which are projected into each other.

The dancing body, a space within space, continually changing and redefining itself. That moving body corresponds to the highest degree of complexity within a defined area. The central perspective is affected and the unequivocal (essentially excluded) position of the spectator is changed into an extraordinarily aggressive engagement between dancers and audience.
I wonder if Anne Teresa De Keersmaeker aims for happiness or misery in her dance. I have the feeling that this is not up for discussion.
I think she wants to use this form of dance to show a new kind of modern man: a very worthy man.
Merciless worth in a visual labyrinth.

Paul Robbrecht

Small hands (out of the lie of no)[2001]

The sublime is not innocent. In that fraction of a second in which you get a glimpse of something both so pure and yet so ineffable, language fails completely. That is quite frustrating for someone whose business is language.

But never mind. Perhaps that is why attempts are made to sing, beat, flog and cajole language away from its meaning ... in order to achieve the impossible one day. Why? Because it is good to reach for the stars, even if you know that they are not there.

There is a purity that bowls me over.

I have heard the unbelievably pure voice of Andreas Scholl. No friction whatsoever.

And I have seen Small hands. The performance filled me with a kind of absolute gratitude.

The facts are simple. There are two *beautiful* dancers (Anne Teresa De Keersmaeker and Cynthia Loemij) in transparant dresses which reveal *beautiful* bodies. There is some *beautiful* music (Purcell). The choreography is *beautiful*, intricately drawn up and yet sustaining the power of improvisation.

The facts are important and, of course, to a large extent they determine the quality of the performance, but they never tell its secret.

The wonder of *Small hands* lies in its intimacy. As a spectator, you are seated in an oval whereby you mark out the dance floor. Sometimes the dancers pass by closely. Sometimes they stand right in front of you. You can see their bodies through their dresses. You can see the sweat gathering. You can smell the dancers. You see them blush. In short, you are literally a witness to the *intimacy of the dancing bodies*. The dancers assume different guises before your eyes: they change into little girls, fragile cherubs, vulnerable women, and into strong and confident ladies. And that is quite impressive.

But there is more.

It continues to affect me if I may catch someone in his or her most naturally vulnerable state: someone who walks along the street deep in thought and winds a lock of hair around a finger, or children so preoccupied with a game that they reveal their true selves simply because they do not know they are being watched. Such states are usually impossible on a stage. Anyone on a stage is inevitably aware of all the surrounding eyes. Yet in *Small hands* you see two dancers so taken up with the joy of a duet that you can, as it were, *catch them in their beauty*: joy combined with great skill. You see two women who are fulfilled. They reach out for beauty until they literally smile with it. They absorb it to the full before your eyes. And then, at that moment, you see a smile welling up which makes you not only a witness to the smile, but, as it were, a partaker of it. This is both pure and irrepressible: you want to put your hands around it to keep it, but it spills between your fingers. Until it causes you to glow yourself. Something like a longing. A gleam. A tiny hand which reaches for a star (which may not even be there). Stubborn. Profuse. Against your better judgement. The result is that you are, as it were, purified and fulfilled so that you don't want to leave the theatre.

Peter Verhelst

(but if a look should) April me[2002]

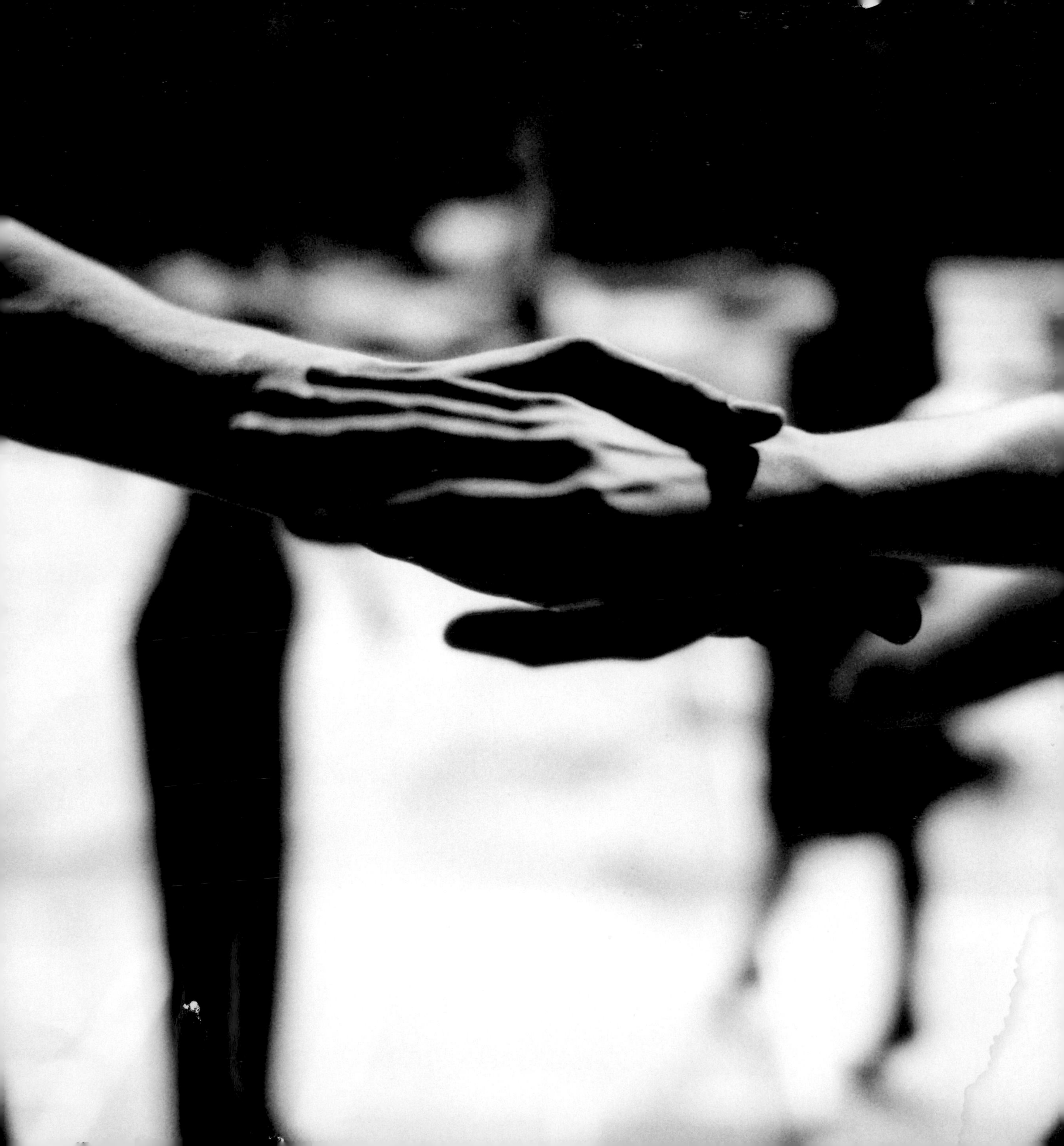

Seeing *April me* was a fascinating and unforgettable experience. What struck me was the musical quality of thought; I saw musical processes with my eyes. In the first place the imaginative use of *noise* was exciting. That is to say, *reject* elements were gathered up in a formal structure and became meaningful and even beautiful. In music composers have used key clicks and multiphonics on wind instruments, bow noise or bow-attacks without the ensuing tone on string instruments – sounds we all hear but most people do not listen to. They are part of the sound but have normally no significative meaning. It is the pitch and its quality of timbre to which we listen – the rest is rejected, put out of mind. But Anne Teresa is a sort of Lachenmann of dance; she has taken the mechanics of rehearsal, theatre, life outside the theatre – and integrated them in a huge sweep of inclusiveness into structures of great formality – structures ultimately of complexity and harmony – structures stretched to the limits. Because the *noise* element is so seamlessly integrated with the more normal choreography (this is such a dangerous and risky enterprise) the unity achieved is more precious, we learn more from it, things belong together in a pattern we never knew existed; a mysterious pattern.

In the second place, Anne Teresa's use of music was so musical. I remember the constraints of the opening sections, with the stage divided with many bars to movement, many obstacles which one would have thought gave no space to swing a cat as we say in English, let alone dance. Yet from this situation there unfolded the most magical erotic, innocent imaginative flowering of a few limited choreographic movements, which echoed across the divided stage from dancer to dancer in musical phrases of great formal precision. As Stravinsky said, in constraint lies freedom. The whole impression of the evening was of symmetrical lines being drawn across the stage, of quasi-musical structures, which echoed and repeated and transformed each other in a defined syntax, giving that depth of underlying structure which makes it possible to listen to music fifty times and still marvel at its subtle and non-trivial form.

I came away excited and enriched by a profound insight, an insight (as with music) too deep for words...and for that am deeply grateful to this art.

Jonathan Harvey

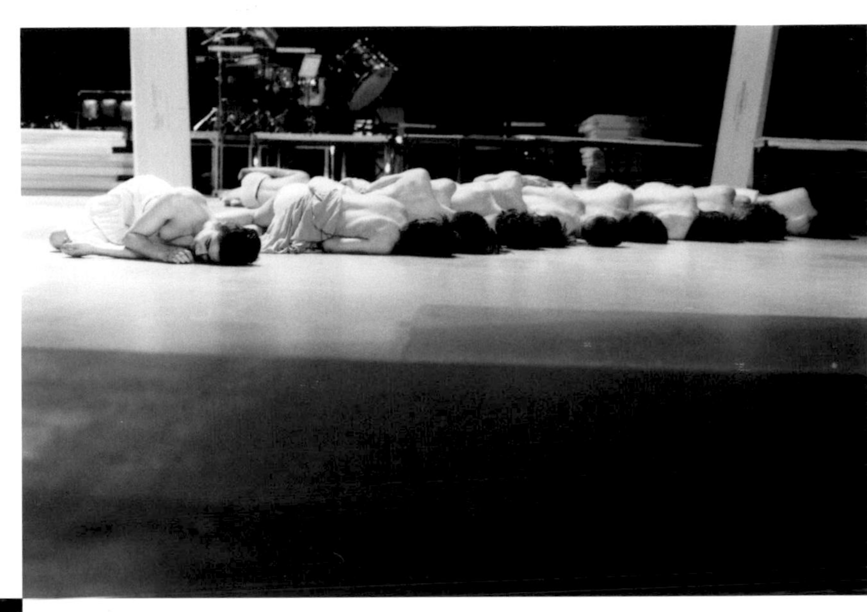

I had the feeling that I was witness to a telluric event (seen through various prisms) – the arrival, the setting up, the peak, the weariness, and finally, the slow and inevitable end. The event seemed to me at first to be made of pure energy, energy produced by the musicality of the bodies in the space, seemingly able to convert sound structures into action.

As soon as this first feeling of surprise had subsided, I could distinguish the lines: although each individual formed part of a polyphonous network, they all seemed to follow their own lines, their own lives, in an apparently spontaneous, self-evident way, instantaneously switching from the one state to the other. And thus they influence the network of which they are a part, rendering the polyphony hypersensitive, changeable, responsive to the least stimulation, like the nervous system of an animal lying in wait for prey.

In these constructions, where the lightning-swift movements are often cut short, as if to fuel our desire, we move from a mental, abstract, and musical world to a world which delves deeper into individual behaviour. In *Noces*, for example, the men and women display themselves to each other in an innocent or mischievous way during the soirée, as if they want to provoke a reaction from the opposite sex, for fun, for a dance, to party, to share the joy and the dangers of being a couple. All these activities are taken up in the music, express the music, and contribute to the great sense of natural movement which continuously propels the terrific energy of this performance, making it seem like one large *body*, irrigated by individual movements and vacillating between order and chaos.

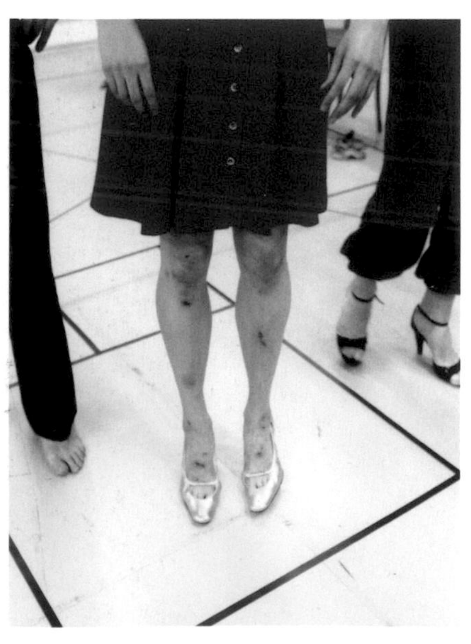

And then, as after an intense life, there is a natural feeling of ending, of chaos, of being too tired to continue in the same way. The piece veers into a spiral – actions are repeated over again as though suddenly devoid of meaning. The space also empties, stripped of its content. We see the fly tower of a theatre, the machinery; we see bodies making one last attempt to mark a few movements. All this revolves slowly between elegance and brutality and finally gives the impression that *eternity* has made its entrance.

It is at that moment when the performance (its sequences, its giddiness, its contrasts) appeared once again like a puzzle in my head, giving me an impression of perpetual, never-ending movement that gave rise to emotion, and a sensation of great elation.

Georges Aperghis

Repertory Evening 2002

The hostess is like a woman in an elegant photograph from *Vogue* in the fifties, She wears a long dress and bustier and her hair in a chignon. She receives her guests in a very intimate twilight, one after the other, as befits an accomplished lady of the house. Then she slips into lassitude, without shedding any of her tension nor relaxing her concentration. At the rear, on the other side of this pictorial, living fresco are luxuriant bouquets, wines in abundance and an opulent buffet. Everything appears like a still life from the 17th century. This is the way Anne Teresa de Keersmaeker celebrates twenty years of creative work and collaboration. She has just performed a fragment from *Fase*. Once they've dressed for the party, she is joined in turn by, the boys from the *Grosse Fuge* by Beethoven; the girls from the *Quartet* by Bartók with their laced boots; the Portuguese friends from *The Lisbon Piece*; the dancers from *Toccata*; and even the children from the interlude. But no one from the audience would dare to join them in their soirée champagne – joy and emotion, nearness but no familiarity, reserve but no coolness. It's like a social ritual celebrating the sensual friendship of a genuine group. The following week brought the opportunity to tumble over and over again on the waves of Steve Reich and *Rain*. 2001. The colours of their flesh pinkened to almost scarlet: dawn would soon be breaking – 2002. *(but if a look should) April me*: the culmination of twenty years' momentum which began with the mechanical precision of a clock, with relentless geometry, with the millimetric work of an architecture – *Fase* – to which you abandoned yourself completely. Demanding pendulum, quizzical clock. Twenty years of music incarnated in movement and bodies that have themselves become music. Streams, floods, waves. Tension, unwinding, swirling in spirals towards *Noces* by Stravinsky. The minimum and the maximum, the intransigence and the joy, the ascetics and the drunkeness. The blue chaos after a disaster: everything lies wild and smashed on the floor in order to emerge even more beautiful, like a phoenix from its ashes. This neither heathen nor sacred dance has something Dionysian; it opens the rite of performance, for it is ultimately theatre. The girls wear a ceremonial uniform in all possible hues of red, from blood to fuchsia. The boys flex their muscles, everything is pulsation, convulsion and earthy energy. It makes you think of a rite of spring. Litanies, Psalms, and rhythmic songs by women and children. The mechanics become soft, almost operatic, the emotion becomes all smiles and the party is consumed – poetry enters. With humour, sensitivity, and secrets. Thierry De Mey's palanquin of sounds. Echoes of Jeroen Bosch or the surrealists, everlasting painting from which Flemings draw their modernity, for it transcends appearances. And then all the living notations: a smile, sketching a movement which is suddenly arrested, a knowing look, an inaudible word, like the traces of a rehearsal consciously preserved. Shared elation and joy. You come outside with youthfulness in your head and in your body; full of vitality and liberated energy; regenerated and reconciled. Over and beyond the obsolete, conventional boundaries of classical and baroque, splendid austerity and spiritual lyricism can be found. You feel at one with others, a little proud and resolved to share the world courageously.

Christian Lacroix

2002: Rosas is celebrating its twentieth anniversary and ten years of residence at La Monnaie. That immediately evokes a whole stream of memories and images: pictures of rehearsals, performances, tours,... *Mozart* in the Palais des Papes in Avignon... Peter Greenaway filming Fumiyo Ikeda in *Rosa*... The counterpoint by the five dancers in *Toccata*, echoing the polyphony of Bach... Anne Teresa De Keersmaeker meeting Klaus Michael Grüber to talk about Schönberg... The serious and splendid text of Quevedo, which gave its title to *Amor constante*... The ever changing spectrum of colours of the Dries Van Noten costumes in *Rain*... Cynthia in *Quartett* by Müller... The mirror relationship between Anne Teresa and Cynthia in *Small hands*...

All along this entire road I see the power and autonomy of an art form which, in the twentieth century, freed itself from the chains which bound it to opera. The fact that Rosas has established itself in La Monnaie perfectly illustrates a relationship between partners who maintain their freedom yet want to combine their strengths. In such a relationship both partners make specific contributions: an opera house must fight constantly against the slackening powers which threaten it, whilst the dynamism of the more flexible and mobile dance company can only stimulate an opera house.

Dance and music: Anne Teresa has chosen to work with the most varied kinds of music. She explores the worlds of Purcell, Bach and Monteverdi, Brahms, Schönberg and Bartók, Ligeti, Steve Reich, and Aka Moon, ... Her latest creation, *April me*, brings together traditional African and Indian music with that of Igor Stravinsky and Thierry De Mey, her close associate from the very beginning. She never uses music as sound decor: her relationship with the music is both structural and emotional. She adapts the music piece's structure and hidden language and in this way she is able to find the material for her choreographic work and develop a suitable form of organisation. The emotion emerges from the special bond between form and expression, between duration and instant, and between the considered movement and the instinctive gesture.

The theatrical dimension appears to me to be constantly present, even in the most abstract works. It is noticeable in the irony of the Bartók quartet; in the laughter of Johanne; in the body of Taka; in the looks of understanding in *Achterland*, and in the image of the newly wed couple who stand on the refrigerator at the end of *Noces*. It is felt even more strongly when the dancers make a text their own: Handke, Müller, Tennessee Williams, Quevedo, Rijnders, etc. The consistent theatrical dimension is due to the fact that the work of the choreographer and her dancers is continually nourished by reality and certain powerful media images that have become part of our lives.

Continuity: the P.A.R.T.S. dance school was founded in 1995. It was quick to acquire an exceptional reputation in the world of contemporary dance. A school which is linked to a company represents, for me, the ideal form of transmission, through creation, nearness, word, example and daily work. This relationship works both ways: the one who passes on often receives much more in return...

Dance and opera: dance has gained its autonomy, but is appearing again on the opera stage in all its strength: its coded gesture, its discipline, the considered way in which it occupies the space, and a physical awareness which differs strongly from that of the world of theatre. Some of the most beautiful opera productions in recent years are the fruits of the work of choreographers. After *Duke Bluebeard's Castle* by Bartók, Anne Teresa will soon direct her second opera *I due Foscari* by Verdi. I am convinced that this adventure is far from over.

Bernard Foccroulle

Annotations

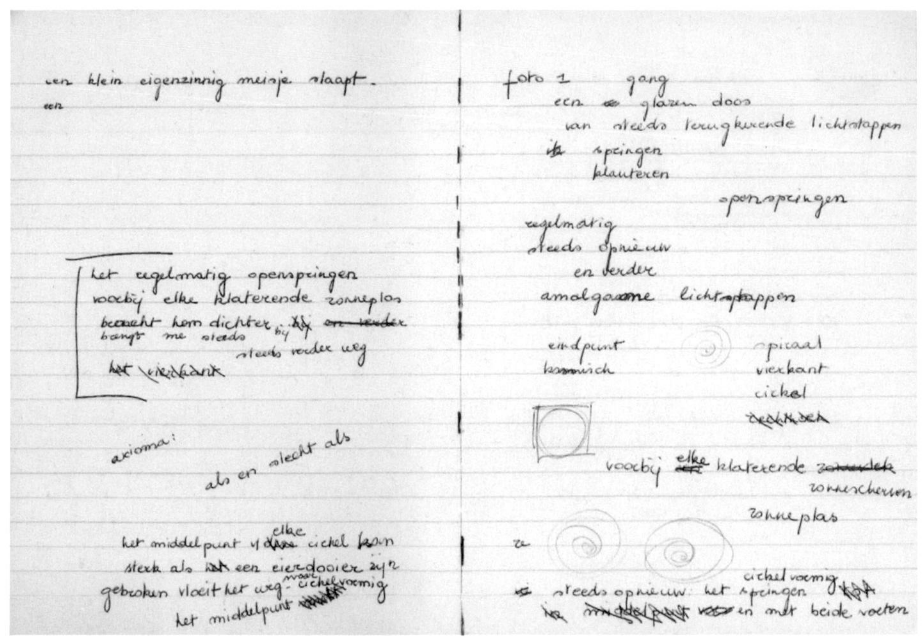

Asch (1980)

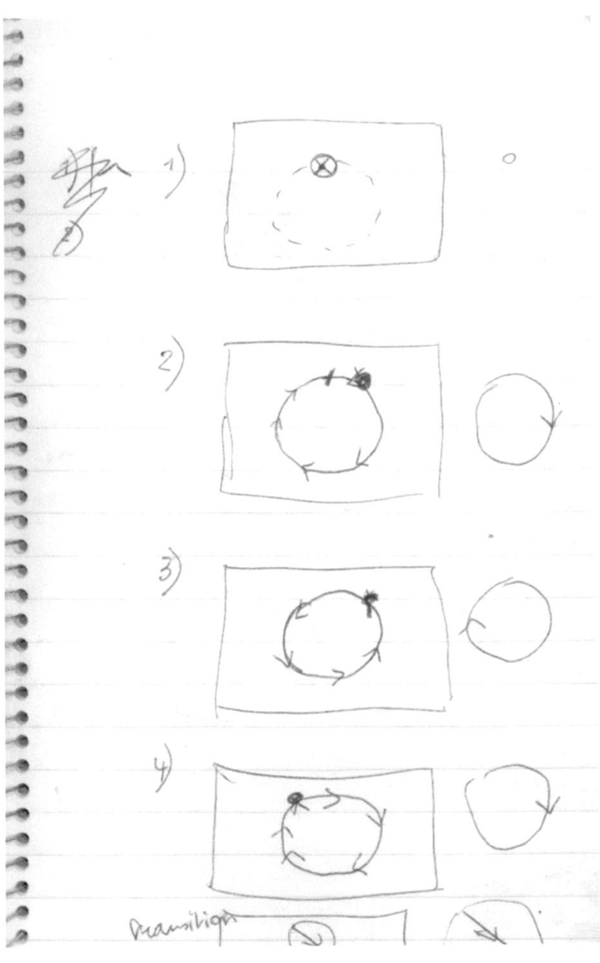

Fase (1982)

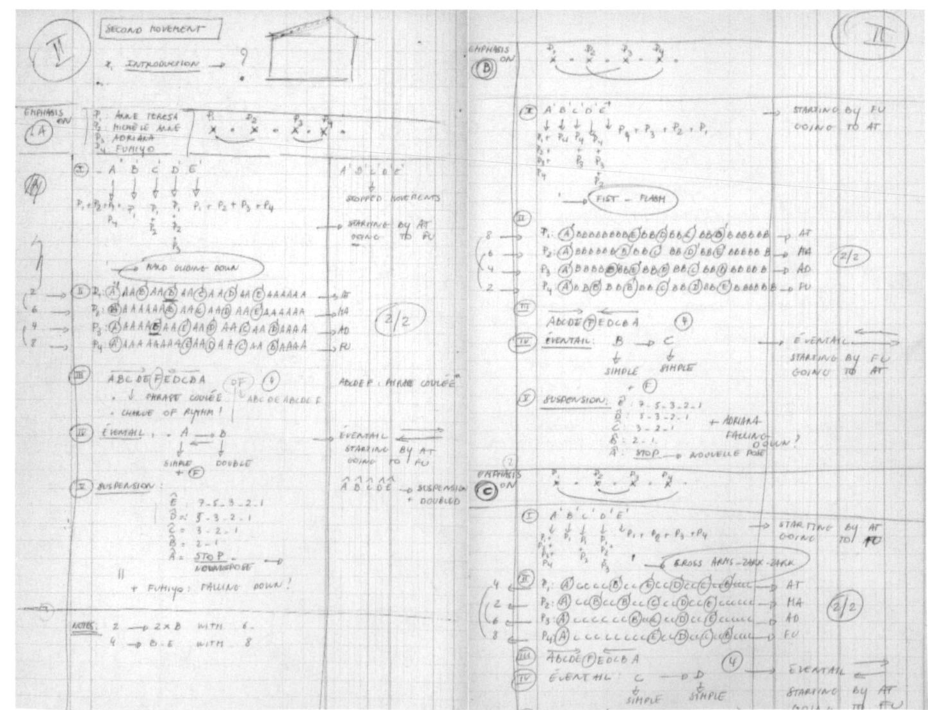

Rosas danst Rosas (1983)

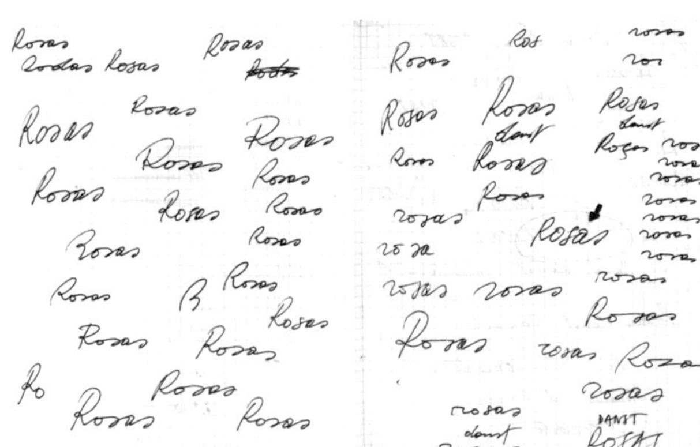

Rosas danst Rosas (1983)

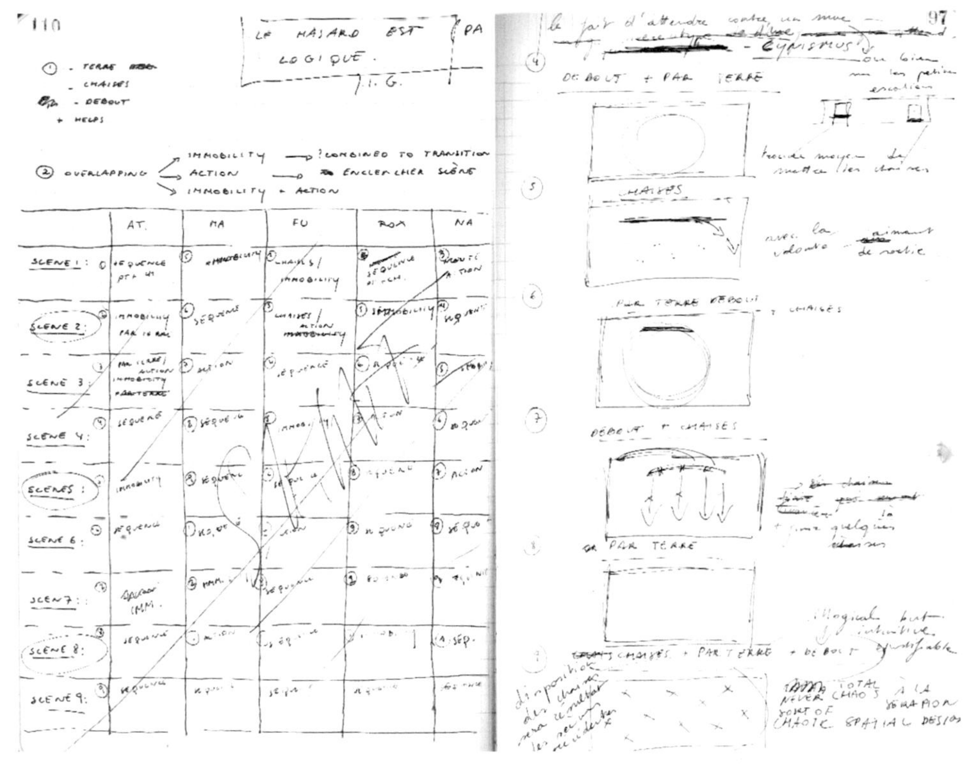

Elena's aria (1984)

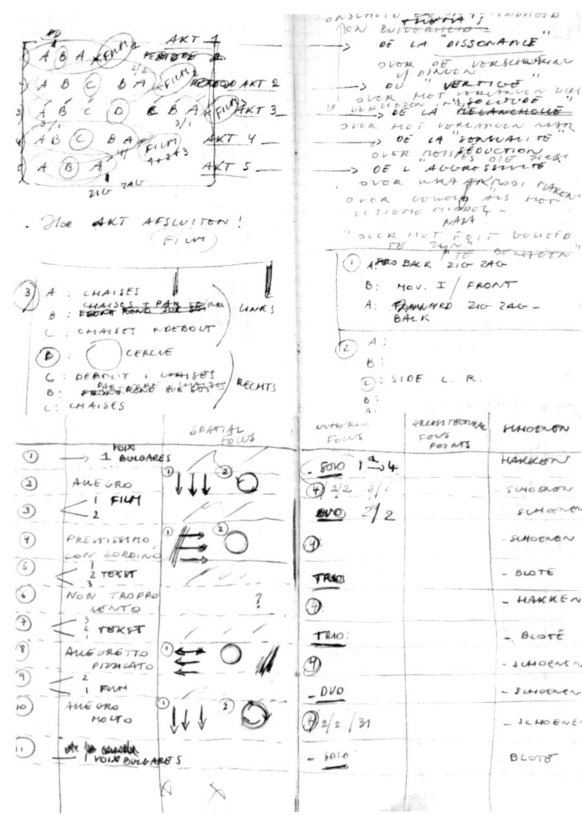

Bartók/aantekeningen (1986)

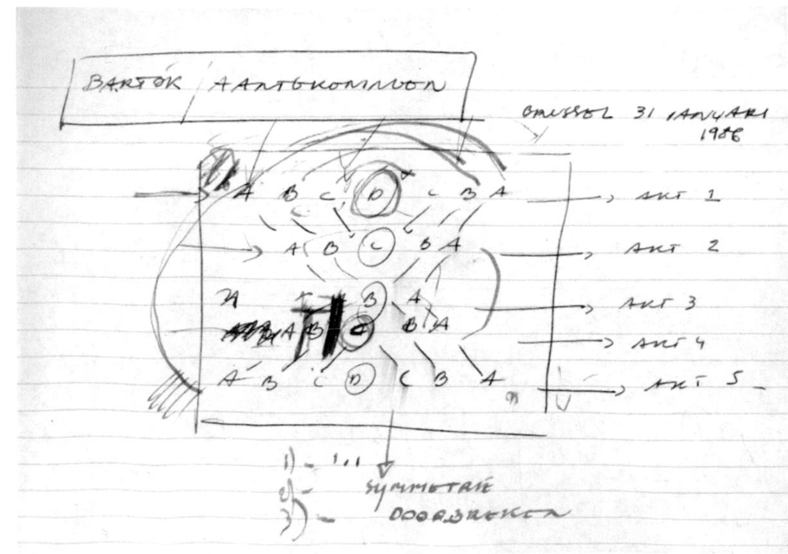

Bartók/aantekeningen (1986)

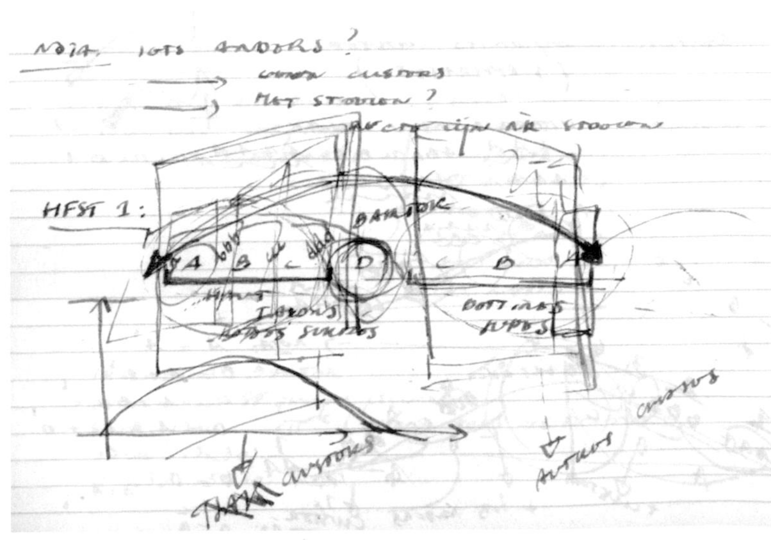

Bartók/aantekeningen (1986)

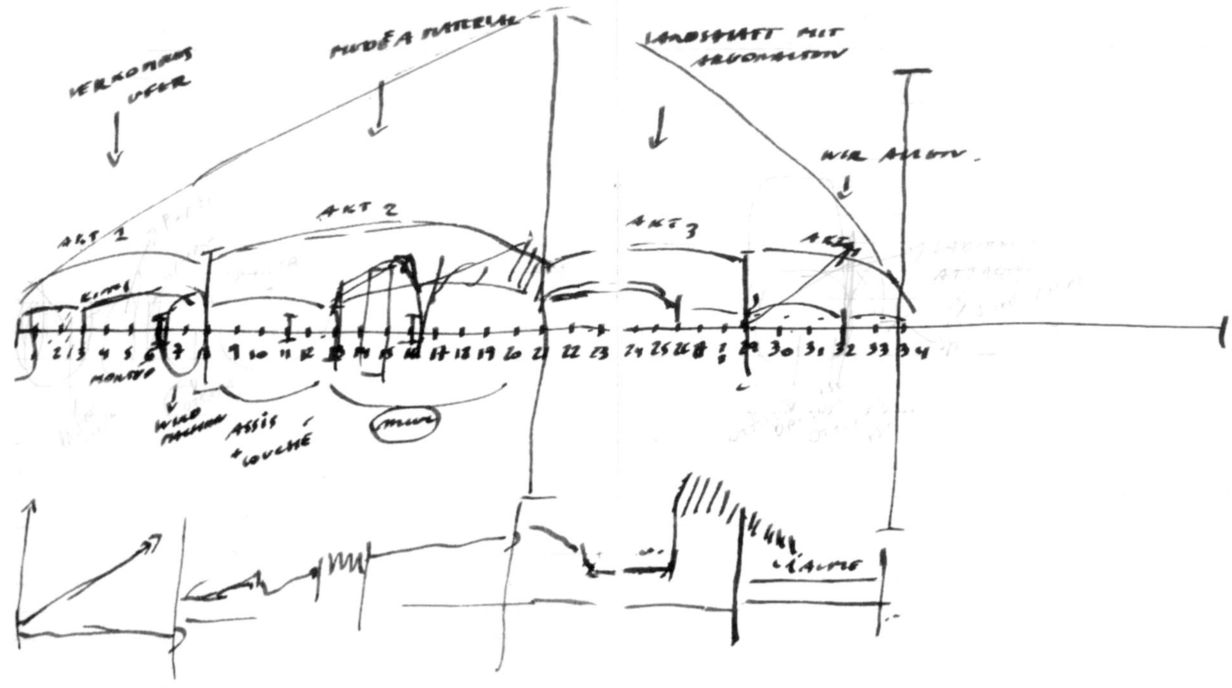

Medeamaterial (1987)

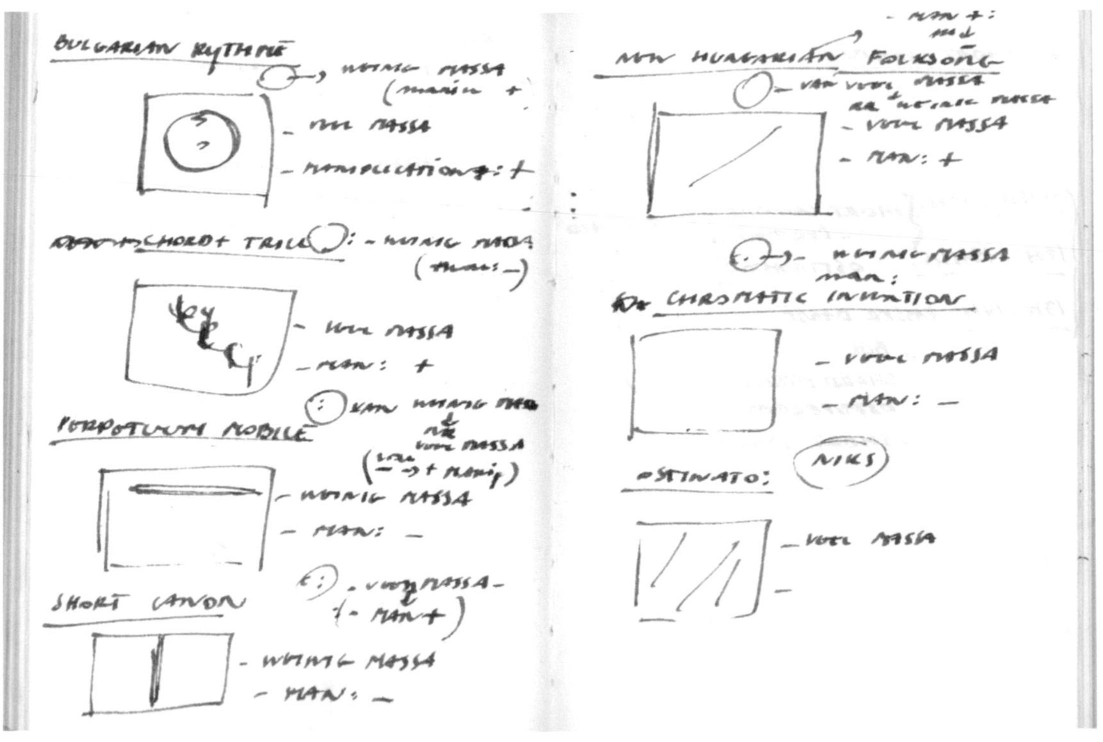

Mikrokosmos (1987)

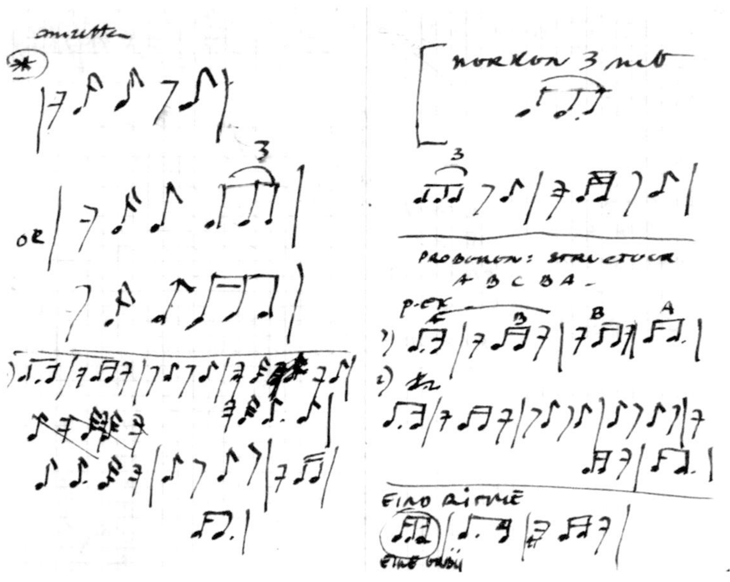

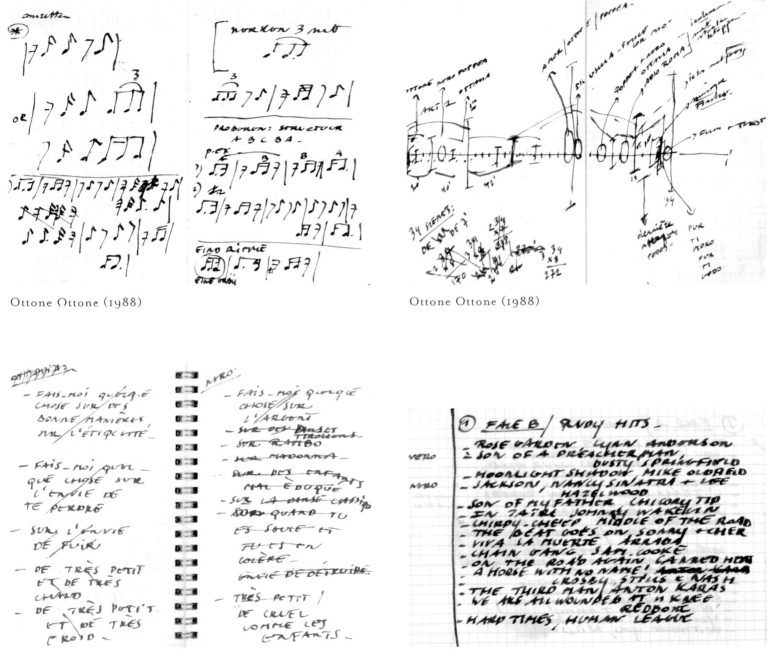

Ottone Ottone (1988)

Ottone Ottone (1988)

Ottone Ottone (1988)

(1) FACE B / RUDY HITS –
– ROSE GARDEN LYNN ANDERSON
– SON OF A PREACHER MAN, DUSTY SPRINGFIELD
– MOONLIGHT SHADOW, MIKE OLDFIELD
– JACKSON, NANCY SINATRA + LEE HAZELWOOD
– SON OF MY FATHER CHICORY TIP
– IN ZAIRE JOHNNY WAKELIN
– CHIRPY-CHEEP MIDDLE OF THE ROAD
– THE BEAT GOES ON, SONNY + CHER
– VIVA LA MUERTE ARRABAL
– CHAIN GANG SAM COOKE
– ON THE ROAD AGAIN CANNED HEAT
– A HORSE WITH NO NAME, CROSBY STILLS & NASH
– THE THIRD MAN / ANTON KARAS
– WE ARE ALL WOUNDED AT W KNEE REDBONE
– HARD TIMES, HUMAN LEAGUE

Ottone Ottone (1988)

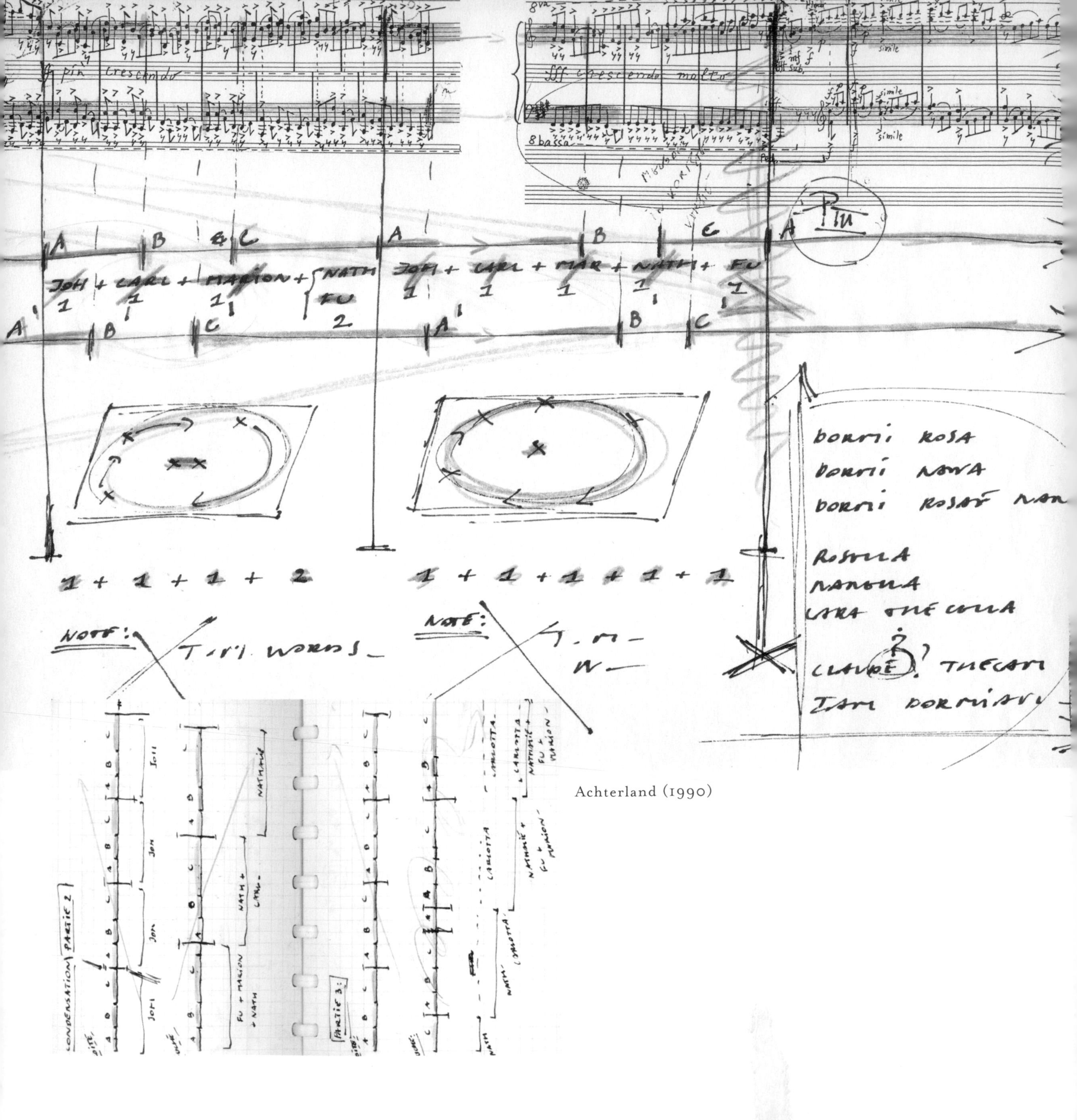

Achterland (1990)

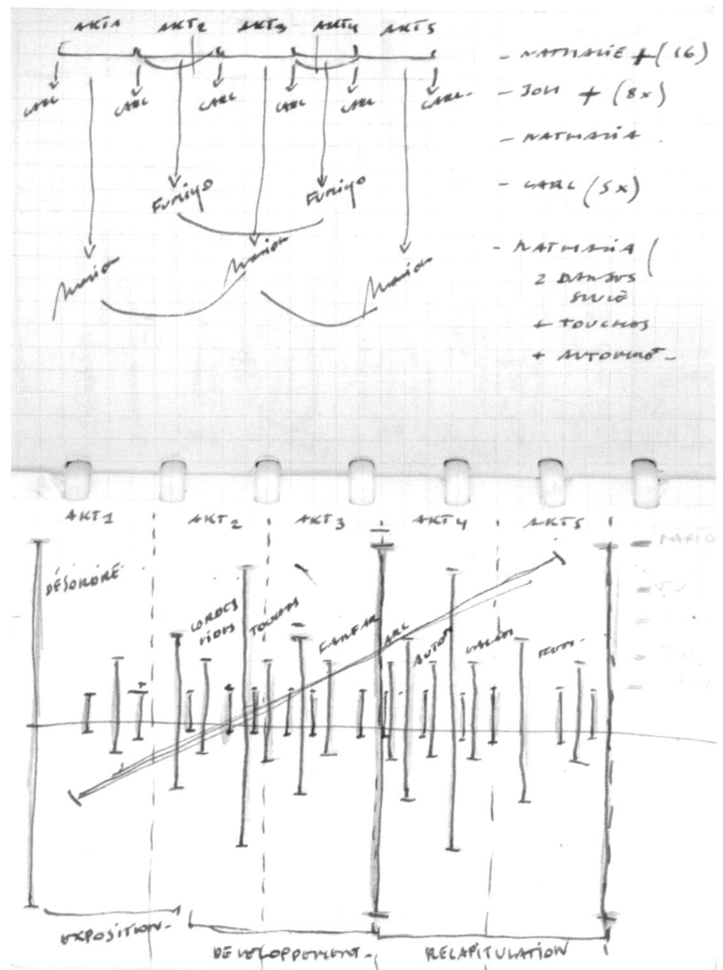

Stella (1990)

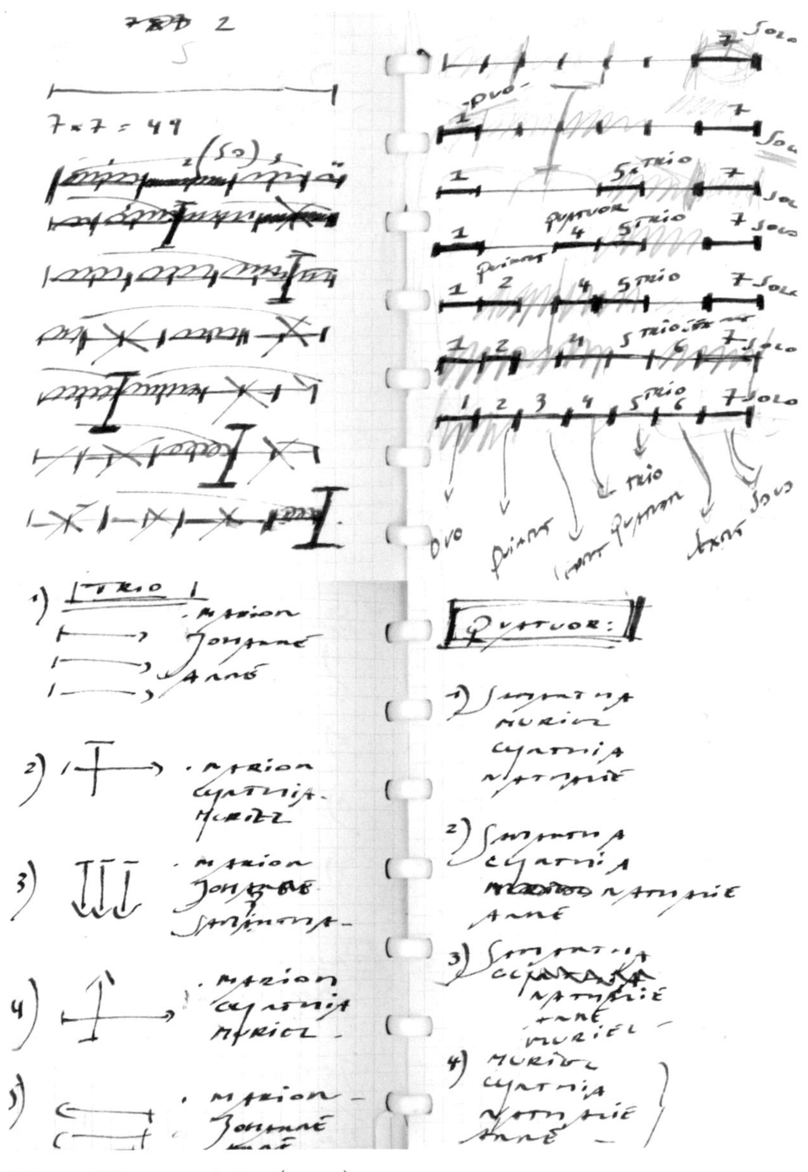

Mozart/Concert Arias (1992)

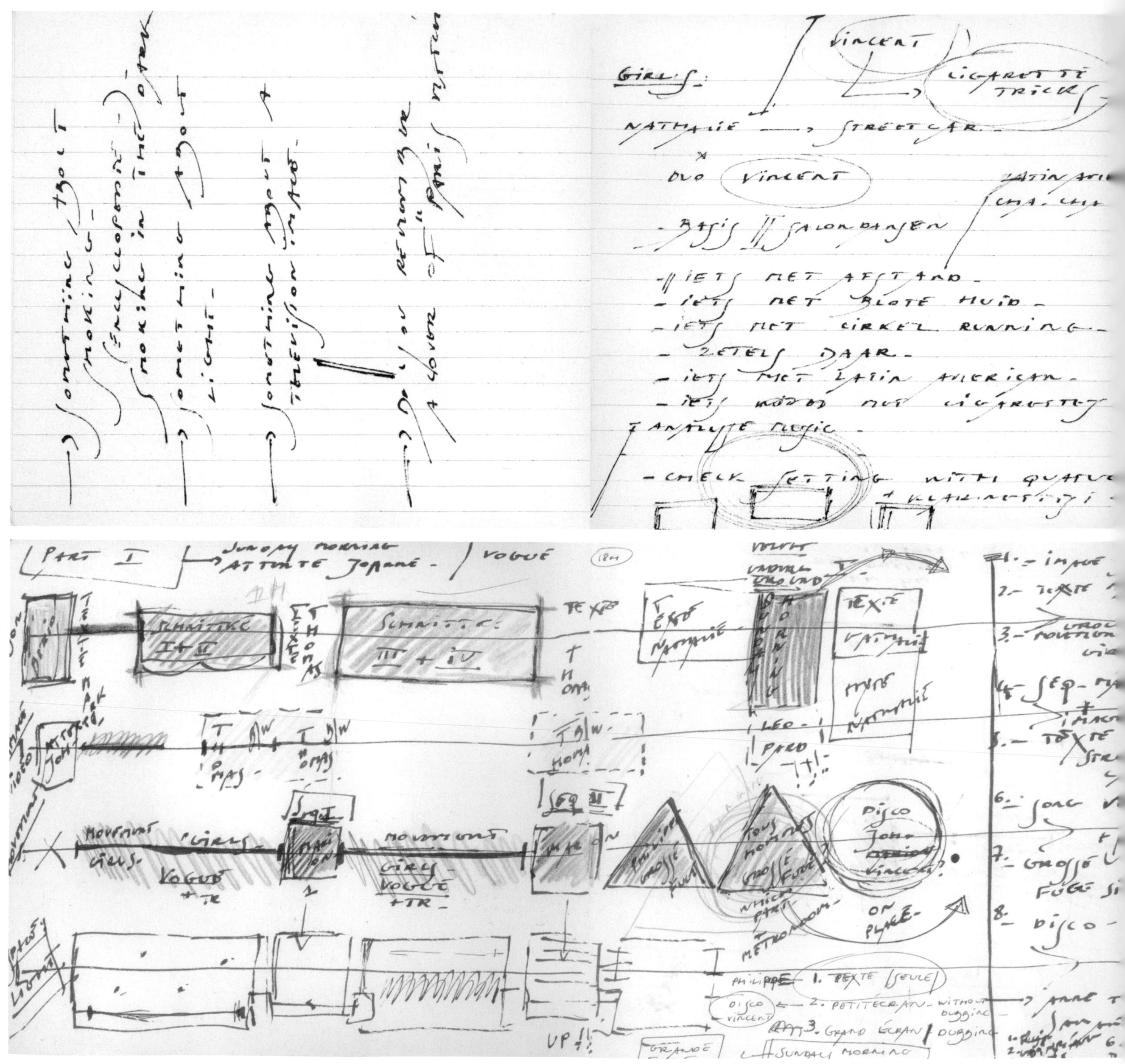

GIRLS:
VINCENT
CIGARETTE TRICKS
NATHALIE → STREETCAR
DUO VINCENT
BASIS II SALONDANSEN
IETS MET AFSTAND
IETS MET BLOTE HUID
IETS MET CIRKEL RUNNING
ZETELS DAAR
IETS MET LATIN AMERICAN
CHECK SETTING WITH QUATUOR
PART I
SUNDAY MORNING
VOGUÉ
TEXTE
DISCO
ON PLACE
PHILIPPE
1. TEXTE
2. PETIT ÉCRAN
3. GRAND ÉCRAN
SUNDAY MORNING

Erts (1992)

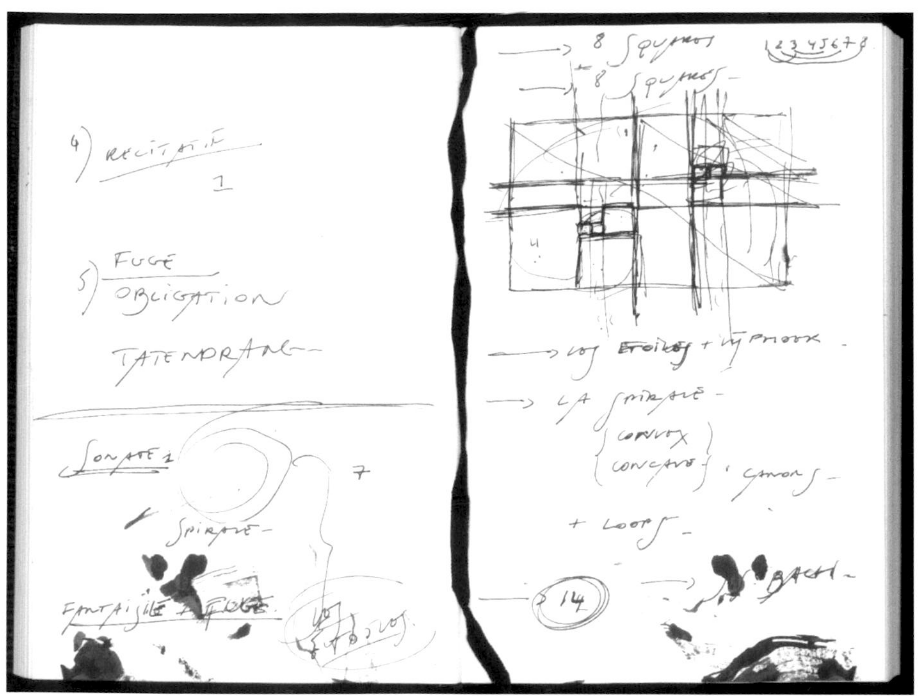

Toccata (1993)

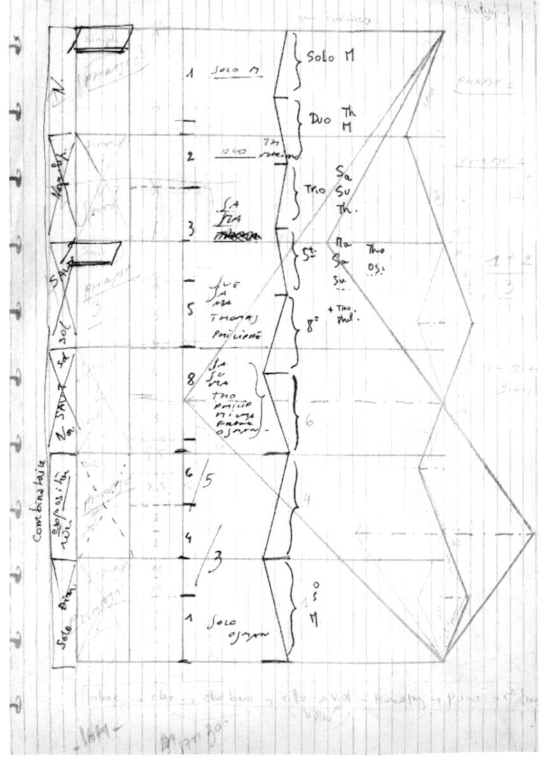

Kinok (1994)

SOLO MATERIAL
MARION
MINIATURES
— CUT UP MANIPULATIONS

SWL 1 — ALL MEN PART PRESTO DELIRANDO
→ MARION KOJ.
SWL 2

MV 1: ALLEGRETTO GIOVALE

SWL 3 → SARA.
SWL 4 →

MV 2: ANDANTE AMOROSO
P1: OK –
– HURZO –
P2: IRIS + SARA: CANON –
P3: COMING IN OF THE 3 MEN –
SWL 5 → MARION + KOJI –
FINISHING – 3 MEN + 3 WOMEN – MARION + KOJ
→ MANIPULATION +

MV 3: ALLEGRO MISTERIOSO

NEGATIVE OF SPACE →
IRIS + OLIVER: DIVIDE UP RETROGRADE OF MANIPULATION → MARION + KOJI
→ SARA + MARK –

→ SILENCE: SARA + MARION + KOJI
COMBINATION IN PHRASE MEN –

MV 4: ADAGIO APPASSIONATO

→ SARA: CONTINUES TO DO PHRASE WOMEN –
OR REPEATS WHAT SHE WAS DOING IN
PREVIOUS MOVEMENT – OR RETROGRADE –

MV 5: PRESTO DELIRANDO
→ GROT TO BIG OVERLAPP –
P: UNISONO'S –

— SOLO MARION
MV 6: LARGO DESOLATO ——

– ALLEGRO GIOVALE: OLIVER + IRIS –
ALLEGRO MISTERIOSO:
PRESTO DELIRANDO:
– IDEA: PERSON REPEATS WHAT HE WAS DOING IN PREVIOUS MOVEMENT –
E.G. SARA

Lyrical Suite (Woud)
(1995)

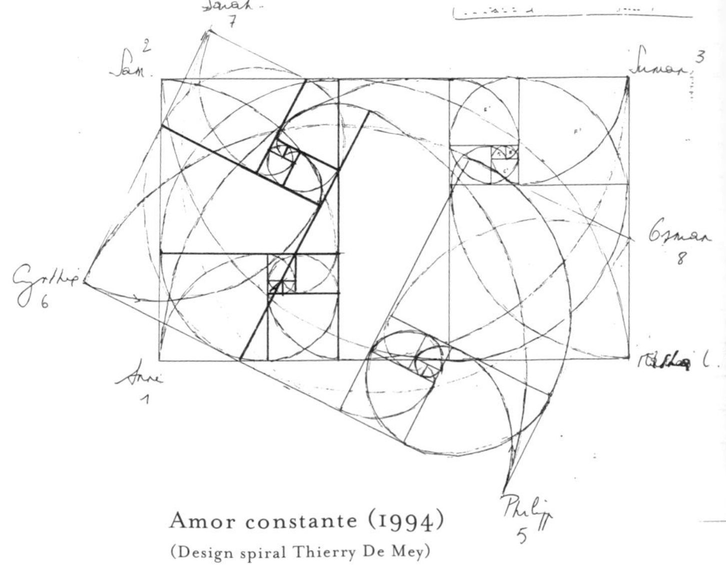

Amor constante (1994)
(Design spiral Thierry De Mey)

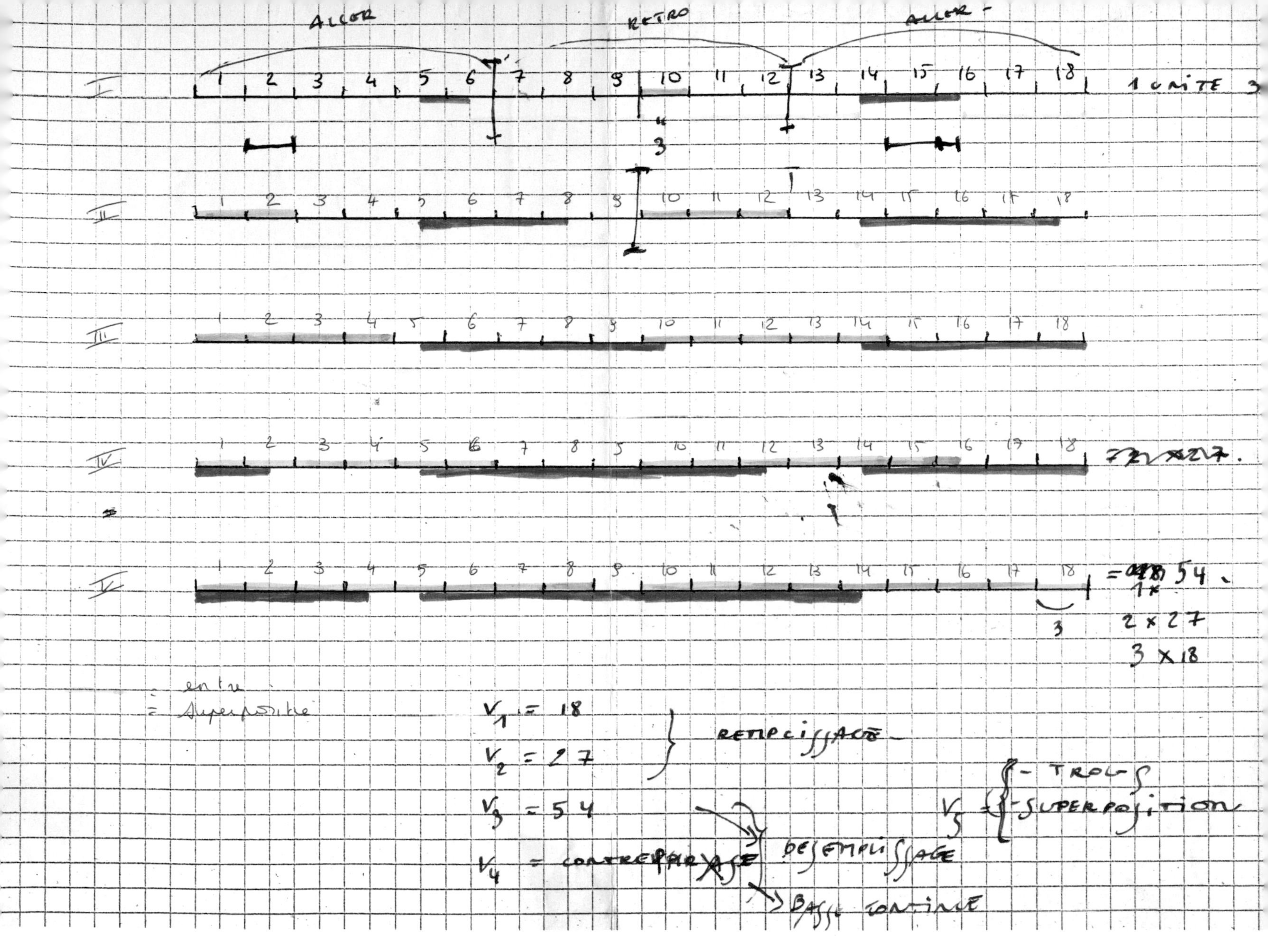

Amor constante (1994)

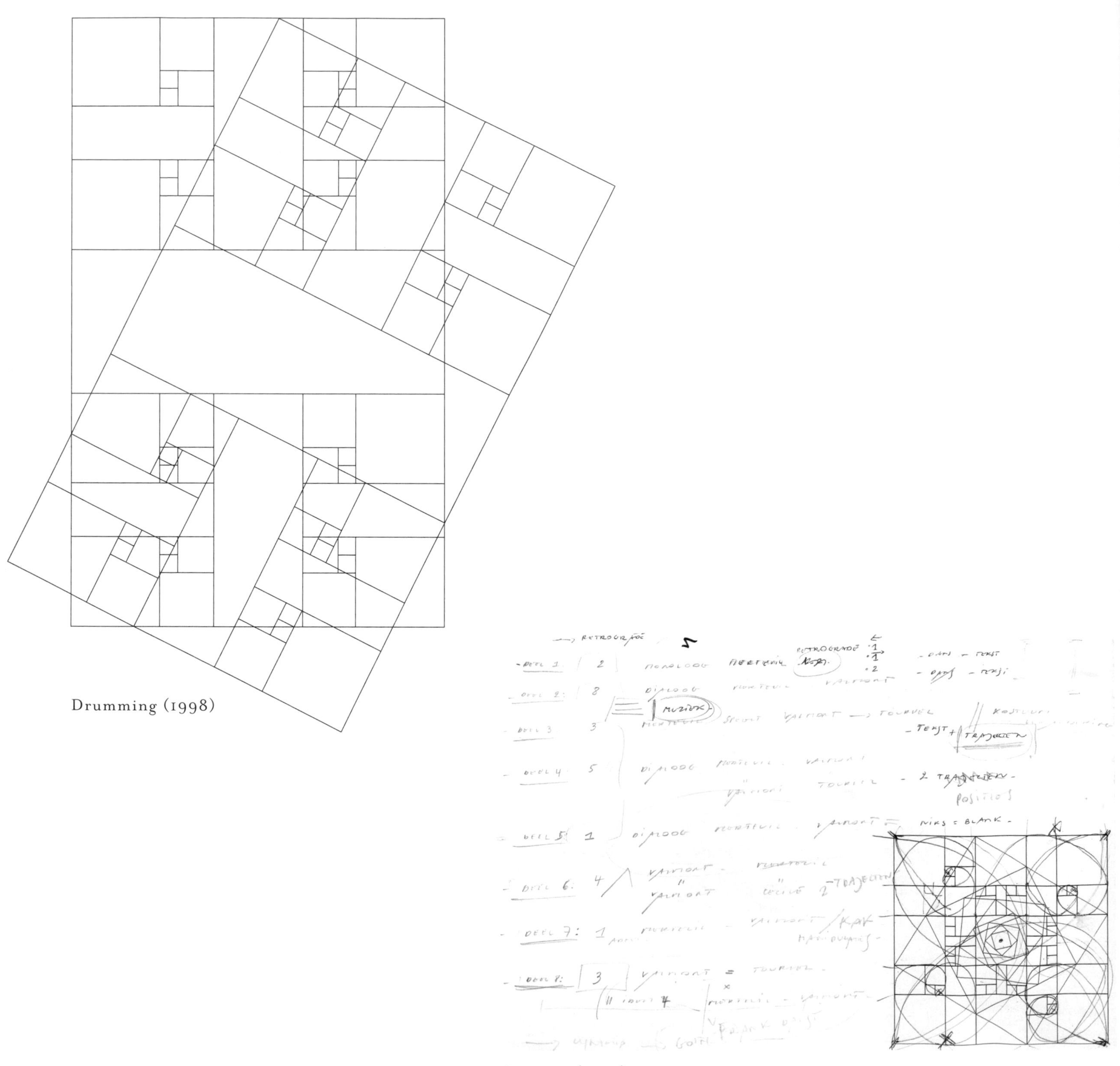

Drumming (1998)

Quartett (1999)

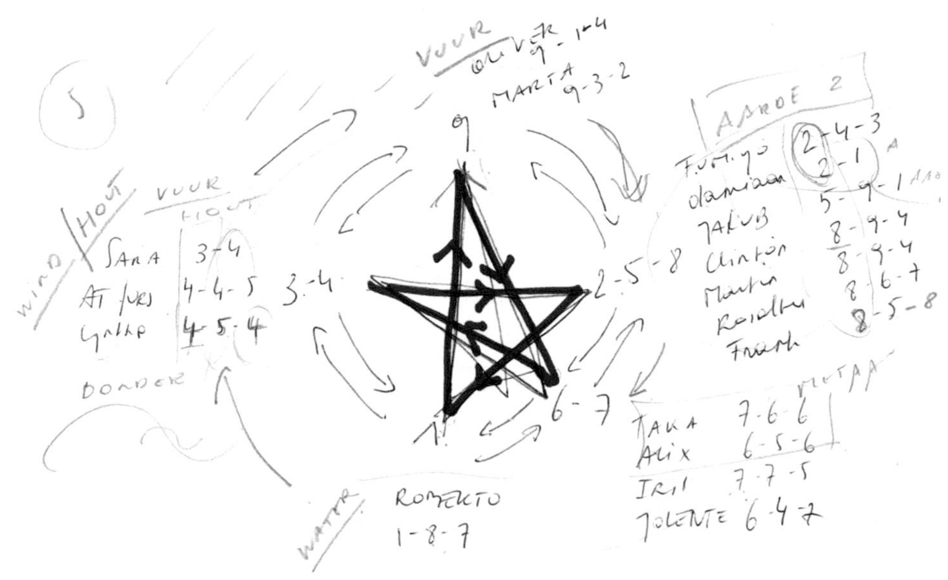

In real time (2000)

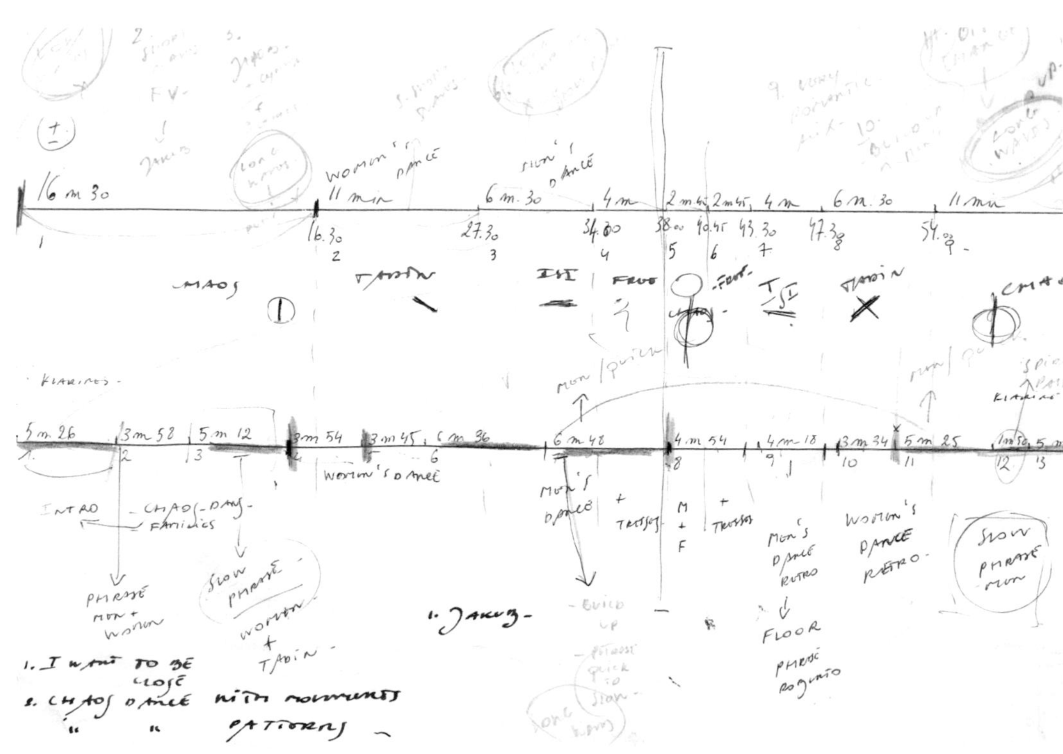

Rain (2001)

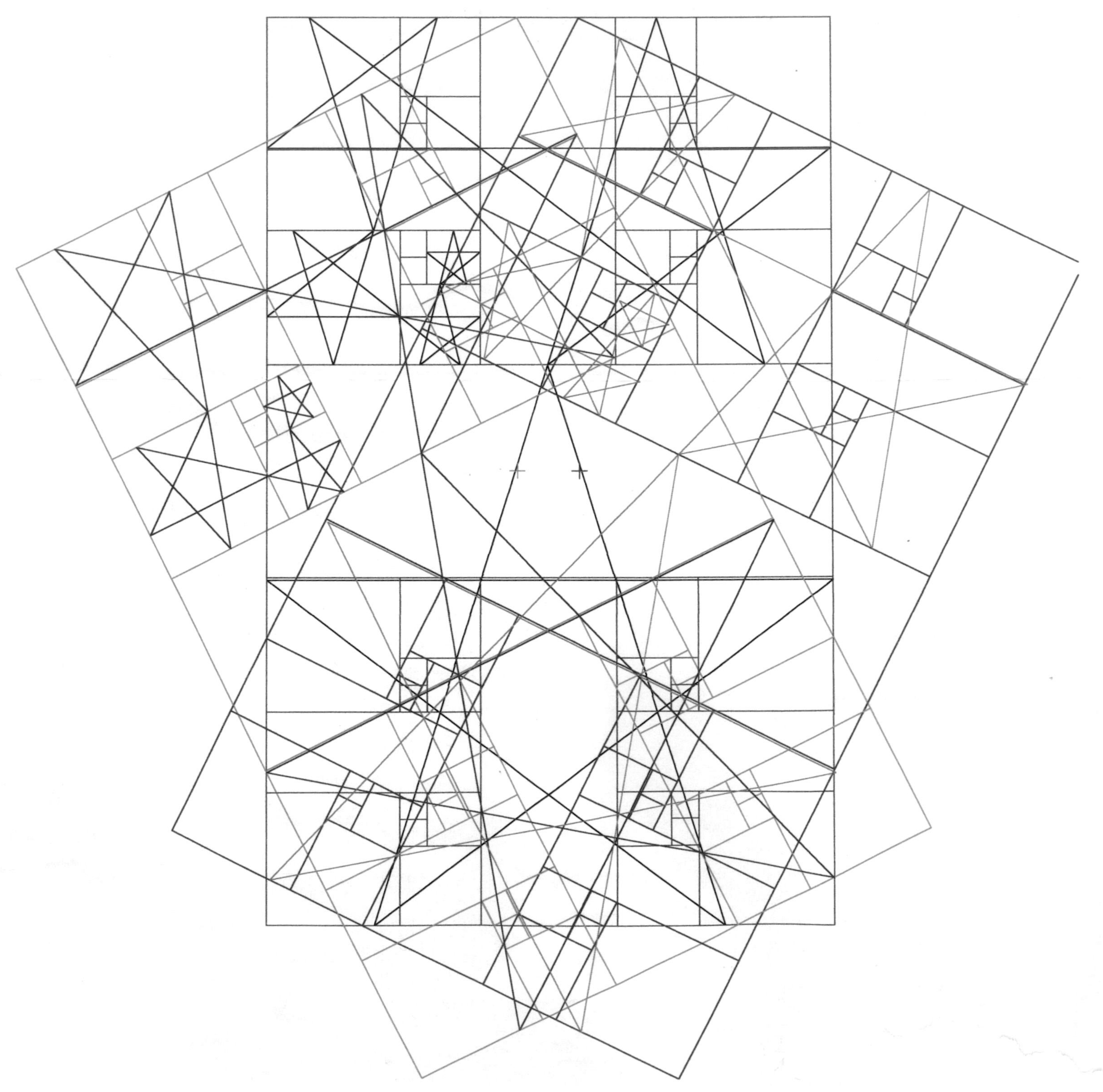

In real time (2000)

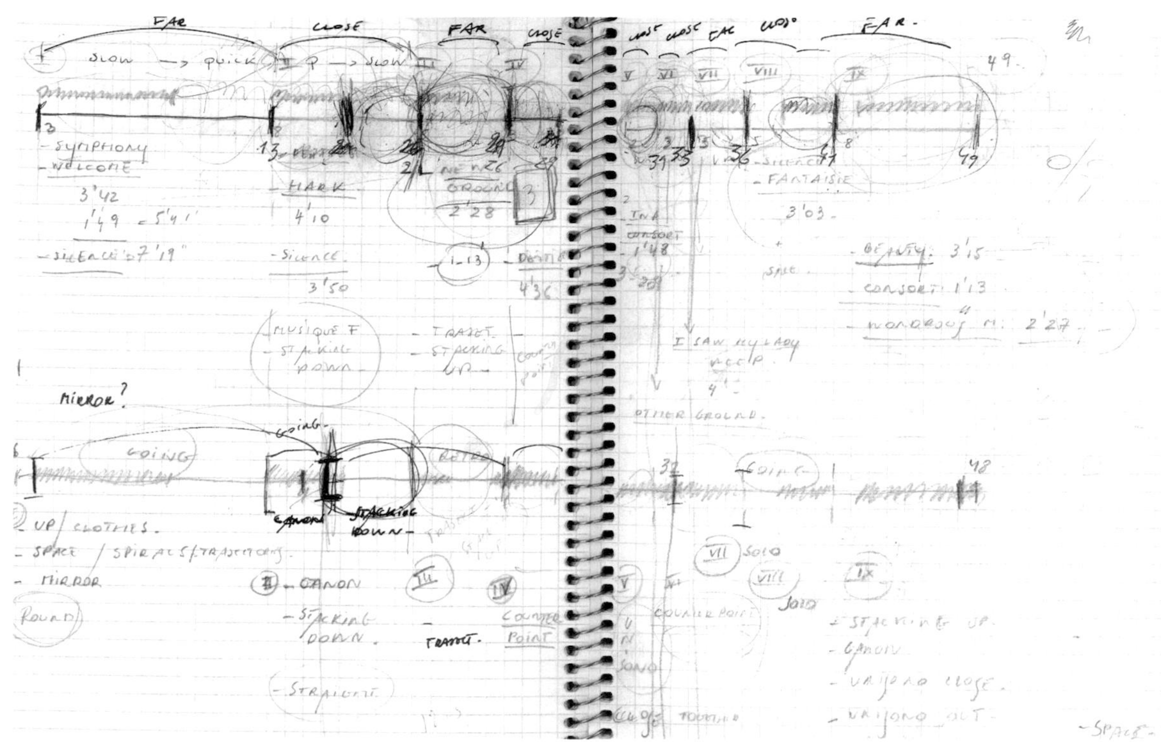

Small hands (2001)

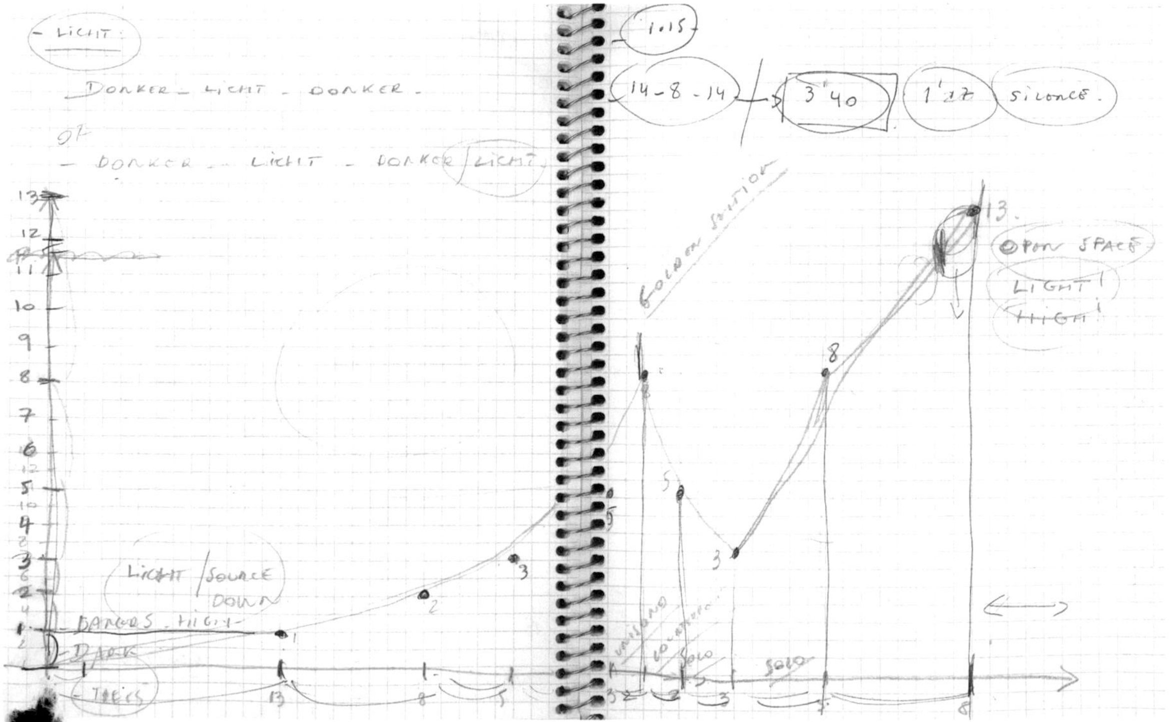

l hands (2001)

Essays

Fibonacci Fragments
Anne Teresa de Keersmaeker and music

Jean-Luc Plouvier

First embrace

In 1983, with the second movement of *Rosas danst Rosas*, Anne Teresa de Keersmaeker and Thierry De Mey invented a completely new relationship between dance and music. In the famous, minimal 'chair quartet', the dance's entire development is completely subservient to the musical structure, sequence by sequence, second to second. The music itself is derived from a number game – at least the core rhythms and tempo – and is forcefully, almost brutally accented. The prevailing atmosphere is very 'rock'. In answer to this doubly merciless music (its sonority and the excruciating counts) the movement material responds with gesture built largely on erotic poses: short and seductive movements – a hand smoothing hair, the covering of a nude shoulder; arms stretched tautly between thighs; heads thrown back in abandonment; breathlessness. There is maximum tension – a war is going on between the driving impulse of the movement and the choreography itself, between the vocabulary (specific to dance) and the use of it (subordinate to the music). This experiment, this first masterpiece of a very young choreographer, set the tone for the adventure Anne Teresa de Keersmaeker would have with music: a story of fascination, of war and peace and of an embrace that is yearned for as much as it is feared.

Too much, too little

So, it's all about finding a connection between music and dance, but there's is no certainty that there is a connection. Nevertheless that doesn't mean we can say that there are many connections , more or less cleverly measured, more or less equal. No, but there is something, something precious and wilful: a special request made by dance to music; a utopian rapport, a fictional relationship. Something that has never really existed, that never will, but that creates a thousand interesting connections by continuing to insist. Excessively. Or by default.

Too much: formalism, analysis, diagrams, schemes; subjection of the body to sums, of time to divisions, of space to limits. Or too little: sense, coherence, unity, an accumulation of events until the space is saturated, sudden outbursts of hysteria [illegible]struction of directing lines in a deluge of anecdotes. This is how they denigrate her work, the restless Rosas detractors – greedy for harmony, precision, humanity and emotion: too much o[illegible]ch disorder. Too much coldness, too much chaos. The art [illegible] and of [illegible], of nerves.

Ultimate resistance

Thierry De Mey recently spoke about his work on *Rosas danst Rosas*.[1] 'In those days we were very into the texts of Georges Bataille. His analyses of the discontinuity language introduces in instinctive continuity, and all attempts for reunification where ecstasy and transgression come together. To achieve this, we first needed an extremely sturdy form, a real structural wall, into which the four dancers would crash with all their might. In this case the structure was a kind of merciless master who enforced limits and imposed speed and effort on the body; the entire choreographic vocabulary on the other hand had more to do with desire and consisted mainly of sexual attitudes and impulses. It was tension and contrast between a cold, predetermined, irreversible form, running towards its logical end, and the physical gift of the dancers, who, through endless repetitions of a small number of highly connotated gestures, became highly erotisised. In the end, it became a [illegible]ification of the body as the ultimate resistance to numbers.'

This experience later caused Thierry De Mey to set up the Maximalist! sextet. Its name brilliantly sums up the project – minimalism with reversed aesthetics. The use of the obvious processes of minimalist music remained, immediately discernable as repetitiveness. However, the soft, almost mystical experience of rolling, cyclical time was discarded, replaced by the exhilaration of boundless physical exertion.

Thierry De Mey's words strike us by their violence. They take us back to a source of creative intuition that has been tamed by time and covered with a 'classical' patina. For this young choreographer and musician creating a ballet, giving dance a form, meant building up a wall, enforcing a master on oneself, using bolts, establishing irreversible rules. And the dancers had to crash into these rules, this wall, this master with all their might in a highly eroticised state, in a gesture of ultimate resistance.

If we are willing to take this statement seriously, we have to know how things were in 1983: basically, music stood for form, which meant numbers, which are violent and limiting for the body. Dance stood for desire, which meant transgression and ultimately exhausted victory over enforced order. (More precisely: on sought for order).

This radicalism has somewhat softened over the years and has become more complex; it has outsmarted itself and looked for more discrete ways and means. We could also say that the music has become melodious, it has learnt how to seduce the seducers, it has broken down all resistance. Yet it is difficult not to see in *Rosas danst Rosas*, the original hallmark of De Keersmaeker's style – and, in accordance with the fiction – music giving dance a numerical key to form. It was for the bodies to submit to it whilst simultaneously resisting it in all possible ways, to produce, in fine, immeasurable and glorious results.

Mythology

One day people will probably rightly say that Anne Teresa de Keersmaeker's greatest merit is the fact that she looked intensely for a new connection between music and dance. It's already almost mythology: I've been surrounded by that myth since I was twenty, before I even knew its heroine. The myth goes that De Keersmaeker is not the type of choreographer who uses music in the background during dinner parties, nor is she a parvenu who wants to prove she was moved by Mahler or has dined with Boulez. To her, music is not décor, nor a pretext or something minor. Her dances really are dialogues with music. She includes its formal foundations, analyses its architecture, illuminates its polyphony. That is what really intrigued me. I was twenty and studying at the Conservatory. I quivered when I heard about Rosas' notorious witchcraft: those beautiful dancers actually knew how to read music, knew what harmony and counterpoint were. In rehearsal, they effortlessly resumed from bar 613, and turned over the violinist's pages in between entrechats.

Great pieces and tiny panties

With more gentleness and humour, the relationship between music and dance in *Rosas danst Rosas* was consolidated by *Mikrokosmos*, in 1987, in the women's quartet, danced to the music of Bartók's *Fourth Quartet*. Anne Teresa and composer Walter Hus had analysed all the score's bars together. She marked each canon with a red pencil, every theme's entry, all the pivotal points linked to the Golden Section (Bartók and de Keersmaeker both being lovers of the Golden Section).[2]
Set precisely on the music up until the last bar (the wonderful way the four girls return to the chairs at the back of the stage and drop down exhaustedly for the last time on the final cord) the style of choreography contradicts the hugeness of the undertaking. The dancers whisper, exchange wicked glances like naughty schoolgirls; show their knickers; behave like untameable, cheeky femmes-enfants. The kind of insolence we see here is, nevertheless, ingenuous: Bartók is not ridiculed and his oeuvre is left in tact. It seems as if the choreographer is making fun of herself and apologising for having the presumptuousness to take on such a great piece and dissect its workings. She seems to challenge her own wisdom and perhaps apologise for it: she plays the culture game, yes, but.

Boum go the women, Hé go the men

As her exegete Marianne Van Kerkhoven puts so well, the evocation of the feminine in Anne Teresa de Keersmaeker's work is always plural, agitated, indecisive.[3] The bold one, the one in love, the crazy one, the striptease dancer, the solemn one. There are lots of women, their masks change and the question of their identity is posed again and again. When I write: music stands for form, dance stands for desire, I am inclined to add systematically: music is a man thing, and dance a woman thing (Rosas was, as we known, a strictly female group until the Ducourt-Saunier duet in *Mikrokosmos* in 1987). A hasty remark of course that doesn't clarify anything. Still, in the meditations, in the words, work, and even in the daily life of Anne Teresa de Keersmaeker (even in the food she eats, I believe) I see the reflection of a perpetual attempt to find contrasts that might conceal, explain, even pacify the exasperating and inextricable duality between men and women.

She believes this passion seized her when she was eighteen during a rhythm lesson with Fernand Schirren at Mudra, who, incidentally, had a very personal philosophy (Thierry De Mey describes him as 'a kind of Zarathustra of the Bara street, a Brussels man through and through'[4]). Schirren taught a kind of universal order that was led by the elementary, rhythmic alternations of *Boum* and *Hé*. Thierry De Mey: 'The *Hé* indicated the start of a rhythmic movement, the ejection, the leap, the bow, and by extension, difference or differentiation. The *Boum* was the finishing point, the rest, and by extension, the same or sharing.' Anne Teresa saw this as a 'variant of Yin and Yang, the feminine and the masculine'.

It is clear that her imagination was stimulated by these countless contradictions, adaptable to all areas of activity. So let us not even try to answer the question why she explicitly worked out a small construction for personal use – a dual opposing the constellation of music-form-number-analysis-masculine against the constellation of dance-desire-body-intuition-feminine. The essential part is, that however passionately she meditated on and laboured with these countless dualities, her dance put them to the test, pulled them apart and put them together again with ever increasing complexity.

The ideal listener

As we known, the work of Merce Cunningham with John Cage completely dismantled the relationship between music and dance. Dance found itself free to develop total autonomy, outside any narrative. The pure thrill of a body able to forget everything it knows at the peak of its technical prowess. Cage made this dichotomy possible through the strange neutral quality of his music, in which no sound, however loud, ever loses contact with the silence it came from. But without Cage who, in his unique madness, toyed with the total evaporation of all possibilities for music, would dance have found another solution to preserve its freedom other than choosing silence once and for all?

Choreographers have continued to use music: not for its narrative, nor for the disjunction with dance. But, all things considered, for its detail: the detail of texture, of density, of a rhythmic frisson, of a suggestion that can resonate with the action on stage. So, all these connections are possible after all.

What is so special about Anne Teresa de Keersmaeker is that she refused the narrative, and the disjunction, and the relation to detail too. She loved beautiful shapes and wanted to grasp the music as a form.[5] That is why she needed to meet 'contemporary music' musicians, who are more sensitive than others to the difficult question: if you listen to a piece of music, do you listen to a form? Must, can listening be homogenous with the structure of a piece?

(We can suppose that Anne Teresa de Keersmaeker is secretly the ideal listener for many musicians. The question: 'Could there be a connection between music and dance? – can dance read music?' is exactly the same as: 'Is there an ideal way of listening to the piece, without distractions, without daydreaming, without disturbing disruptions?')

A certain disruption

In a beautiful book that appeared last year, musicologist Peter Szendy talks about the paradoxes of order: 'You have to listen!' – be it exteriorised or interiorised.[6] I quote: 'While the command in this imperative does not permit questions (you have to!), the activity it commands (listening) seems less easy to define: what is listening, what is listening if you do it because you have to? Is this an activity at all?' In his analysis of what historically, in the light of the quasi-religious cult devoted to Beethoven, has become the listening duty of the modern music lover, he speaks of his doubt about the idea of *completely adequate listening*, what Adorno called *structural listening*. He asks this question by throwing the ball back to his preachers through a comic reference to Beethoven's deafness: 'We for our part can wonder if this total listening is perhaps a form deafness on the part of the of the listener. Listening without any thoughts, without being distracted by 'the sounds of life', can we still call this listening? Does listening not also mean being aware of a certain disruption outside?'

Throughout the entire book loneliness is a recurrent theme – we are oh so alone when contemplating the oeuvre. How can we let others listen to the way we listen?, he wonders. 'Indeed, I would love to claim ownership and undersign my way of listening. (...) What I would like to do is mark it, identify it and share such an auditory experience that no one but me – I am convinced of this- has ever heard the way I have. There is no doubt about it. I am even convinced that the experience of listening to music is comparable to this desire and conviction. In other words: listening – and not hearing or perception – begins with this legitimate desire to own and offer it to others.'

I believe the two theories advanced by Peter Szendy – the question of one perfect form of listening and the desire to enhance listening by communicating it to others – are also entwined in Anne Teresa de Keersmaeker's work, in a less 'magisterial', more fragile way than one might think. By putting the musicians on stage, by never being overawed by the prestige of the pieces (not even the *Grosse Fuge* of Beethoven, which surprised quite a few people) by refusing to cut (she has never made a choreography on a 'second movement', for example, always complete works) she has broken with ballet's traditions and invented a type of performance that immediately states that the music will be taken seriously, that it has to be listened to as if it were being played at a concert (attentive listening). The dance that slips into the centre of this unexpected concert (if we look at it this way) now appears as a music-lovers declaration, the flesh and blood incarnation of a special listening experience: undersigned listening as Szendy calls it, to a piece not just chosen according to the choreographer's taste, or the feelings it evokes, but is specifically chosen for what it can make the listener hear.

What has personally touched me is that this form of listening, Anne Teresa's temperamental, formalistic yet disparate, passionate and slightly mocking way of listening seems to be offered first and foremost to the musicians, to all those who are torn apart by the music. Because all musicians are torn apart: between the conscientious practice and the secret desire to get carried away, between good listening and the risky pleasure of detail, between respect and desire, form and fragment. Her ideal audience is probably a musician.

Thierry's notebooks

Art historian Esteban Buch writes the following about Peter Szendy's book: 'Structural, global, teleological, no pausing, no favourites, no zapping, no sampling or being led astray – this is compulsory listening and I want to get rid of it. I often want to get rid of it in order to dream of a world of sound where everything is a favourite of mine, or not there at all. (...) But as soon as the trend is reversed, a retro club might have to be set up, which would then in fact be a club for utopians, fans of structural listening, drunk on continuity, direction, happy endings, perfect rhythms (...) Discovering a structure can also be moment of jubilation.'[7]

I want to give this last sentence a moment's thought, it sounds familiar, it has a face: it could be a sentence by Thierry De Mey, and it probably is. Many of Anne Teresa's intellectual pleasures remain unclear unless you know about her long and passionate friendship with Thierry De Mey. It is interesting to have seen him showing his notebooks of renaissance paintings, full of beautiful shapes: paradoxical numeral series, magic squares, reversible processes, extensive, deceptive, spiral shaped, plaited, in a Mobius band... And to have seen her, bent over her sketches, already working out a choreography, never forgoing the benevolent irony directed towards the dishevelled, shambolic older brother. The entire experience of *Kinok* was about : 'Discovering a structure can also a be moment of jubilation. To put it in the words of Szendy: the mutual pleasure Anne Teresa and Thierry give each other.

Chronometrics (1)

In several recent pieces she borrows a typical Cage-Cunningham object: the chronometer. It is in *In Real Time* that it is most visible (it is impossible for the audience not to follow it) and is also used in the most ambiguous way. In one way it strengthens the Rosas mythology and reminds the audience they are in a highbrow place of serious learning, where there is a whole cult around the power of the Form. Time is strictly divided, the interventions are precisely measured, and the musicians are saving their best piece for the Golden Section moment. However, the fact that the chronometer is counting backwards (from three hours to nought) in a situation of improvisation means a very different kind of suspense is generated – we have 180 minutes for something to happen, for the grace of the dance improvisations to meet that of the musicians and for some unexpected sparks to fly – or not. The paradoxical message of *In Real Time*, which would also fit a large part of Anne Teresa's oeuvre since *Violin Phase* and would express both measure and loss, is perhaps this: time is limited.

Chronometrics (2)

Rosas dancers have always had to count a lot. Trusting musical cues or partners is rarely sufficient to perform Anne Teresa de Keersmaeker's elaborate counterpoints that pass through a spectrum ranging from strict unison to the unbridled multiplication of danced voices. Counting the repetitions of a movement, counting pulsations before a canon entry, counting the time needed to cover a distance... and then to do it with ease... probably the hardest thing that is asked of them (sometimes, they say, it's unbearable).

There is an amazing scene in *I said I* where dancer Martin Kilvády begins to count, *one, two, three...* into the microphone, softly measuring the tangle of paths paced by his partners. What in fact is he counting? It's hard to say: the music in this scene is improvised live by DJ Grazzhoppa, the tempo is simple... We assume that a more discrete element, an artifice hidden in the music, could have just as well structured this scene. Nothing repetitive or hypnotic like in *Einstein on the Beach*. No: he is counting time, enumerating the space; and it has to really resound as the music simply carries on...

Pretending

A hypothesis: it is the experience of improvisation, meeting improvisers, that changed her. Throughout Anne Teresa de Keersmaeker's work, there are sometimes painful, unexpected swings between the confinement of numbers and the refusal of any stable form, in other words – an oscillation between the duty to read musical compositions and respect their coherence and the desire to secretly love them and escape, just by chance. All this toeing and froing is gradually becoming less frantic. Not thanks to harmony or synthesis, but thanks to a softer, more confident, pendular movement. New savoir-faire has gradually crept into her choreographic technique: the art of pretending.

It was already visible in the choreography of the *Suite Lyrique* by Alban Berg (in *Woud*, from 1997) and was recently consolidated in *Drumming* and after that in *Rain* (to *Music for Eighteen Musicians* by Steve Reich): the music is no longer a structural wall and the dancers no longer – to come back to the words of Thierry De Mey – crash into it with all their might. Slowly but surely De Keersmaeker seems to have stopped reading the music through dance and has accepted, whether she likes it or not, interpretation, in order to be able to add a layer to the counterpoint. Not submission, not transgression, not neglect, but a higher bid. You could say her uncertainty is slowly disappearing, and her irony with it. Although something does remain from past experiences, from a former, more obedient (and more cheeky) relationship with the music; it is made of meticulousness, formal correspondences, temporal concordances, and, inevitably, bold slip-ups (such as in the recent *Noces*, an almost autonomous fragment from *April Me* and a virtuoso replica of the style of *Mikrokosmos*). But all this is only fiction right now. Nothing seems to remain of the Rosas mythology that has to be believed or denied because the tables have turned: it seems as if the music, in its unfolding, in its advancing and retreating, through its anticipations, through its symmetries and in its imperious taking up of time, sets off the dancers' movements, leads their variations, canons, spirals, etc. But at the same time we can see clearly that this is not the case: the dance is elsewhere, always already elsewhere, ready to provoke new shifts, tap new logics... endlessly. I find the *Suite Lyrique* and *Drumming* are the best Rosas moments for me, ones that bring about genuine amazement: an absurd equation of time and space that goes mad and is annihilated in a furious desire for limitlessness. The polyphony begins; it is no longer a form; it becomes a thousand voices, ready to welcome a thousand other ones.

A vague memory

Throughout *Drumming*, just like in *Music for Eighteen Musicians*, Steve Reich uses the very precise counterpoint technique in which he excels: short musical figures are defracted by multiple canons, squeezed together until they form an inextricable texture, a polyphonic block. The composer then makes a cut in this block and extracts a new figure from it, a 'resultant' that seems to be loosening itself from the texture like a snake shedding its skin. What is the similarity between this procedure and the entwined stars and spirals drawn on the dancefloor that guide the dancers' movements in *Drumming* (the ballet)? And what links this process with the sections of *Rain*, in which the nine elements of Chinese astrology are hidden, themselves connected to a game of colours [illegible]nd characters which, in turn, is contradicted by the persistent presen[illegible]f the Golden Section and Fibonacci's series?[8] And I don't dare even [illegible]ntion the exploration [illegible]f the dualities (masculine and feminine ph[illegible], Yin and Ya[illegible] moveme[illegible] and so on). In short – this mess, these [illegible]or less auton[illegible]us, structural layers – what do they have in comm[illegible]thing, as far [illegible] know.

Some may be tempted to say that Anne Teresa de Keersmaeker, a keeper of the form from the start, has, thanks to much diligence and mischief, study and refusal, admiration and provocation, at the end of a fascinating tête-à-tête with the music, eventually reinvented the Cage-Cunningham solution. The separation of disciplines, each in its own kingdom. This is how she treats Purcell in *Small hands*: she leaves him royally alone. Nonc, or few structural similarities in this collage of short pieces, no History or baroque, no more jokes, but instead a floating ear open to the play of disharmonies shaken by rhythm. Not even that: behind the rhythm – a tremble of joy and behind that – nothing; a beat, almost as inaudible as silence. Now that would be quite a story, would it not? A moral epic: the slow conquest of her freedom by the freedom of the other, or some such similar.

If only it was not the pretending that gives her latest style special appeal. This vague memory of having dreamed of true equality, of concordance, of a real meeting. And of having fled the dream, of having urgently devised an escape route. I can imagine she will never completely give it up, her dream and her torment. That she wants to fight a duel with the music, red pencil in hand. Theatre diverted her from it, then she returned. After all, Anne Teresa has no taste for 'open work' where the artist is happy to propose several chance outcomes and trusts that the audience will appreciate the pertinence of them. Just look at the extreme care with which she works out the opening and final scenes of an outstandingly sharp performance, often set right on the music, undeniable proof of how premeditated the piece is right through to its end.

Enjoy the party

In the light of the anniversary celebrations that coincide with the publication of this book, it is interesting to know that Anne Teresa will soon make a choreography to her old Joan Baez tapes, 'a reminder of her teens'.

During your teens: you put on music, close your eyes, and pretend the music will guide all your movements now and forever. You let go of it later on: the time then comes for learning, building, knowing.

Rosas celebrates its twentieth anniversary, Anne Teresa her twentieth year as a choreographer. Forty-two and two children. Her second adolescence.

1 Thierry De Mey, conversation with J.-L. Plouvier. Programme of the 2001 Musica festival, Strasbourg.

2 This preceding analysis later became more professional with conductor Georges-Elie Octors, whose fifteenth 'syllabus' for music analysis, which he systematically publishes before each new production, is out now.

3 Marianne Van Kerkhoven and Rudi Laermans, *Anne Teresa de Keersmaeker. Kritisch Theater Lexicon*, Vlaams Theater Instituut, 1998.

4 Thierry De Mey, quoted text.

5 These few words are used to clarify the most specific characteristics of Anne Teresa de Keersmaeker's relationship with music: the three-part relationship between music, dance and form, form meaning all procedures for musical pieces throughout time, which can be analysed or even made mathematical. No matter how obstinate, this relationship was never absolute in a naive way, it has in fact always been immoral to a various extent – and this is precisely why there is style. Other 'nodes' have been tried out, I will not elaborate on them: the music-dance-sense for example, where the disciplines meet through poetry used in vocal music, which conjures up analogies in the danced material (in *Mozart/Concert Aria's*), or the composer's literary, programmatic or bibliographical words (like in *Verklärte Nacht* about Arnold Schönberg's music).

6 Peter Szendy, *Écoute. Une histoire de nos oreilles*. Éditions de Minuit, 2001.

7 Text published on the site of Entretemps: www.entretemps.asso.fr

8 Fibonacci's series begins with 1 and 1 and continues this way, in which each number is the sum of the two previous ones: 1, 1, 2, 3, 5, 8, 13... The further one goes in the series, the more the quotient of two successive numbers give a precise approximation of the Golden Section, an approximation alternately rounded up and down. In her choreographies, Anne Teresa de Keersmaeker makes plentiful use of this series, for example when structuring the irregular canon.

The Trajectory of a Hand

Sara Jansen

To mark the 20th anniversary of Anne Teresa de Keersmaeker's *Fase, four movements to the music of Steve Reich* (1982), long term collaborator Thierry De Mey created a video installation featuring the third part of this ground breaking performance, a short solo piece entitled *Violin Phase*. The video shows De Keersmaeker dancing the solo from an aerial perspective, tracing her choreography in a fragile surface of white sand. As the dark ground underneath the sand begins to reveal itself, her feet begin to inscribe a circle onto this pristine surface. She subsequently starts to traverse this circle, dividing it initially into four equal parts, then eight. The *phasing* in the choreography and the constant shifting of the dancer's torso as she continues to travel around it, cause the circle and the eight lines emanating from its center to be jagged and slightly undulating. The drawing in the white surface reveals a flower, a rose, *rosas*. As the performance continues, the repetition of the movements, the traveling along the same trajectory over and over again, begins to blur the figure traced in the sand. The dance effaces its own tracings, and only fragments of the (rose) pattern remain.

The image is extremely provocative, as it reveals choreography as an act of *writing*, writing that embodies a tremendous sense of ephemerality, and is in a state of constant transformation, always vulnerable to erasure – the inscription of a trajectory on the volatile surface of fine white sand. Superimposing both the movement of the writing and that of effacing the same writing, the video piece not only visualizes how dance writes in space but also highlights its intimate involvement with time/temporality. The remarkable writing and *un-writing* of the trajectory drawn by the dancer's feet concretizes the tension, inherent to the medium of dance, that is found between the extremely powerful physical presence of the dancer's body (its materiality) and the imminent disappearance of the event (its ephemerality).1

This extraordinary video piece reflects also on choreographic notation. It characterizes notation as a sort of tracing or marking, as a form of writing that is direct, unedited, still very much connected with the physical gestures of the writer, and as writing that is incomplete (a draft, sketch, or trace) but extremely rich (pregnant) at the same time. The writing is simultaneously very close to and far removed from the dance. This tension is equally manifest in Anne Teresa de Keersmaeker's personal archive, a remarkable collection, an excessive one hundred notebooks accumulated over the last twenty years that hold an abundance of choreographic notation, musical analysis, dramaturgical notes, lists, and ideas. In its totality, this archive offers invaluable insight into how a performance is developed, what its (literary, cinematic, musical) sources are, how these sources are transformed and translated into movement, and how movement phrases and performances in turn are transcribed and recorded. It also reveals how an oeuvre takes shape over the years, what evolution takes place, what kind of elements recur, and how different performances are internally connected. Taking a closer look at this material also raises a myriad of questions about the connections and intersections between dance/choreography and writing.

The notebooks are full of sketches and jottings, with fragments of writing. Even though the collection offers itself as one large text (and I am approaching it that way here), this is not a finished text and is not intended to become one. The notebooks are not meant for the public eye. Intimate and hermetic, the writing remains largely *illegible* to the outsider. The emphasis is on an activity (the writer at work), on the thinking, planning, and developing process. More than on the text, the emphasis is on what precedes it, how it came into being, its history and its context. The reader is also drawn to the texture of the *text* and its figurative qualities. The notebooks are quite beautiful as objects, and the writing is infused with the passion, the pleasure, the desire to move that a performance such as *Violin Phase* exudes – the endless repetition, looping, whirling to the point of exhaustion, exaltation, exhilaration. The text is interspersed with graphics, accompanied by elaborate multi-colored drawings and diagrams. Parts of the writing are crossed out or covered with blotches of ink or coffee. Including a variety of writing styles and colors, the collection in its entirety acquires a graphic, *visual* dimension. The careful selection of old-fashioned marbled notebooks and calligraphy pens reveals the interest of the writer in this aspect.

The books contain a large variety of information: from traces of everyday life (phone numbers, 'to do' lists); drafts for personal and official letters; notes taken during rehearsals, to records of auditions; citations of literary work, poetry, and film; textual analysis; lists of options for music; designs for costumes and sets; lists of names of dancers and their possible divisions in solos, duos, and trios; drawings of floor patterns; tour schedules; technical information; and incurred expenses. The writing is often interrupted: a draft of a letter to a funding institution is encroached upon by a series of letters or numbers, outlining the sequence of a chain of movement phrases. Words and spirals spill into the margins and spread out onto the inside and outside covers of the notebooks. At times whole sections are crossed out, 'shit', 'merde', and 'stront' written all over them. In one of the first notebooks, De Keersmaeker, in search of a name for her company, inscribes page upon page with *Rosas*, in all directions, in a variety of writing styles, over and over again. French, Flemish, English, and German appear in an eclectic mix. Internal conversations ('trying to combine systems of acceleration,' 'verder gericht werken – het totale schema in het hoofd houden!!!') and external dialogues ('Quelle syteme? Eh, Oui!' 'I think this is shit! So do I') happen on and between the pages. De Keersmaeker takes on different roles, different voices: the dancer, the choreographer, the director ('plaats vrijlaten, be careful with your chairs'), the private person.

The repetition, revision, and crossing out reveal a restlessness, an intensity, at times a real struggle. The writing, especially in the notebooks Anne Teresa De Keersmaeker completed while working on the first ten or so performances, reflects an intense process of brainstorming, rumination, and calculation. For *Ottone Ottone* (1988) alone, she filled up almost thirty notebooks, trying to organize the (new) elements of the performance – this was the first time she had worked with an opera, with a story, with colorful costumes – and had had to tackle the challenges involved in making the leap from working with five dancers to working with a diverse group of sixteen dancers and actors. This particular selection includes separate booklets for textual analysis, music (musical analysis of the opera, Monteverdi's *L'Incoronazione de Poppea*, as well as numerous lists of popular songs, from Dolly Parton to Prince), the divisions of performers into smaller groups, clues used in improvisation exercises, and so on. The veritable explosion of notebooks show De Keersmaeker wrestle with this material, her searching for solutions for each element individually and for a structure for the performance as a whole. It points toward an insatiable hunger and voracity, and toward an underestimating, perhaps, of the difficulty of an ambitious project such as *Ottone Ottone*.

Looking at the collection of notebooks as a whole, the connections between the different performances become very clear. The story of the Rosas oeuvre reflects frequent returns to previously visited places as well as giant leaps forward. New challenges are confronted in many performances; elements from previous performances are countered or further developed or refined in new pieces. Movement phrases are repeated, transformed, translated and presented in a different context or a more *pure* dance form in another choreography. Charting the oeuvre as a whole, one sees it develop very clear lines that follow a spiral-shaped trajectory or make full circle.

In a notebook from 1980, when De Keersmaeker is preparing *Asch*, the young choreographer mentions her desire to 'work continuously with gaps.' She is referring to her intent to experiment with a variety of disparate elements and media (acting, dance, light, space, voice, sound), allowing them to speak for themselves and hold on to their own specificities, while pushing their limits by combining or juxtaposing them, allowing for something new to develop in *the space between*. She writes: 'every sentence, every bundle of words, taken from an existing text and placed in a new context, acquires additional value because of its place in a new language structure.' The dossier she compiles to apply for funding for this first production includes a provocative combination of photographs, drawings, poems, and an extremely eclectic bibliography.[2] The combination of a variety of elements lies at the basis of the creation process of every performance since Asch. These elements – organizing structures or systems, musical compositions, literary or cinematic sources, movement phrases – form the anchor points of a performance. Both the nature of these elements and the way in which they link together differ widely depending on a variety of aspects, including the characteristics of the music or the main text (in the case of an opera or text performance) used; and its central themes or structure, or the atmosphere or emotions it evokes. The dossier on *Asch* already outlines such explorations of the use of a variety of media as part of a search for an individual language, and of a continuous questioning and challenging of the possibilities of the medium of dance as 'a writing, a language, an art.' All of the material brought together is written into the fabric of a performance and shapes its language, its aesthetic, its movement vocabulary.

Anne Teresa De keersmaeker speaks about writing a choreography.[3] Since *Woud* (1996), but more prominently since *Just before* (1997), she starts the creation process of a new performance by writing a phrase, a movement sentence, which, especially in the most recent performances, including *Drumming* (1998), *Rain* (2001), and *Small hands* (2001), becomes the basis of an entire choreography. This movement phrase, is, much like the way in which music is composed, subsequently developed and transformed using a variety of technical devices, and returns in different guises throughout the choreography. It is in constant transformation, deconstructed and reconstructed, as the dancers in the company work on reversing ('retrograde'), accelerating or decelerating the movement phrase, executing it facing left or facing right, transposing it to the floor ('shadow'), cutting parts of it or adding other elements to it ('counting down' or 'filling up'), making it larger or smaller, performing it while isolating one part of the body, while working with a partner ('manipulations'), while traversing the stage in a particular way (adding 'traveling steps'), and so on. The different versions of the original movement phrase form the grammar, the syntax of a performance, and the center of its movement vocabulary.

Techniques used to develop a movement vocabulary, such as the ones mentioned above, are often complemented with words, images, or sentences connected with the central idea(s) of the performance. In *Mozart/Concert Arias* (1992), for instance, the narrative aspect of the music is contrasted with a highly structured movement vocabulary. In this case, *point phrases* (phrases dancers develop in pairs, one dancer pointing to a place on the others body, their bodies always touching) are subsequently pulled apart (leaving the dancers to perform their half of the phrase independently) to develop a movement vocabulary tied in with the main theme of the performance, the love between a man and a woman despite the distance between them, in turn derived from the theme of the Mozart aria at the heart of the performance, *Ch'io mi scordi di te*. The notes demonstrate how movements are also generated by examining characters in famous operas; dance scenes in films featuring Cyd Charisse, Fred

Astaire, and Ginger Rogers; and the movements of animals ('Marion: poule, chien', 'Nathalie: canard, sardine'). In *Toccata*, connections between J.S. Bach's music and the choreography are made by using the letters of the composer's name to develop a movement vocabulary. For this production, the company studied numerological systems presumably hidden in Bach's compositions. *Amor constante*, in turn, is developed around the number seven (seven days of the week, visible planets, colors of the rainbow, ...), and for *Woud*, movements are derived from images as diverse as sculptures by Auguste Rodin and stick drawings found in an article on birthing positions. Words and images used to generate a movement vocabulary are often retained and used to refer to sections of the production. Such terms begin to lead a life of their own and form an (hermetic) internal language, another layer beneath the visible language of the choreography.[4]

The notebooks are packed full of citations from literature, poems, popular songs, and films. Frequently literary and filmic sources are used to help create, deepen, and define an idea for a performance. The program notes for *Bartók/aantekeningen* (1986) include an innumerable amount of literary citations, artwork, and images.[5] The selection of the texts in this program reveals an interest in the layer(s) beneath these texts, a reading for feeling, surface (the tactility or texture of texts, and what they do to the body of the reader) or underlying emotions. They talk about death, war, inhumanity, grief, solitude, and pain in a style that emphasizes smells, sounds, and bodily experiences.[6] The same physical, visceral vocabulary typifies Heiner Müller's *Verkomenes Ufer/ Medeamaterial/ Landshaft mit Argonauten*, the first theater play Anne Teresa De Keersmaeker directed (1987). She approaches Müller's dialogue much in the same way she approaches a musical composition, by dividing it up in segments and linking these segments with specific actions and levels of movement, for instance ('laying down', 'sitting up', 'crawling'). About this process, she writes: 'One week of rehearsals have passed. With Kitty. My question was: how do I give shape to this text, to any text? Again, I am forced to conclude that in the end it is the coming together of sensibilities and movements that shape the form, carried by the text and its development. It is an unusual coinciding of form and emotion – of letting oneself be guided by movements that are the carriers of states of mind.'

In *Elena's aria* (1984) the dancers first speak text on stage (fragments from work by Tolstoy and Brecht). In *Stella* (1990) ample use is made of dialogue derived from Tennessee Williams' *A Streetcar Named Desire* and Akira Kurosawa's *Rashomon*. However, until recently, with the exception of *Medeamaterial*, such literary and filmic sources were part of the dramaturgical preparations of a piece but remained in the background in the actual performance. For *Just before*, Anne Teresa De Keersmaeker starts collaborating with her sister Jolente, a member of the theater collective Stan, and subsequently creates a series of text-centered performances: *I said I*, based on Peter Handke's Self-Accusation, Heiner Müller's *Quartett*, and *In real time*, based on texts by Gerardjan Reynders and others. For *Just before*, an entirely new text was created and developed (transformed, manipulated) with the dancers in a way similar to the techniques employed to develop a basic dance phrase.

From the very first notebooks, directional lines and spatial patterns – designs traced on the floor by the dancer's movements – abound: circles and straight lines in *Fase*, straight frontal and lateral lines in *Rosas danst Rosas*; star-shaped patterns in *Kinok*; spirals in *Amor constante* (1994). Many notebooks additionally include pages filled with small boxes, one for each scene, with dots and crosses indicating the shifts in the positions of the dancers in space, tracing their pathways, from one segment of the choreography to the next. These forms of notation, in combination with the innumerable grids and diagrams linking such shifts in the spatial positions of the dancers with gestures, objects, or actions, immediately reveal the importance of organization and structure in this oeuvre. In *Bartók/aantekeningen*, for instance, one such diagram contains columns listing 'spatial focus' (frontal, lateral, diagonal, circular, zigzag), 'numerical focus' (solo, duo, trio), 'architectural focus points', and 'shoes' (high heels, shoes, bare feet) for each scene. As a whole, *Bartók/aantekeningen* is divided into five parts (ABCBA), following the division in the music. Each segment of the musical composition is analyzed in great detail, the emotions or feelings (including seduction, desire, innocence, dissonance, aggression, and revenge) that characterize each part are pinpointed and in turn associated with other pieces of music (Bulgarian folksongs, Russian Partisan songs), written texts (the words of Corday in Weiss' *Marat/Sade*), images (family portraits, crashing cars), actions, movement phrases, spatial shapes, set design, and costumes. The non-movement elements in this performance are utilized to break up the presentation in five clear-cut segments. *Rosas danst Rosas* consists of four segments, organized around the progress of a normal day. For this performance, a musical composition in four movements was especially created by Thierry De Mey, simultaneously with the development of the choreography. *Toccata* (1993) is the first piece choreographed around spiral-shaped trajectories, developed according to the proportions of the Golden Section and Fibonacci series. This (invisible) writing on the floor, the structure and organization of the dancers' pathways, has become especially significant in recent work. Thierry De Mey has played an important role in the exploration of new possibilities in the use of floor patterns. He designed the complex star and spiral-shaped structures used in *Just before*, *Duke Bluebeard's castle* and *Drumming*, for instance, as well as the *tresses* employed in *Rain*. Since the beginning, mathematical systems regulate both time and space, and function as guiding or framing principles. Movement sentences are executed in symmetry, mirror image, or canon; cells are arranged to mirror the overall structure of the performance; spirals open and close.[7]

Anne Teresa De Keersmaeker's personal archi[illegible] contains different systems for taking note of movements in t[illegible] space, a variety of mnemonic devices that record these move[illegible] l become the basis for their recreation or transformation. [illegible]ence of movement phrases or cells, their variations and repeti[illegible] documented using letters and numbers. Their dynamics and timing are, especially for the first performances, marked directly on musical scores, or, more recently, on special charts. Sometimes references are made to movement ideas, actions ('tourner les doigts dans les cheveux', 'enlever larme avec main' – *Elena's aria*) or gestures ('sauter de la chaise pour stopper musique', 'essayer de siffler' – *Elena's aria*) with which a particular phrase is associated, but movements remain part of the dancer's body and memory. Movement phrases themselves are not described or recorded. In this sense, these notebooks evoke the enormous absence of the live performance itself, and of the dancer's body.

The notes also contain precursors to performances, new elements and ideas – germs of performances. In this second sense, the writing is not a trace of something that has since disappeared, but, on the contrary, a *sketch*, a temporary shape on its way to becoming or transforming into something else, something new. The choreography takes shape through the writing. In this sense too, the absence of the dancing body and the *finished* choreography as a whole is felt. The reader of this *text* is always conscious of the difference or the gap between the two: the choreography and the writing. It is not possible to read these notebooks without constantly linking them back to a dance, a dancer, a performance. Like a third element, the missing performance links the writer and the reader. It is a reality that is not present in the writing but also not lost. It exists both before and after the writing.

It is the unfinished, fragmented nature of these notebooks that makes them so fascinating as a collective text/object. While they offer a wealth of information, they do not offer a fixed narrative. The numerous different elements these notes contain remain in suspension, they still have to be connected, and will be (re)combined, organized, crossed out, repeated, and transformed. This text eludes a definitive interpretation or analysis. Its eclectic combination of categories (drawings, citations, letters, lists, diagrams, texts), writing styles, and languages promotes this its illegibility. Various systems and (dynamic, variable) rhythms of reading and making connection are possible. By maintaining a sense of fragility and instability, these notes mirror the choreography's (appearance and) imminent disappearance and transformation. This, and the fact that the writing appears to maintain a connection with its writer – the writer is present in the work, we see her movements as she traces a figure on paper, the trajectory of a hand – perhaps makes these notes more evocative and better capable of grasping, recording, and representing choreographic work than a complete text (or even a video or photography).

In recent years the [illegible]ed to write has apparently subsided. The number of notebooks per p[illegible]formance has gradually decreased to almost none in the last five ye[illegible]. This reveals a shift in the way in which a choreography com[illegible]ing. While working on her early performances, De Keers[illegible]plored and developed small parts of the performance separ[illegible]eparate notebooks. The writing is very fragmented. An excess of lists and grids are compiled in which different aspects of the choreography are brought together in endless possible combinations: divisions of the piece in segments, ways of combining gestures or actions, directional lines, trajectories, movement phrases, levels of movement. Long hours of organizing, structuring and restructuring made a performance come together and eventually shaped the ultimate structure of the work as a whole. These early notebooks reveal a kind of restlessness and extensive internal conversation, a need to go through every element and every aspect of the preparation or rehearsal process over and over again. In contrast, De Keersmaeker now starts out with an overall structure for the performance in mind, and then gradually fills in the details during the creation process. Numerous little notebooks and pads are replaced with increasingly longer and more elaborate charts – timelines almost – on which she marks temporal shifts, evolutions and breaks in the music and the choreography, as one interlacing whole. The rather fragmented approach of the early years – a movement from the development of many small elements to one large, overarching organizing structure – has made place for the inverse movement from one large, overarching structure to filling in the details.

The intensity and difficulty of the search for a balance between the ideas or (often very direct, raw) emotions at the basis of a performance and the formal aspect of a piece are reflected in the (large) number and the (fragmented, clashing, combative) nature of the notebooks kept by De Keersmaeker in the eighties. In her early performances, the emotional aspect and the structural aspect of the performance were more separate entities, there was almost friction between them. Now it seems that these two aspects have come together, have become more interwoven than ever- one almost folds into the other. Similarly, the development of the oeuvre demonstrates less and less concern with confronting an existing but limiting dance vocabulary in order to develop a new, more suitable or personal one; or with fighting an established, stifling system in order to work outside of it or create a new, more liberating one. The environment in which she works has drastically changed, and the restlessness, the anxiety demonstrated in the notebooks she kept in her twenties has made place for a sense of confidence in the moment.

A shift takes place in Anne Teresa De Keersmaeker's more recent performances to reveal the internal organizing structure(s) of her choreography. In the recent video version of *Violin Phase*, the new aerial perspective together with the contrast between the white sand and the dark ground that surfaces from underneath, expose the pattern that forms the basis of this choreography. It makes visible an aspect or element that remained largely invisible to the audience over the last twenty years. This particular performance of *Violin Phase* makes its internal structure legible. Something similar happens in recent performances, such as *Just before*, *Drumming*, and *Rain*, for instance, in which the trajectories followed by the dancers are (partially) drawn on the floor for the audience to see. These performances visualize the writing aspect of choreo-graphy. They make clear how much this choreography really is about writing, about developing a movement phrase, and combining, calculating, and organizing its many transformations in time and space. *Small hands* not only reveals the dancers' trajectories but also practically offers the audience a catalogue of Rosas movement vocabulary. In this remarkable duet, Anne Teresa De Keersmaker and Cynthia Loemij make transparent the elements and organization of the movement sentences they execute (quite literally, naked underneath their simple, white, see-through dresses). The choreography cuts trough time, as references are made to earlier performances (movements and youthfulness reminiscent of *Fase* and *Tippeke*, for instance), and is immediately placed in its historical context. The audience, seated close to the event, on all sides of the large elliptical stage, is made conscious of the theatrical space and able to clearly observe every shift in movement. The transformation from heavy period dresses in the beginning of the performance to plain everyday clothing at the end, as well as the alternation of segments performed to Purcell's heavenly baroque music with segments danced in complete silence, successfully shift the context in which the dance is viewed. The translation at the very end of *Small hands* of the lyrics of a Purcell song heard earlier in the performance into sign language completes this philosophy of dance.

Part of what previously remained the property of the (secret) notebooks – the construction or structuring, the marking, charting, or sketching process – is transposed into the performance itself and becomes an integral part of it. The choreographer offers the viewer a glimpse of the creation process, an insight into the internal structures of the choreography, and new tools for reading the performance. This externalization of the structure of a performance and of its formal and formative elements reveals a sense of confidence, of mastery, and freedom. While in performances such as *Drumming* or *Rain*, movements and trajectories are precisely calculated, and the structure/characteristics of the music inform the structure of the dance very closely, the engagement with the structure of the music appears to be no longer as combative as it was in some of the early performances, such as *Fase*. The erasing of the rose pattern towards the end of the video version of *Violin Phase*, is indicative of the fight with Reich's music that is taking place: the struggle to work with and express its repetition, its (rondo) form, the feelings it evokes, while also challenging it in some way. In the early performances, a physical struggle with the music appeared necessary to formulate something, to develop a personal language. *Drumming* and *Rain*, also choreographed to music by Steve Reich, are less a struggle with structure (and/or frameworks or limitations introduced by the music or other elements of the choreography) than an inspired and, maybe ironically, more free interaction with structure. The choreographer is at ease with structure, with structured-ness, she enjoys it – it has become the trademark of her work. In the process, the structure of the choreography has come more and more to the surface, it has become part of the performance, transparent, legible.

1 The video installation *Violin Phase* is also historically significant. De Keersmaeker wrote *Violin Phase* while she was a young exchange student in New York City. Together with three other short pieces choreographed to and named after short compositions by Steve Reich, *Piano Phase*, *Come Out*, and *Clapping Music*, it later became an evening length performance. *Fase, four movement to the music of Steve Reich* announced De Keersmaeker's entrance onto the international dance scene, and continued to occupy a special place within the choreographer's oeuvre. Throughout the years, the original cast of Anne Teresa De Keersmaeker and Michèle Anne De Mey continued to perform this monumental piece. With the video installation and Thierry De Mey's film *Fase*, released in 2002, twenty years after the debut of the performance, it has made a full circle.

2 The bibliography includes books on dance, theater, film, and art; schoolbooks; poetry; fairy tails; songs and literature published by the catholic church; treatises on war; personal family documents, and so on.

3 The form this writing takes has evolved significantly (while it never really entails the physical act of writing, of transcribing a complete movement phrase onto a page using words or drawings).

4 The vocabulary encountered in the notebooks as part of the notation of the movement phrases as well is eclectic and at times humorous. Levels of movement, for example, are frequently described in terms of shoes (bare feet, high heels) or chairs. *Elena's aria* is choreographed as a bow-shaped structure with each segment described in terms of 'chairs', 'on the floor', 'standing up', or a combination. The duet between Johanne Saunier and Jean-Luc Ducourt in *Mikrokosmos* is expressed in terms of 'wanting' and 'not wanting', with 'wanting = instigating movement' and 'not wanting = obstructing movement'. De Keersmaeker describes the dance segments in terms of: 'she wants to – he wants to', 'she doesn't want to – he doesn't want to', 'she doesn't want to – he wants to', 'she wants to – he doesn't want to'.

5 *Aantekeningen*, or annotations in English, refers to the personal interpretation by the choreographer of Béla Bartók's music.

6 Authors cited in the program notes include Weiss *(Marat/Sade)*, Rilke, Buchner *(Lenz)*, Kafka, Müller, Brecht, Duras, Calvino, Handke, Schönberg, and Barthes. Many of these authors, together with poets such as e.e. cummings and Quevedo, returr repeatedly throughout the notebooks and the oeuvre.

7 This interest in mathematical designs, sy ms that arrange objects in space, explain evolutions and structures in nature (Golden Sections, Fit nacci Series), or guide relationships with other people (I Ching, Nine Star Ki) or foods (macrobiotics) has become more pronounced over the years. This might be related to the need for a sense of control/ frame in a field, an art, which is extremely difficult to grasp or record. To the extent that many of these systems are also life structuring ones and speak of the relationships between man and nature, rationality and emotion, the fascination with such systems can be connected to the relationship between structure and emotion De Keersmaeker identifies as a concern central to her work.

About the Empty Workspace and the Cosmos

Pieter T'Jonck

Choreography comes into being through the arrangement of bodies in time and space. The tendency is, therefore, to analyse the oeuvre of a choreographer by looking at how this is done. In the case of Anne Teresa De Keersmaeker's oeuvre such an analysis only tells part of the story because it doesn't really take into account that a dance performance is not presented just anywhere, but is devised and created for a particular setting, the theatrical stage. This setting has, since the renaissance, been designed to focus the gaze of the spectator and to therefore emphasise whatever is happening on stage. De Keersmaeker is the choreographer par excellence who not only made this a theme in her work – this is also true for theatre directors such as Jan Fabre, for example – but also deployed it as a means to convey the content of the work. This explains the hermeneutical relevance of an investigation into the use of the theatrical space in this œuvre.

In reviews about Anne Teresa De Keersmaeker's work, reference is often made to the tension between more theatrical productions and the dance-centred ones. However, this dichotomy is not very fruitful as a tool to interpret the work. Indeed, closer examination shows that material from the first group is often worked into the second. De Keersmaeker's movement vocabulary, like a spiral (an image she often evokes herself), describes an increasingly larger circumference from one production to the next, while the same original impulse remains at the core. The movements, which have a particular meaning in the 'theatrical' productions, become more ambiguous when they return in 'dance-centred' works. This alternation brings to light different aspects of the same basic material. The alternation between 'theatrical' and 'pure dance' productions is therefore not a coincidence: where a theatrical production often stays close to the (personal) experiences of the choreographer, a dance-centred production focuses on the work, on the 'impersonal' task of structuring and organising. The dance productions express the joy of dancing. They suggest the possibility, for a moment, to turn the chaos and indeterminacy of human existence into an image that suggest a supra-personal connection between things. In other words: the theatrical performances are concerned mainly with subjective experience, while the pure dance pieces evoke an almost impersonal 'drive', an undercurrent of life force. This alternation finds its expression at times in chaotic performances and at other times in extremely structured ones.

De Keersmaeker's oeuvre comes together the way it does because of the importance she attaches to how the theatrical stage is used. Originally, the stage was foremost an 'empty space', a screen onto which desire was projected. As an empty space, the stage was also very clearly a workspace, a place where serious work took place. The productions came together through a fight with the always looming chaos or collapse. This becomes clear in *Stella*: the set unambiguously represents the studio in which the choreography was created. Later on, the stage became a signified space. *Mozart/Concert Arias* marks a moment of transition: for the first time the stage represents a place of encounters (a meeting place). In it, a flash of desire transforms into a concrete shape. Later on, in performances such as *Toccata* or *Amor constante más allá de la muerte*, the scenic design increasingly suggests aspirations for a more harmonious organisation. The stage is then not only a meeting place (a house, a square, or even a battlefield), but also the allegorical representation of a larger, even cosmic unity hidden behind the sometimes unsettling emptiness on the stage. This development is however not linear. De Keersmaeker would not be herself if she did not periodically breach this allegory in order to return to the initial rawness of the empty place. The later work is not a negation of the earlier performances, but shows the relationship the choreographer has developed with emotions, which in earlier work appeared in a raw form and were contained by a rigid choreographic structure.

Fase, the work that heralded the choreographer's international breakthrough, is at first sight a meticulous transcription of Steve Reich's hypnotic, abstract, minimalist music. However, the analogy between score and choreography hides a different intention. While Reich's musical structure is, as it were, without perspective, part of an infinitely extendable whole, the choreography produces a coercive perspective for the dancers, for the stage. The stage is not one point on an endless screen, but the focal point where the dancer seeks out the spectator's gaze and locks it onto her self. Reich's music hypnotises because it cancels out all sense of time and space. The dance, on the other hand, holds the gaze and makes the viewer conscious of the duration of the monotonous and precise repetition in a tactile way. This difference in intention is revealed by small details in the set. In *Come Out*, Anne Teresa De Keersmaeker and Michèle Anne De Mey sit on stools in a very compact circle of light so that even the most insignificant action is emphasised for maximum effect. Formally, we are talking about two dance phrases which are identical but are shifted in time. It is only because of the way in which two very different women embody this dance phrase that the performance works. Therefore, the abstract quality of the movements is not the key here but rather the concrete embodiment of the phrase by the individual dancers. De Keersmaeker conquers the space with a rigid structure of calculated circles and lines. There is something defensive about it: the gaze is captured and cast back. There are only a few cracks in the choreography's armour. Only the solo *Violin Phase* appears to be an exception: it defies the gaze of the spectator in a direct way. Unexpectedly, in the coda, De Keersmaeker looks straight into the eyes of the audience, her fist clenched in front of her chest. As if with the snap of a finger the hypnosis is lifted.

In a dramatic fashion, *Rosas danst Rosas* introduces a new dimension to the movement structures developed in *Fase*. The dancers now also occupy the space in a vertical sense. In the first movement, the dancers, now four instead of two, lie on the floor, rolling from side to side. Even though, it appears as if suddenly the dancers are overcome with doubt. Do they no longer want to show themselves? Do they intend to keep the spectators waiting? Because of this hesitation, the audience can no longer be absorbed from the very first second by the virtuoso staccato experienced in *Fase*. On the contrary, the audience becomes painfully aware of its gaze. When the music of Thierry De Mey and Peter Vermeersch does finally get the dance moving, it is stopped once again. The dancers do not move their entire bodies, but sit on the chairs arbitrarily placed on the empty stage. The chairs seem to act as points of reference for the dancers in a space with which they do not know what to do. The implicit question – 'We are on display here, but what are we going to do?' – became the subject of many later works, including *Stella*. Only when the chairs are pushed to the side does the dance really gets going. It then begins to conquer the entire stage and the audience with an astonishing exhausting performance. The movement vocabulary of this choreography differs slightly from that of *Fase*. Rolling on the floor, running fingers through the hair, suddenly moving the hips: despite their stylisation these are recognisable everyday movements and refer to the way in which women show or conceal themselves from the gaze of others. This highlights the individual interpretation of the movements by each dancer. What the movements suggest finds its most important metaphor in the set design.

Elena's aria radicalises the hesitation in the first part of *Rosas danst Rosas*. In this performance again the movements are repetitive and make reference to women's actions of everyday life. More straight lines and circles, more chairs. However, the coercive perfection, the expansively conquering repetitiveness has now turned into its opposite. The choreography seems to absolutely want to prevent the gaze from being hypnotised by the same movement to the same beat over and over again. Instead, children's games visibly exhaust the dancers, to the point that they stumble and fall. Not actions that generally belong on a stage... This increasingly confuses the spectators and even embarrasses them, and all the more since there seems to be no end in sight. Nor does the movement phrase develop into increasingly longer lines. Quite on the contrary. In the end it implodes. The dancers sink into their chairs, gasping for air, and stare blankly into space. At that moment, one feels very strongly the absence of the music, which propelled the actions forward in previous pieces. In this segment, sound is faint and appears to arrive from far away: an aria, a speech by Castro. These fragments of sound do not structure anything. They are and continue to be fragments, just like the performance itself. In such dead moments, time weighs especially heavy. This produces a sensation of enormous alienation: the effect of the set is deployed against itself. The stage directs the spectator's gaze towards events which obviously do not concern him. He is forced to look at something he did not expect to see and which does not appear to be worthy of his attention. The reactions to the first few performances were predictable: these dancers were putting on airs! They stand indeed on a stage, but – and no-one was expecting this – they are also making a scene. The entire theatrical construction of *Elena's aria* was developed as a metaphor for a desire that moves back and forth between the desire to be looked at, to catch the spectator's gaze – and thus to stand on the stage – and an overwhelming doubt, the refusal even to meet that desire. The end of the performance drives this to a head. In front of a lowered safety curtain, the four dancers look straight into the eyes of the audience. The set design allows for the simultaneous aggression and vulnerability of this gesture to find a clear and simple shape. This is why the spectator is made to feel part of a frighteningly direct emotional landscape. This is all the more disturbing because these emotions are not named, and the spectator is left wondering about their nature or cause.

Bartók/aantekeningen makes the radical alienation effect of the stage in *Elena's aria* more recognisable. The set, designed by Gisbert Jäkel, is a large box with cold, shadow-less lighting. The grey walls, the worn velvet folding chairs and a stuffed deer evoke the meagre and all too familiar sight of deserted local village reception halls and school cafeterias. Places where a combination of too much space and too harsh lighting undermine any kind of drama and mercilessly highlight every imperfection. The space makes the desire to be at the centre of attention turn into its opposite, the fear of being seen. *Bartók/aantekeningen* is characterised by the buried tension between the awareness of the objective gaze of the spectator, reflected in a heightened notion of imperfection, and the desire to seduce the spectator's gaze. There is only one remedy: conspire, trick the spectator. It is no coincidence that in *Bartók/aantekeningen* the dance is performed explicitly in unison. Details, such as the rather girly school uniforms worn by the dancers, provide more references to women's childhood memories. Attracting and refusing the gaze – the basic structure of *Elena's aria* – acquires specific meaning in this performance, as if it is meant for someone who is not (yet) there. Yet the choreography is not about the anecdotes of a schoolgirl, if only because of the intense relationship with the music. *Bartók/aantekeningen* carefully constructs a theatrical look through recognisable, but, due to their lack of glamour, alienating movements. This theatrical gaze is a metaphor for the gaze itself, in which the other remains impossible to grasp. The 'I' becomes conscious of its dependence on, and desire for, such a look, but cannot be fully available for it. A gap remains between what is seen and what can be or should be seen.

Stella takes this notion further. In this performance the dancers no longer form a united front against the outside world. Instead, the individual personality of each dancer comes to the fore. Each dancer follows her own 'score', and attempts to attract all the attention, as if she wants to conform to the imaginary requirements of the gaze she knows is always focussed on her. This situation escalates constantly. To find a sense of unity within all this diversity becomes the theme of the production. It is therefore not a coincidence that the set represents a workplace, the studio. The performance reveals the reverse side of the studied appearance the dancers are trying to make. The studio and the stage are metaphors for the real situation of women in the world. The production is a masterpiece: through a nearly invisible basic choreographic structure, De Keersmaeker manages to introduce, within this chaos, the unity that can reveal the common denominator of the very diverse actions of the women. This performance provided the basic material or many others to come.

The extent to which De Keersmaeker consciously manipulates the implicit meaning and effect of the stage as a focal point is revealed in an almost exaggerated way in her staging of *Verkommenes Ufer/ Medeamaterial/ Landshaft mit Argonauten*, a theatre production based on a text by Heiner Müller. De Keersmaeker pays careful attention to rhythm and intonation and treats the text almost as a musical score. What is special about this performance is that De Keersmaeker, contrary to her approach in previous work, annihilates the workings of the stage as a focal point. The actors stand on an extremely elongated plateau. The spectators are seated very close to the action on narrow benches along the entire length of the stage. This means that it is impossible for the spectators to see the whole stage at once, and that it is equally impossible for the actors to keep the attention focused on themselves at all times. This unusual setting is also a metaphor for the theme of the performance. The extremely destructive emotions in the text throw the characters off balance. The body of the actor can no longer present one unified meaning and can not absorb all the verbal abuse. In this way, there can no longer be any spatial unity and consequently not one single focal point. The set designed by Herman Sorgeloos removes every last shred of an illusion of cohesion: bare walls and a floor covered with small, loose pieces of hard board, laid out in a pattern severely disturbed by a visible wind machine. This set is the first in a long series developed for Rosas by Sorgeloos, who is also the company's in house photographer. One can hardly overestimate his contributions to the productions of this period: even though it seems as if he tries to efface himself with his minimal, and often elementary constructions, this frugality of means is literally and metaphorically the ideal basis for how De Keersmaeker tells her story. It is by no means a design quirk: when the oeuvre takes a new turn where content is concerned, with performances such as *Mozart/Concert Arias* or *Toccata*, Sorgeloos also develops entire new spatial tools and shapes.

In the film version, created with Walter Verdin, of *Ottone Ottone*, her adaptation of Monteverdi's baroque opera *L'incoronazione di Poppeia*, De Keersmaeker achieves a similar effect by not filming the theatre performance chronologically, but instead cutting up the action completely. A variety of camera shots rip apart the image, and repetitions make the image stammer at moments when the brutality of the story becomes unfathomable. Only the music remains more or less coherent. This causes an inversion of the usual operatic logic. If in opera the music carries the emotion, in this performance it is the image that expresses what remains hidden in the music. The music is balm to a never healing wound, a guarantee that it is possible to express what appears to be unutterable. The stammering black and white close-up of Fumiyo Ikeda screaming without making a sound, while Monteverdi's ceremonious music builds up to its climax, is the grand finale of this brilliant use of the medium of video. This experiment also alludes to other important experiments with scenic space. When De Keersmaeker uses video, in *Erts*, for example, it immediately becomes an important organising element. The use of close-ups, especially of faces, subtly undermines the clarity of the scenic action because the faces are impossible to grasp. While they appear at first to bear the complete emotional content of an action, the close-ups instead reveal fully the impossibility to read the face. In this respect, De Keersmaeker has no doubt been a forerunner of later work by other artists.

From the 90s onwards, the deployment of the stage became less prominent in De Keersmaeker's oeuvre as a tool to question the workings of the gaze. However, the awareness of its effects never really disappears. A performance such as *I said I* (1999), which she created together with her sister Jolente, and based on the text of *Selbstbezichtigung* (Self-Accusation) by Peter Handke, even revolves entirely around the insight that we never coincide with ourselves, but instead can only relate to ourselves via language or through others. This realisation is completely analogous to the friction between the dancer and the spectator's gaze in the early works. The performance also produces a social dialectic within the space of the stage: there is no longer only the movement from audience to the stage and vice versa. The first production in which such a social dialectic is developed is *Mozart/Concert Arias*, in 1992. The company at that time already consisted of thirteen dancers, including six men. Rosas was no longer an all-female company. The gaze the women on the stage wanted to receive from the audience in earlier performances is in *Mozart/Concert Arias* already present on stage. This results in a new interpretation of the stage space. The stage for *Mozart/Concert Arias* is an enormous elliptical hard wood floor. The symbolism is obvious: a figure with two centres replaces the circle, the form with only one centre, as used in *Fase*. In this way, the stage becomes the representation of an entire world. Since the axis of the event is no longer only oriented from the audience to the stage, but lies mainly on the stage itself, the relationship between being present on the stage, showing oneself to the world, and being absent, leaving the stage, becomes important. The complex variations of dance phrases cutting through each other reveals a pattern (formally) reminiscent of court dances. Entering and exiting the stage acquires double meaning because of the subtle set design. It is not only about literally entering and exiting the stage, but also refers to a solemn act: the dancers make their entrance into the world, an entrance which, sadly, can be followed by a humiliating exit. The elliptical set becomes the stage for a wonderful, but precarious drama. In *Mozart/Concert Arias*, Anne Teresa De Keersmaeker plays on the theatre's original magic as the place where the mundane receives a solemn aura.

Toccata (1993) without a doubt demonstrates the other new meanings the stage would acquire in the years ahead. The performance consists of five short choreographic sketches, created to as many short pieces of music by Johann Sebastian Bach, and interpreted on a grand piano by Jos Van Immerseel. The company's dance vocabulary had already become much more complex than in the early productions, when the choreographer created dance phrases written for her own body. The construction of the performance as a series of short pieces results in a rather mannered style. The attributes and tools used in the choreography are presented to the audience one by one: elements of the dance vocabulary, composition techniques, the influence of other choreographers, and the music... The set itself has become emblematic of the careful attention to musical structure in this oeuvre: an enormous chunk of the rectangular stage has been removed to create a space for Van Immerseel's piano. The music is very literally brought to the fore as the most important element of the performance, as if the choreographer wants to convey that maybe she does not have very much to add to it. The result is that the surface of the stage itself is shaped like an upside down grand piano and considerably slopes down towards the audience on both sides. This for dancers is an unusual and difficult set up and underlines once again that the purpose is to display things. The most remarkable aspect of the set design is, however, that the stage surface is made extremely visible in order to show thé allegory of classical proportionality, the Golden Section. All these features together point to one thing: De Keersmaeker acknowledges with emphasis that she is part of a larger tradition, of a system in the world at large, which as Bach's music solemnly suggests, foreshadows salvation. There is nothing mystical about this: the choreographer continues to work with her dancers in a very concrete way. But contrary to the destructive exposure of the peep-show aspect of the theatrical stage in her earlier performances, she now seems to accept the rules and regulations of this extraordinary invention. This acceptance introduces a certain melancholy: acknowledging the rules also implies an awareness of the relativity, the illusionary character of the world evoked on stage. The final image of the second version of the performance, Marion Ballester's solo to *Nun komm der Heiden Heiland*, emphasises this aspect. While until that moment the stage floor was lit and the rest of the space remained dark, the rear wall is now bathed in bright light. The mechanics, the make-believe of the performance becomes visible and dismantles at once the magic of the theatre. Marion Ballester stands alone against the rear wall. With great elegance she inscribes beautiful arabesques. Even after the music has faded, she continues to dance in the dimming light, like a muse who works on, even when the magic of the drama has disappeared.

Woud plays the same game with illusion and reality. This production is a collage of four fragments. The first part is a film, *Tippeke*, directed by Thierry De Mey, who also wrote the music. De Keersmaeker herself dances and acts in this film. The following three sections are independent choreographies, created to music by Alban Berg, Arnold Schönberg, and Richard Wagner. The three musical compositions are linked by the fact that a secret love inspired each one of them. Anne Teresa De Keersmaeker's choreography to this music is not a repetition of the story behind the music, but explores powerful passions and deep suffering in its own way. These emotions are not shown literally, but appear as scenes from a dream. This becomes clear through the abrupt switches between the different pieces, like sudden awakenings. With each switch, the theatrical illusion is disrupted by raising either the backdrop or the trees that evoke a nocturnal forest and are part of the set designed by Gilles Aillaud, so that the desolate feeling of an empty stage becomes visible. The last part comes back to the film *Tippeke*. At first sight, *Tippeke* has no connection with the three sections of choreography and their common theme. Anne Teresa De Keersmaeker is running through a forest while singing and dancing and reciting the nursery rhyme *Tippeke*. The rhyme itself is not important, but the way in which De Keersmaeker presents it is. As though she is totally unaware of the camera. The inventive gestures she makes while excitedly finding a way through the forest are disarming and childlike: the film shows flights of imagination, the barely formulated desire of a young woman, and in this way already hints at the dance. While the film continues, the two female dancers who danced the last section of the choreography copy De Keersmaeker's movements in the film live on stage, announcing in this way the last section of the performance created to Wagner's music. There is a second structural link between the film and the dance production: the trip through the forest comes to an unexpected end in the film when De Keersmaeker reaches the edge of the forest. Its is abruptly interrupted by the noise of a highway at her feet. The brusque interruption of the dream after each section of the performance is therefore already present in the film. The last image of the piece, when the set of *Verklärte Nacht* is completely cleared away and Cynthia Loemij is left all alone, is analogous. Slowly, the dance runs out of steam and finally comes to a complete halt. Quietly, with an ordinary, everyday stride Loemij exits the stage, while a faint image of the film *Tippeke* is projected onto the stage as a vague reminder of a wild dream that has been irrevocably lost.

The work of the 90s onwa[illegible] as far as the *mise-en-scène* is concerned, continue with and furth[illegible]elop what was first introduced in performances such as *Mozart/C*[illegible]*ias*, *Toccata*, and *Woud*. The contribution of Jan Versweyveld bec[illegible]isive in the developments in the set design, especially from *Just*[illegible]wards: using apparently simple and obvious materials and light[illegible] Versweyveld always manages to create a powerful image, which supports and clarifies the increasingly complex choreographic patterns. In these performances, the stage floor plays an increasingly clearly allegorical part. Directional lines and pathways are combined into complex geometrical patterns, which refer to historically important organising systems and figures, such as the Golden Section and spirals (a pattern that emerged for the first time in *Amor Constante más allá de la muerte*). The stage becomes then an allegory of the basic structure of the world itself which the choreographer writes on; although not without realising the ambiguity inherent to any allegory. Where, at first sight, such harmonising figures suggest the image of an exalted view of the world, they appear in many performances also to express of the fragility of the constructions we design in order to help us understand the world. The collage performance *In real time* in which as well as Rosas dancers, actors from the theatre collective Stan and musicians from the jazz ensemble Aka Moon participate, demonstrates this division. While at one moment the chairs on the stage are arranged by the choreographer to form two interwoven spirals, large sections of the performance are plagued by intense quarrelling, debate, and even complete chaos. Destructive and constructive moments alternate in a performance with hidden but strong constructive ingenuity. It is no coincidence that the production is about the meaning and place of the work of performing artists in confusing and turbulent times. Every performance De Keersmaeker created in this period explores new basic moods. The fact that she expresses these basic moods not through titles, texts or explanations, but mainly – inspired by the costumes designed by Dries Van Noten – through the use of specific colour schemes, suggests perhaps the choreographer's hesitance to express emotions in a too direct way. In *Drumming*, orange and white dominate, in *Rain* the principal colour is pink, almost magenta, *Small hands* is bathed in deep blue and *April me* in light blue, except for the last section of the performance. Apart from *April me*, the productions in which colour plays such a prominent part are all dance-centred performances like *Drumming* and *Rain* which have grown from *Just before* and *In real time* respectively.

The fact that the set design continues to function as a bearer of meaning even today becomes clear in the recent choreography: *Small hands (out of the lie of no)*, the duet the choreographer performs together with Cynthia Loemij. It is framed as a reassessment of the trajectory she has followed since *Fase* twenty years earlier. The space of the piece is unusually large and its set up is eccentric: the choreography is performed on a surface of 18 by 36 meters demarcated by an oval shaped seating construction. This set up overturns the spatial premises of *Fase* which was conceived as a frontal confrontation with the spectator who had to be conquered. There is no longer such a coercive perspective. Sometimes it is even impossible to see everything at the same time because of the large distances between the dancers. The dancers on their part cannot see the entire audience at one time. They can also not entirely assess the impact of the choreography because of this 'all-around' set up. This is also not the fragmentation of *Medeamaterial*. The oval inside which the women dance is, with their first circling of the space, immediately seized, as if it were a new world, entirely separated from that of everyday life. A somewhat solemn, elevated world (i.e. the world of the theatre) – ma non troppo –, suggests the music of Purcell. This world touches that of the spectators seated all around it. However, they are also separated from it, precisely by the first circumscribing movement. At the end of the performance, these two worlds will once again come together as the women change into everyday clothing for the final scene. The contrast with *Fase* is also maximised in the dance itself. Although it is built on equally as precise geometrical shapes, there is nothing left of the syncopated, precise swinging movements of the arms and legs that drew their strength from their endless repetition as seen in *Fase*. On the contrary, the movements in *Small hands* are capricious and fluid, like a response to the music improvised on the spot. Elegance, playfulness, seriousness, and sometimes plain silliness alternate in an unpredictable manner. In contrast with the rigid unison of *Fase*, the differences in the way in which both dancers execute the movements can be considerable, at times very large, even when they are performing essentially identical movements. The production is more of a refined game than a tough fight. That is true also in the psychological sense: the rich pallet of emotions and fantasies are reminiscent of the film *Tippeke*, even if the spectrum here is more mature and broader. The result is a performance which turns the closed, clenched, and conquering style of *Fase* into its opposite: a performance with a fluid, open, and porous structure. The 'all-round' construction is the clearest expression of this revolution and of how the use of space of the stage, despite all developments, continues to be a basic theme in the work of Anne Teresa De Keersmaeker.

The Poetry of the Invisible

Elke Van Campenhout

'No, I can't explain dance to you. If I could say it, I wouldn't have to dance it.' This statement by Isadora Duncan says a lot about the relationship between word and dance. Choreography and language seem incompatible in some way or other. Ideally, language should be an unequivocal reference system for meanings. Dance is often referred to as, to use Martha Graham's expression, 'the hidden language of the soul.' Moralists in every generation have fiercely opposed the evil influences of dance which can only subvert and undermine the social ethos because of its intangibility and its direct relation to the dark caves of the subconscious. Conversely, numerous romantic souls – and therapists – cite dance as the ultimate antidote to a state of mind lost in its own rationality.

This is the classical dichotomy between body and soul. The Platonic ideal of the perfection of pure reason that denies any kind of hesitation. Nevertheless, in debates about dance we often come across arguments that once again bring word and dance closer together. Choreography is often regarded as a linguistic system. Dance movements are phrases, part of a larger text, choreography is written, a performance is 'read', and one talks about the vocabulary of dance. Sir Francis Bacon said that 'a dance is a measured pace, as a verse is a measured speech.' In his book *The principles of Art* philosopher R.G. Collingwood even refers to dance as the mother of all languages. According to him, speech is no more than a system of gestures which are unique only in so far as each one produces a characteristic sound. And thus, speech is only a special form of movement in so far as it can be perceived by both the ear as well as the eye. 'Listening to a speaker instead of looking at him tends to make us think of speech as essentially a system of sounds, but it is not. Essentially it is a system of gestures made with the lungs and larynx, and the cavities of the mouth and nose.' In his view, writing down these sounds and reading them also demonstrates a fundamental misunderstanding of the basic fact that speech is essentially a movement. This means that in our notations, only a small part of speech can be recorded and pitch, stress, tempo, and rhythm are almost completely ignored.

'Every language is in this way a specialised form of bodily gesture, and in this sense it may be said that the dance is the mother of all languages.' This curious statement by Collingwood belongs to a broader epistemological theory that is not possible to analyse in depth here. However, considering the generally accepted hierarchical relationship between word and movement, he is certainly making a surprising statement.

If we assume a separation between body and soul, dance and word appear to be irreconcilable in their basic antithesis. If, however, we assume that words are the distilled notation of a movement and that dance is an essentially linguistic system, our discussion takes on a completely different nature. It is no longer about a hierarchy, but a complex relationship with a different meaning. In this context, word and dance acquire a complicity which is difficult to grasp.

Things become more specific if we examine the classical dances of the East. Here the connection between language and dance is clearly in evidence and can probably help to throw more light onto the relationship between the two. In Japanese kabuki theatre, the story is backed up by the actors' gestures. As the drama develops, the acting becomes more stylised and therefore more dance- like. Each gesture becomes a sign, then a symbol, and eventually, becomes completely abstract. The actors' movements end up being detached from and even irrelevant to the role's rational interpretation. Much more than an illustrative note in the spoken text, dance is rooted in the origins of the performance itself. Each new actor bases his performance not on the text, but on the performance of his predecessor. This means that dance has a very formal, aesthetic quality. Speech is likewise stylised, it becomes something between singing and speaking.
What we are witnessing in the development of kabuki is a mutual exchange between word and dance. First of all in terms of illustration, dance is liberated from meaning and, in turn, the spoken word is liberated from its unequivocal condition. Originally kabuki was an art form with a major political and social significance, but in modern Japan the content of this form of drama no longer has the same impact. Dance has elevated the meaning of words to such a level of abstraction that any direct claim to social relevance is futile.

A similar process is occurring in the development of the North Indian dance form kathak, which literally means 'to tell a story'. Originally, kathak was a temple dance that brought to life the mythology of Radha Krishna. Later on, during the time of Mogul rule, kathak became a court dance and incorporated aesthetic elements from the Muslim tradition. In this context, kathak evolved into a sophisticated art form whose aesthetic development was more in evidence than that of its narrative. This gave rise to an infinite number nuances in the dance. Often these dances render the stories superfluous or, at least, they completely undermine the direct relation between language and meaning.

It seems from both accounts that word and dance have difficulty in keeping in balance. The question of hierarchy arises continually. If we examine the history of modern western dance, we cannot escape the conclusion that language all too often surfaces as an inappropriate accessory in the development of dance theatre or that dance's function, alongside text is purely illustrative. A balanced and in-depth co-operation between the two is seldom explored. In the work of Anne Teresa De Keersmaeker, we have seen over the years, an increasing number of attempts to address the issue. Here is a brief overview.

In 1984, in the performance of *Elena's aria*, she introduced text by Tolstoy, Brecht, and Botho Strauss. Later on come *Bartók/aantekeningen* and *Verkommenes Ufer/Medeamaterial/Landschaft mit Argonauten*, and, in 1996, *Stella*, which relates as much to the book of the same title by Goethe as to the character from Tennessee Williams' play *A Streetcar Named Desire*. In *Amor constante*, a poem is recounted in sign-language, and from 1997 onwards Rosas worked closely with Anne Teresa's sister Jolente De Keersmaeker, member of the theatre collective Stan. From that moment, Anne Teresa and Jolente worked regularly together on the search for the relationship between theatre and dance. Sometimes both the artistes' voices alternate with each other, and sometimes they fuse into spontaneous, exceptionally beautiful cries from the heart. In *Just before*, the dancers worked on their own reminiscences, on the gaps in their memories. *Quartett* is the Heiner Müller adaptation of *Les liaisons dangereuses* by Choderlos de Laclos. Actor Frank Vercruyssen and dancer Cynthia Loemij play together in a sparring match of temptation, betrayal, passion and reason. In 1999 came *I said I*, based on the text of *Selbstbezichtigung (Self-Accusation)* by Peter Handke, and in 2000, *In real time*, which was based on texts including those by the Dutch theatre director and writer, Gerardjan Rijnders.

Language has always had its place in Rosas' work. This was true of *Elena's aria*, but also of more dance-oriented pieces such as *Bartók/aantekeningen*, *Asch* and *Ottone Ottone* that have a strong textual element. Moreover, there are also the danced sections of performances which arose directly from the adaptation process of texts like in *Just before*, and which carry an intensity which would be missing if the initial intention had been purely choreographic. Anna Teresa's decision to work together with her sister was a logical consequence of Jolente De Keersmaeker's work as a lecturer at P.A.R.T.S. During the rehearsals for *Just before* Jolente provided essential feedback to the dancers on how to deliver their texts. The result of the shared experience was a mutual curiosity that grew between choreographer and theatre director for each others disciplines.

Jolente De Keersmaeker : 'Originally, in my work with the dancers, I always began with a very separate, purely theatrical approach. It has only been since working on *Just before* that I became intrigued by the potential of dance that doesn't try to explain anything. In theatre, the body always works to support the text. You stamp your feet to express fury, you don't immediately lift your leg in the air.'

'With *Just before* you have a completely different relationship. You tell a story and at the same time you see dance which is actually completely unrelated. The movement emanates from the basic choreographic phrase of *Just before* which has nothing to do with the content of the text.'

In *Just before*, the dancers worked with their own memories. A certain object, a place, or an experience which was infinitely personal was explored and passed from dancer to dancer. There are small gems of emotion: the story of a broken teapot or of a meeting with an unknown southern beauty that didn't quite take place.

Anne Teresa De Keersmaeker : 'For *Just before*, dancers described, as precise as possible, something which they had loved and which had lost. It was a memory related to a scene, an object, a person, or an experience. The beauty appeared in the moment a subtext emerged from the confrontation between text and dance. For example at a certain moment in the performance there's a duet by Bruce Campbell and Taka Shamoto where only a faint odour of dance remains, only a tiny quotation.'

JDK: 'At a different moment you have a dialogue between Roberto Oliván and Iris Bouche who at, one point, stops speaking. The dance which takes place at that moment is heavily charged with meaning, there is an invisible layer of tension that flows under the movement and makes the dance more compelling, even if it is impossible to pinpoint exactly what it evokes. The word gains in significance and a new layer appears through the coming together of dance and text. All of a sudden it becomes possible to look at the text in a different way and for it to generate another meaning.'

ATDK: 'For me, it is also about secrets and mystery. There is a great deal of material which the dancers possess within them but do not reveal. This means that a performance can never be interpreted in only one way. What is special about the independence of text in relation to dance is that the movement does not have to follow the words. If movement is in opposition to the meaning of the text it creates a particular kind of tension. Although, one has to always remain consciously aware of the danger of imposing artificial limitations.'

Each of the performances which have emerged from the partnership between Jolente and Anne Teresa De Keersmaeker possesses a characteristic sensitivity in the relationship between word and dance. As personal as the generated text material is in *Just before*, in the text by Handke in *I said I*, the focus shifts to what is happening in the group. *Quartett* is a dialogue which physically forces both performers to confront each other and *I said I* is a monologue performed by ten dancers. Sometimes, the dance is independent of the written text, and at others they are inextricably interwoven. There exists throughout a constant quest for different possibilities, as well as for prerogatives inherent in the content of the text.

JDK: 'The difference also lies in the subject matter of the text. The text by Handke, for example, revolves around self accusation, a completely different sort of theme than the antagonism between men and women dealt with in *Quartett*. *I said I* is more universal and poses different questions: ones about the relationship between the individual and society, about the gradual conforming of the individual to his or her surroundings. This is on a different scale than the personal account of *Just before* or the intimate dialogue of *Quartett*. In *I said I*, the text is carried by the entire group. Even if only one person is speaking, the group is always present. The choreography emerges in the relationship between the individual and the group.'

ATDK: *Self-Accusation* is a text which is very explicit in its message. In *I said I* there is a more marked separation of pure dance and blocks of text. There is less interaction between the two elements. In the beginning you have pure text, then there is movement and activity, and finally dance takes over. The text is never the starting point for the movement, there are always two different sets of logic which are combined. It was only with *Quartett*, that my choice of movement was, to some extent, influenced by the fact that knew from the beginning that Cynthia Loemij would be playing the role of the woman.

It is in *Quartett*, that text and movement confront each other in the most obvious way. A female dancer stands opposing an actor, whose only weapons are his words, and is subjected to her dance which is as capricious as it is seductive. Cynthia Loemij works with a choreography which is made up of succession of set sequences of which the direction and speed can be improvised. Moreover, the movements can be performed forwards or backwards. This produces unexpected connections between text and dance which vary with each new performance. Movements take on a different flavour according to their relation to the text and vice versa.
JDK: In *Quartett* you can feel quite clearly how text and dance begin to rub up against each other. Cynthia has both dance and language at her disposal so she has a trump card to use against Frank. And so, the relationship between them is not played out only at the level of the text, but also at the level of the relationship between dancer and actor. It is a trial of strength which is developed more concretely in *In real time*. At that point the actors also begin to move.'

For this performance the actors from Stan worked for four months with dance material under the direction of David Zambrano. The improvisation sessions were aimed at developing a greater awareness of the body and at exploring how it could be used as an instrument to communicate without words. It was during this rehearsal period that actors and dancers came together more closely than ever before.
ATDK: 'For a dancer, words are a completely different method of communication, connected to everyday life, which you can use to express things which are impossible to express so precisely with movement. At the same time, they represent an unknown world in which you can only find your way around by searching and experimenting a lot. Language and dance both work according to their own logic. In certain situations you feel restricted by using exclusively words and in others by using only dance. If you combine both dance and speech, you arrive at something which can only work if it is propelled by a poetic force.'
JDK: 'At that moment you enter a new territory, another country with no set borders. A completely new language emerges from the association of word and dance, an undercurrent whose substance is difficult to determine and which changes constantly. In *Quartett*, it summons up such enormous vulnerability that you end up with an emotional memory of the experience. With other performances these are moments when you think: that's it; that is exactly what I want to express.'
ATDK: 'In *Quartett*, dance illuminated the text by means of the delay which it imposed upon the speech. The music of the text is changed by the dance. It's literally with her hands and feet that the dancer expresses the content of the text, yet this relationship is never direct, and content and movement rarely go the in same direction. The word *bal* (ball) is accompanied by a square dance to make the ball even rounder. And that's what makes it poetic.'

Friction of skin against skin – the language as movement and movement as word. An infinite allusion to meaning. It is the visual poetry of an invisible current of references and sensitivities. From personal stories to invisible appointments. It is something which the maker cannot attain and which the spectator cannot pinpoint. And it emerges very occasionally, for a moment, in an endless search. One moment it is there, and then it has gone. It is fleetingness itself, the moment when what is missing can speak.
In contrast to the classical dance theatre forms which we have focused earlier, the Rosas' performances are not about purified abstraction which has completely separated itself from its content or the individual personality of the dancer. The individual and irreplaceable body of each of the artists is the place where language and dance meet each other. Where text and dance are given an increasingly specific form. It is a communicative field, a constant search, which cannot conclusively be put in formal terminology. This means that both word and dance always contain a certain urgency. The tension brought about by their juxtaposition is engendered by individuals with a voice and a body of their own. They each have their own story which is revealed and concealed throughout the course of the performance.
At this point, word and dance have called a cease-fire. The supremacy of one or the other is of negligible importance. Rather than their power struggle it is their kinship which thrusts itself upon us. The linguistics of dance, the tentativeness of language, and the infinite field of cross-fertilisation are in the midst.

Another Colour on Every Horizon
The International Dimension in the Work of Rosas

Michel Uytterhoeven

I. At a time where the worldwide exchange of images is growing at a fantastic rate via the media (television and, even more so, via the Internet) it is somewhat surprising that there is still an equally strong, universal desire to see live dance on stage: Rosas travels from Brussels and Paris to Adelaide and Brasilia, Trisha Brown to China, Pina Bausch to India, Buenos Aires, and Palermo, but also Indian dance in deSingel (Antwerp), old Korean court dances at the Paris Festival d'Automne, African rituals in the Zuiderpershuis in Antwerp, and the Turkish dervishes as a global export.

There is neither a film nor a video which can replace a live experience. It costs a lot of money and effort, but we still want to witness something as archaic and unpredictable as dance, as if it belonged to an ephemeral heritage that art lovers want to experience, hold on to, and keep. Perhaps it is because dancers, through their bodies, reveal a strand of unuttered truth about our universal human condition that reaches through to the fibres of our being.

II. Anne Teresa De Keersmaeker and Rosas emerged and became successful on an international level immediately. Nowadays that surprises no one, but before then it had been very un-Belgian. Belgium was not really a part of the international arts scene twenty years ago. International performing arts producers did not call in on this little corner of Europe to look for budding talent for the major festivals. Belgium certainly did not have a prominent dance tradition like France, Britain, or Germany.

Belgian theatre makers were seldom seen on stages abroad. *Mistero Buffo* by the Internationale Nieuwe Scene, which appeared in Avignon in 1973, was an exception to the rule. And more on the fringe: the third world theatre of Tone Brulin's Tie Drie, which made an impression internationally, but only flourished in Flanders itself later on.

De Keersmaeker and Rosas' international success story has much more in common with the very early artistic movements, such as that of the talented Flemish painters (and polyphonists) and the medieval alliances or networks. A survey of the primitive Flemings or baroque painters (Van Eyck, Van der Weyden, Breughel, Rubens, and Van Dyck) shows that their exceptional talent was quickly discovered by the sponsors of art of the epoch ie. the sovereign, of any nationality, who controlled the region. Up to that moment though, the novice artists spent their time studying diligently under harsh, strict conditions. Firstly, in accordance with the medieval guild custom, they became an apprentice in the workshop of a recognised master and then undertook a study trip to Italy or Spain to gain the necessary expertise and authority to take part in the European painters' forum.

So in the Middle Ages there were networks as there are today, albeit without the speed of a click on the mouse button. Nonetheless, they existed and they worked – note the Hansa towns or the network of universities. The work of scientists such as Vesalius, Mercator, and Erasmus echoed very quickly all over Europe and a generation of printers like Plantin & Moretus were able to serve a truly universal clientele in this way.

III. The history of Rosas runs almost parallel to the story of the emancipation of contemporary dance in Belgium. What was the cultural landscape like in Flanders, Brussels, and Belgium in those days?

In Belgian dance, we can regard the pre-Rosas period (of the 1960's and 70's) as a continuation of the modernistic movement: extremely successful in the case of Maurice Béjart and his Ballet of the XXth Century and also, albeit with less artistic daring and public approval, with Jeanne Brabants' Ballet van Vlaanderen, which was more orientated towards the so called Central European school of Rudolf von Laban and Kurt Jooss. In retrospect, one can ask whether or not the Ballet de Wallonie ever wanted to move on to modernism and if it was able to take that step.

Béjart's impact was enormous. His tactics of what would be referred to today as 'audience development' effectively touched masses of spectators who came to see his shows in the Cirque Royal or Forest National. He captivated a new and enthusiastic public at a moment when hitherto, contemporary dance was only being seen within small elitist (opera) circles. Furthermore, by establishing the dance school Mudra, he created a stimulating environment for dance in Brussels, which attracted a young generation of dancers from all over Europe.

A less positive aspect however, was Béjart's urge to maintain a monopoly. Although he himself must have been aware of the international developments in dance, he and the director of the national opera at the time, did not attempt to present them in Brussels or indeed, allow their influence to infiltrate his own work.

By way of illustration, here are some programme details from the Paris Festival d'Automne. 1972: Bob Wilson, Yvonne Rainer, Merce Cunningham, and Richard Schechner; 1973: Richard Foreman, Trisha Brown, Simone Forti, Joan Jonas, and Béjart himself; 1974: Peter Brook, Meredith Monk, and Het Nederlands Danstheater. In Belgium, it was not until the 1980's that we were able to see work by these artists in our theatres. Even then, we still see no reference to what was happening on the performing arts scene in Germany at that time, namely *Café Müller*, the breakthrough by Pina Bausch in 1976.

In Flemish theatre, the sclerosis hit hardest in the repertory theatres in the big cities. The alternative movement of 'chamber theatre' drew to a close and political theatre was unable to breath new life into itself

despite endless revivals of *Mistero Buffo* and some experiments with audience participation by theatre company *Het Trojaanse Paard*, inspired by the social emancipatory methods of the Brazilian Augusto Boal.
Despite this, the ever increasing circle of cultural centres, together with the initiation of the Festival van Vlaanderen, facilitated, in a practical way, the presentation of culture and live performance. The idea was that everyone in Flanders, even outside the cities, was entitled to have access to this kind of art. Europalia focused each year on a different European Union member state in order to give cultural expression to the concept of European unification.
At the same time though, there were other things happening: on the sidelines, away from the glare of politics and the subsidy watchdogs. Things born of artistic inspiration and cultural commitment, and often based on a brand new approach to cities and urban identities.
With the Beursschouwburg in Brussels leading the way, the end of the 1970's saw the emergence in Flanders of a number of initiatives driven by individuals or organisations which were later to come together to form 'Art Centres'. The well-known pioneers are Kaaitheater in Brussels, Stuc/Klapstuk in Leuven, deSingel in Antwerp, Limelight in Kortrijk, and Vooruit in Ghent. They found inspiration and kindred spirits in the Shaffytheater, Mickery, and the Festival of Fools in Amsterdam, the theatre festival in Nancy (led by Jack Lang, later French cultural minister), and the Festival d'Avignon recently transformed under Bernard Faivre d'Arcier, who quite expressly returned to the original objectives of Jean Vilar, the great left-wing reviver of French theatre in the fifties.

This group did not receive any significant government support, yet succeeded in organising Mallemunt, the first Kaaitheater festival in 1977, the animation interventions of Grasgroen in Leuven, the first productions by Radeis ('theatre without much cinema') and a programme based on video and new media in the Nieuwe Workshop at the Oude Graanmarkt in Brussels. The Acienne Belgique was beginning a new life as a concert hall and thus was bringing Flanders into contact with rock music and the roughness and *street credibility* of emerging punk rock.

In short: at the beginning of the eighties a new artistic effervescence could be felt and the cultural *avant-garde* imagined that there would soon be a revolution. Somewhat later, we realised that post-modernism had reached Flanders: not only in the performing arts (Jan Decorte, Ivo van Hove, and Jan Fabre), but also in architecture (bOb Van Reeth, Robbrecht & Daem, and Stéphane Beel), music (the late Karel Goeyvaerts, Peter Vermeersch & Thierry De Mey, and Wim Mertens), literature (Tom Lanoye, Stefan Hertmans, and Dirk Van Bastelaere), and video and film (the Theys brothers, Walter Verdin, Dominique Deruddere, and Marc Didden).
In French speaking Brussels and Wallonia, the post-modern *Zeitgeist* had found homes in places such as Théâtre 140, Les Halles de Schaerbeek, La Raffinerie du Plan K (where Frédéric Flamand was the first to offer Rosas rehearsal facilities), and in the circles of Henri Pousseur at the Music Academy in Liège, where composers and musicians such as Philippe Boesmans, Frederic Rzewski, and Bernard Foccroulle were also working. The first Brussels festival of new music, Ars Musica, led by Paul Dujardin, was held in 1988.

IV. This was the cultural climate in which Anne Teresa De Keersmaeker embarked upon her career as a young dancer at the end of the 1970's. She described herself as 'a stubborn little girl' in a poem that was included in the subsidy dossier for *Asch*, her first production.
During her studies at grammar school, she took dancing lessons with Lieve Curias, herself a student under Jeanne Brabants at the Antwerp Stedelijk Instituut voor Ballet, and from Lilian Lambert, through whom she met Michèle Anne and Thierry De Mey. Thierry was to open her world to Antonin Artaud, Georges Bataille, Steve Reich, and Rainer Werner Fassbinder.
She felt such an intense compulsion to make dance her career and her life's mission that she decided to do an audition for Mudra, the school of Maurice Béjart. There, she was impressed and influenced by the old master Fernand Schirren the rhythm teacher, and Alfons Goris the theatre lecturer. She ended up in a markedly international student community in which the following people stood out: Michèle Anne De Mey, Maguy Marin, Pierre Droulers, Nicole Mossoux, Bernardo Montet, François Hiffler, Nacho Duato, Bernard Glandier, Michèle Noiret, and Catherine Diverrès.
The trip to Italy of the apprentice Flemish painters was replaced, for a young choreographer at the end of the 20th century, by a period of study in New York. New York was then the absolute Mecca of contemporary dance, the place where Martha Graham, José Limon, George Balanchine, Merce Cunningham, and the post-modernists of the Judson Church (Trisha Brown, Lucinda Childs, and Steve Paxton) had set-up studios and created communities with other artists. Anne Teresa was able to go there thanks to a scholarship from the Stichting Roeping. She studied for one year at the Tisch School of the Arts, New York University. There she had lessons at the Experimental Theatre Wing and the Department of Performance Studies lead by Richard Schechner. She wrote an article about the German 1930's dancer Valeska Gert for *The Drama Review*. She then returned to Europe with *Violin Phase* a solo to music by Steve Reich, the start of *Fase* and, as it turned out, of an impressive career.

V. She worked on *Fase* together with Michèle Anne De Mey and turned it into a full length performance consisting of a solo and three duets, all to the powerful music of Steve Reich. She took her ideas to Hugo De Greef and thus entered the world of networks. De Gre[illegible]f, initiator of the Kaaitheater festival and the driving force be[illegible]d Sch[illegible]mte, the artists' co-operative, had just organised some [illegible]articularly successful tours for Radeis, theatre without words and th[illegible]ore promotable worldwide. In *Fase* he saw at once a qual[illegible]hat would unanimously enthuse a new public, eager for a diff[illegible]nd of dance and another (more feminine) kind of sensitivit[illegible]

But there was more. Together with some cultural centres, the ambitious Arts Centres had set up the Vlaams Theatercircuit led by Guido Minne. This was the precursor of the Vlaams Theater Instituut. In the initial period, this organisation ensured that De Keersmaeker's work was established and became widely known in Flanders.
And there was more networking: Hugo De Greef and Guido Minne were among the initiators of the Informal European Theatre Meeting (IETM). This brought Flemish producers and programmers naturally and spontaneously together with their European partners and 'comrades in arms'. This in turn facilitated co-production agreements (which were a financial necessity for Rosas) with the Théâtre de la Ville of Gérard Violette in Paris, the Hebbel-Theater of Nele Hertling in Berlin, the Rotterdamse Schouwburg of Carel Alons, the Springdance Festival of George Brugmans in Utrecht, the Festival d'Avignon of Bernard Faivre d'Arcier, octobre en normandie of Laurent Langlois, and contacts with the Brooklyn Academy of Music of Harvey Liechtenstein, and with almost all theatre and dance producers of the European cultural capitals and many others.

VI. Enter Mortier
It was 1981 and Gerard Mortier from Ghent was appointed director of La Monnaie, Belgium's National Opera. The changes he instigated were immediately revolutionary and fundamental, and of a radical nature not previously seen in the Belgian cultural sector. Mortier exhibited pugnacity and developed a strategy that had the successive ministers in charge gasping for breath. He sought and found a new public for opera and gave the young protagonists of the 'Flemish Wave'' opportunities to show their work in La Monnaie (Rosas' *Elena's aria* and *Bartók/aantekeningen* were shown.) However, the politicians did not always want to follow this lead financially and in the first round of reforms Mortier scrapped the Ballet of the XXth Century from his programme and forced Maurice Béjart into a humiliating exile in Lausanne. Mark Morris and his dancers came from New York to take up residence at La Monnaie. The Belgian dance public found this a very controversial choice and it turned out not to be the most successful episode of the Mortier saga.
Mortier's legendary interlude in La Monnaie was also important to Rosas directly. He co-produced *Ottone Ottone*, with music by Claudio Monteverdi's *L'incoronazione di Poppea* and encouraged Anne Teresa to make *Mozart/Concert Arias*, which was performed for the first time in the Palais des Papes at the Festival of Avignon, two key productions in the De Keersmaeker œuvre which both draw upon opera repertoire.
This brought Anne Teresa De Keersmaeker into closer contact with the highly organised, international opera milieu and she learnt about the workings of a large house, an experience from which she would later reap the benefit[illegible] wher[illegible]n 1992, Bernard Foccroulle, as Mortier's successor, asked Rosas to beco[illegible]e the resident dance company of La Monnaie. After the controve[illegible]urrounding Mark Morris, it was courageous of Foccroulle to opt for [illegible] manifestly contemporary profile of Rosas. The artistic connect[illegible] mutual commitment between Foccroulle and De Keersmaeke[illegible]unt and Rosas, proved to be as strong as iron. She requested, and received three things: the chance to perform with live music regularly, to expand the Rosas repertory, and help from La Monnaie in establishing her own dance school. That became P.A.R.T.S. (Performing Arts Research and Training Studios).

VII. Here are some statistics about Rosas: since the collaboration with Michèle Anne De Mey for *Fase* 71 dancers have been involved with the company. They came together from 19 countries. And, as the credit lists for the various productions have consistently quoted the words 'danced by and created with' in front of the names of the dancers for some time now, it means not only their personal history, but also the history of their own culture has contributed to the creative output of the company. Over the past 20 years, Rosas has given 1728 performances in 37 countries and 202 towns and cities. By the same token, this extensive involvement in the world through performing becomes visible in the work.
As regards P.A.R.T.S, the pedagogical team have held auditions in 28 towns and cities from 21 countries in 3 continents. They have selected 212 students from 37 countries in the past 7 years.

VIII. All this intercultural activity needed its own space in Brussels, not to create a closed international enclave, but as a launching pad for those residing, working, and living in Brussels or Belgium or anywhere else in the world for that matter.
After a lot of searching, which in itself helped to establish a definition of the ideal place of work, and thanks to the clear-headed Dutch business sense of Kees Eijrond (General Director of Rosas since 1990), an old factory building was purchased in the Van Volxemlaan in forest. Gradually, the powerful administrative triangle of Kees Eijrond, Guy Gypens, and Anne Teresa De Keersmaeker ensured the necessary finance to house not only the Rosas studios and offices, but also the rehearsal rooms of Ictus, who became the Rosas' musical spouse. Architect Paul Van Aerschot renovated an adjoining warehouse that was used for P.A.R.T.S.
P.A.R.T.S established a worldwide reputation in no time, thanks not least to the artistic and pedagogical alliances that were established with William Forsythe, Pina Bausch, and Trisha Brown. With P.A.R.T.S. De Keersmaeker built a bridge between the legacy of classical ballet, German expressionism and American post-modern dance. Perhaps this was a unique healing moment of synthesis in the history of Belgian ballet and contemporary dance.
The history of Rosas proves that the way from the periphery to the centre is long and bumpy. However, the intrinsic quality of the work continued to earn the support of people both inside and outside the government, thus guaranteeing the possibility of maintaining the basic infrastructure indispensable to the creative work. The site on the Van Volxemlaan has become a place where a hundred or so people from all continents learn, perform and create art every day. This fact alone justifies Brussels being the self-appointed dance capital of Europe in 2000.

IX. The creative world of Anne Teresa De Keersmaeker resembles a house with several doors, all of which are open. Some are always wide open, others are opened and closed by the wind, and still others are left ajar. This openness to other stimuli from art, life, the wider world, others, and the 'Other' provides a fundamental source of creativity the choreographer can draw upon artistically.

It awakens her to the music of Reich, Ligeti, Bartók, Bach, Monteverdi, Stravinsky, Mozart, Aka Moon, and Purcell, the texts of Müller, Weiss, Handke, Rijnders, and Tsjechov, the films of Kurosawa, Fassbinder, and Greenaway, the scenographic invention of Sorgeloos, Versweyveld, and Lamers, the popular sounds of Bulgarian female choirs, Velvet Underground, dj Grazzhoppa, Italian folk tunes, Joan Baez. It makes her curious about the most diverse musicians, costume designers, film makers, the depths of Eastern philosophy, eating habits and ways of life; and keeps her permeable to the bombardment of images and experiences which make up life in a truly intercultural, forever changing setting.

X. It is intellectually difficult to untangle the knot between local attachments, Flemish sensibilities, and Belgian openness to intercultural experience, knowledge of languages, experimental drive, European sympathy, historical awareness, aspiration for recognition and timeless aesthetics. Yet this is the knot that supplies us with a figure like Anne Teresa De Keersmaeker as an example of how art and culture can operate together both locally and globally.

Laurent Busine e.a., *Opera, tastbare emotie*, Gemeentekrediet, Brussels, 2000.

Hildegard De Vuyst et al., *Alles is rustig. Het verhaal van de kunstencentra*, Vlaams Theaterinstituut, Brussels, 1999.

Herman Sorgeloos, Eric De Kuyper et al., *Rosas Album*, Theater Instituut Nederland, Amsterdam, 1993.

Ritsaert Ten Cate, Jef De Roeck et al., *Humus. 15 jaar Kaaitheater*, Kaaitheater, Brussels, 1993.

Marianne Van Kerkhoven, An-Marie Lambrechts & Katie Verstockt, *Dans in Vlaanderen*, Stichting Kunstboek, Brugge, 1996.

P.A.R.T.S.
How to 'School' in the 21st Century

Jean-Marc Adolphe

School. Can art be taught? This question has become more poignant and the answers more divers throughout the course of the 20th century. The surge of modernity caused attitudes to become more individualized and to differentiate themselves from the religious and monarchist dogmas that had, 'til then, been the cement of thought. Naturally this had far reaching repercussions in the sphere of the arts. The teaching of 'fine arts' as split disciplines was severely shaken by the different aesthetic revolutions, from expressionism to surrealism, from the Bauhaus school to the Dada movement. Academic learning fell apart as the question of 'technique' was radically challenged by the 'strategies' of collage, montage and fragmentation. This didn't mean that the techniques disappeared urbi ed orbi but 'the' technique could no longer remain the only reference of value for artistic mastery. This current touched all the arts, and dance was obviously not excluded from the radical overhaul of methods of creation.

Dance's relationship to 'classical technique' ('Classical dance, the only true dance the dance of the West' wrote Pierre Gaxotte in a famous work on the history of dance) also encompasses the notion of a control of the body in a political sense. We mustn't forget that classical dance was born in the heart of the Royal Academy of Dance, in France at the beginning of the reign of Louis XIV. At exactly the same moment, the public performing of folk and regional dances was prohibited. In its ideal of 'elevation', classical dances claims divine inspiration. 'God creates, I assemble' declared George Balanchine to a journalist in the 50's who had asked him how he choreographed his ballets. Modernity in dance was to be a reversal of its submission to a unique and superior model and would precipitate the emergence of the 'subject' as author of his or her own dance. We know the story of the pioneers of modern dance (Isadora Duncan, Ruth Saint-Denis, Mary Wigman) that, with no other technical basis other than that which they invented as they went along, planted the first seeds of 'free dance'. But the revolution also sprang from within the classical 'fortress' with Nijinsky's fabulous act of defiance in 1913, with the creation of the *Rite of Spring*.

Nevertheless, the bastion of classical dance in Europe remained an obstacle to the spread of modern dance for a long time. Even today 'classical technique' remains dominant in teaching structures such as 'conservatories'. It was in these circumstances that modern dance gradually became accepted thanks to the filter of 'techniques'. Graham technique, Cunningham technique etc. This said, when she was asked at the end of her life about the proliferation of techniques that carried her name, Martha Graham claimed to have never developed a rigidly set technique and to still be at a stage of research. She was 95 at the time! If we can imagine art without technique (be it contested, experimental or vague) it goes without saying that technique alone doesn't make art. It goes without saying but it's better to say it nevertheless, especially in dance where 'technical virtuosity' often acts as a fig leaf to the poverty of many a choreographic work. So this said, it's clear that a school of dance should not just be a place for the learning of technique but a place for the awakening of sensibilities in order to produce, if possible, intelligent artists. This might seem presumptuous; but under the pretext that dance is a 'non-verbal' art, dance drags with it tiresome presuppositions based on the old Western split between body and spirit. An intelligent dancer is not necessarily someone with a degree in philosophy; he is simply someone who is not content to reproduce a standard form and who is capable of questioning, with his body (including his head), the form that he is dancing. This fact, which was still strongly contested 'til some years ago, has now become integrated into contemporary dance. Even though the demiurgical status of the author/choreographer vacillates (if there is or is not 'collective choreographing'), the performer can hardly still be compared with an 'executer'. When he is not author of a piece de facto, he is the living material, that the choreographer of course 'manipulates' (there should be a whole eulogy here to 'manipulation' in art that shouldn't be confused with 'instrumentalisation') but that is invested in the work in a consenting, engaged and creative way. It's no surprise, all the great contemporary choreographers (Merce Cunningham, Trisha Brown, Pina Bausch, William Forsythe, Anne Teresa de Keersmaeker,...) forged their creative identities with dancers with strong personalities. It is, moreover, because of this that the expression 'dance company' is much more appropriate than 'corps de ballet'.

In Europe, the change took place with Maurice Béjart and the Ballet of the XXth Century, precisely because, unbeknownst to Béjart (who had clearly seen that the 20th century would be that of dance but couldn't predict how it would take shape) in the 20th century, the very notion of ballet became obsolete, or at least a museum piece (though there are exceptions to all rules and we can't ignore the Frankfurt Ballet, directed by William Forsythe). Logically the transformation took place in a school that had become, more or less against its own volition, a place of creation. Mudra, which Béjart set up in Brussels, was this vital pivot. What was needed, as well as a new generation of dancers aware of the trends that where emerging in New York, was a catalyst – and that was the person of Fernand Schirren, percussionist and composer to whom Béjart delegated the teaching of rhythm. The rest of the story is sufficiently well known not to make it necessary to explain it here.

In the thirst for discovery and innovation that characterised, in Europe, dance of the 80's and 90's, transmission of knowledge or education was quickly relegated to minor status. In the role of inventor and explorer, choreographers were not yet thinking about handing things over. It was essential, especially at the time, to train dancers that were *trained in new ways.*
In order to harness the energy of the wave of individuals journeying to and from Europe and the United States, the French Ministry of Culture created a new school the Centre national de danse contemporaine d'Angers, the direction of which was naturally given first to an American, Alwin Nikolaïs, who was succeeded by another American, Viola Faber. These American influences were certainly determining, but inevitably had to gradually diminish as a 'new dance' began at last to take root in Europe. Few artists however, felt the real necessity to take over the job of transmission that had been left in abandonment since the 'great masters'. In France, only the post-Cunninghamist Michel Hallet-Eghayan and Dominique Bagouet in Montpellier were attached to the idea of teaching in an open way, not purely teaching how to mimic. In creating P.A.R.T.S. in Brussels, Anne Teresa de Keersmaker, has, in turn, acted upon this necessity to transmit an art of which no script, except that of 'shared experience', can guarantee the durability. She did it without making concessions, with determination, rigorousness and the radicality that we know from the development of her choreographic work. She refused the tutelage of the Ministry of Culture in order to avoid the obligation that all the classes be given in Flemish. Despite being a figurehead of the 'new Flemish wave', Anne Teresa didn't see herself as a mistress of a Flemish school, albeit of dance.

We can understand her. She ostentatiously turned her back on small minded nationalism, the P.A.R.T.S. project wanted to be open to the world from the start, like the happily cosmopolitan town of Brussels, that has largely replaced Paris as the artists' capital of Europe! Rosas' choreographer found the necessary funding that the 'public powers' hesitated to give her, through private partners. Roughly renovating an old industrial laundry building, she opened P.A.R.T.S. in 1995, and, without having quite means enough, she turned it into a place of luxury. Gold and red velvet? No, space and time, the real luxuries of dance.

There is already a promise in the title P.A.R.T.S.: *Performance Arts Training and Research Studios.* You have to weigh each word, savor their association in order to understand that P.A.R.T.S. is not quite a school like any other. Or more exactly, P.A.R.T.S. is the prototype for the schools of the 21st century, and not only schools of dance.
So everything is said, or almost. Today P.A.R.T.S. offers to its students from all over the world, first and foremost, a highly specialized training in dance. Classical classes, classes and workshops with pedagogues experienced in the 'vocabularies' of William Forsythe, Trisha Brown and Pina Bausch, study of the Rosas 'repertory' that constitutes the pedagogical back bone of a curriculum that is also open to musical analysis, dramaturgy, theatre, history of art, sociology and philosophy. 'If a student wants one day to make a work of art, if he or she wants to be more than a simple executant, he has to train his mental faculties as well as his body.' In this way P.A.R.T.S. is more than a school, it is in itself an artistic project. Far from considering education as a 'cold and strict system', it is about 'giving space to chance, to the intangible, to fantasy' by linking 'intuition and reflection.' Throughout their studies the P.A.R.T.S. students are encouraged to produce their 'personal work' on their own or in groups. P.A.R.T.S. also aims to be a place 'where critical and creative art can take root.' Alongside Rosas and the music ensemble Ictus with whom the school cohabits, P.A.R.T.S. functions in a complex of around 10 studios, a performance space, a cafeteria and a bit of greenery – an exemplary setting.

Seven years after the opening of P.A.R.T.S., the school has already become the home base of a new generation of choreographic artists. Equipped with the diverse techniques which shaped contemporary dance in the second half of the 20th century, open to the current pluridisciplinarity of performance art, these young artists are beginning to appear on the more discerning European stages. P.A.R.T.S. is, furthermore, concerned with the future of these emerging artists and has initiated DEPARTS which has brought together the following organizations: Théâtre de la Bastille (Paris), Dançás na cidade (Lisbon), the Künstlerhaus Mousonturm (Frankfurt), the Choreographisches Zentrum (Essen) and Tanzquartier (Viena) in order to support the first professional steps of the ex-P.A.R.T.S. students.

In September 2002, when I was artistic advisor for the Théâtre de la Bastille, I had the pleasure of inviting to Paris, in partnership with the Festival d'Automne, the project Parts@Paris The first initiative of its kind, it presented, over a period of five weeks, about fifteen choreographic works, all strong, dense and original. I wrote a few lines for the occasion which I would like to repeat here:

Today some people play Cassandra and deplore the dissipation of styles and techniques that renders all rational attempts at education futile. Is it not the only safe thing to do: frenzied teaching of techniques in order to render the contemporary dancer as efficient, impressive and malleable as possible?
Anne Teresa and Bernard Foccroule, director of La Monnaie in Brussels, jointly took the initiative in 1995 to open a new school. In a few short years P.A.R.T.S. has become proof of the pertinence of a project that aims at marrying the transmission of know-how and expertise with the encouragement of creative incentive. Moreover, certain first generation P.A.R.T.S. students have not wasted any time in making their presence felt on European stages.
Each one of them could adopt this phrase of South African ex-student George Khumalo. 'We inherit, use, reuse and throw away, and that which we know and think takes c new forms and meaning.'
What will become. This v ne title I gave the text. Simply because in the 21st century a school c ne based on what has been, but must stay receptive to the worlc o give a chance to what will become.

Album

Ursula Robb, Beniamin Boar and Cynthia Loemij filming *Counterphrases*, Brussels (2002). Photo Anne Van Aerschot.

Julia Sugranyes filming *Counterphrases*, Heers (2002). Photo Anne Van Aerschot.

Thierry De Mey, Aliocha Van der Avoort, Pascale Gigon and Anne-Catherine Kunz filming *Counterphrases*, Hofstade (2002). Photo Anne Van Aerschot.

Jordi Galí and Julia Sugranyes filming *Counterphrases*, Loppem (2002). Photo Anne Van Aerschot.

Anne Teresa De Keersmaeker, Alix Eynaudi, Fumiyo Ikeda, Julia Sugranyes, Taka Shamoto, Jakub Truszkowski, Rosalba Torres, Clinton Stringer, Cynthia Loemij, Beniamin Boar, rehearsal *April me* (2002). Photo Herman Sorgeloos (HS).

Jan Versweyveld and Anne Teresa De Keersmaeker, rehearsal *April me* (2002). Photo HS.

Ursula Robb, Julia Sugranyes, Jakub Truszkowski, Jordi Galí, Taka Shamoto, Igor Shyshko, Anne Teresa De Keersmaeker and Marta Coronado, rehearsal *April me* (2002). Photo HS.

Cynthia Loemij and Clinton Stringer, rehearsal *April me* (2002). Photo HS.

Igor Shyshko, rehearsal *April me* (2002). Photo HS.

Anne-Catherine Kunz and Anne Van Aerschot, filming *Fase*, Brussel (2002). Photo HS.

Ictus Ensemble with Steve Reich, New York (2001). Photo Elena Olivo.

es Eijrond and Anne Teresa De Keersmaeker
on and Anna Franziska Jäger, Venice (2001).
Photo Fumiyo Ikeda.

Lorimer, Igor Shyshko, Taka Shamoto, Anne Teresa De Keersmaeker, Cynthia
emij, Anna Franziska Jäger, Veerle Francke, Jakub Truszkowski, Anton Jäger,
mantha Van Wissen, Rosalba Torres, Anne-Catherine Kunz, Kees Eijrond,
Alix Eynaudi and Clinton Stringer, Venice (2001). Photo Fumiyo Ikeda.

Mark Lorimer and Taka Shamoto, Tokyo (2001).
Photo Anne Van Aerschot.

Martin Kilvády, DJ Grazzhoppa, Alix Eynaudi, Oliver Koch, Jakub Truszkowski, Roberto Oliván de la Iglesia, Rosalba Torres, Ursula Robb, Cynthia Loemij and Mark Lorimer, Porto (2001). Photo Fumiyo Ikeda.

Rosalba Torres and Roberto Oliván de la Iglesia, Prague (2000). Photo Anne Van Aerschot.

Anne Teresa De Keersmaeker, Hannover (2000).
Photo Frank Vandezande.

Cynthia Loemij, Iris Bouche, Damiaan De Schrijver and Rosalba Torres, rehearsal *In real time* (2000). Photo HS.

Marta Coronado, Ursula Robb, Taka Shamoto, Alix Eynaudi and Frank Vercruyssen, rehearsal *In real time* (2000). Photo HS.

Aka Moon, rehearsal *In real time* (2000).
Photo Frank Vandezande.

Taka Shamoto, Fumiyo Ikeda, Bruce Campbell, Oliver Koch, Cynthia Loemij and Marta Coronado, Adelaide (2000). Photo Roberto Oliván de la Iglesia.

Marta Coronado, Ottawa (1999).
Photo Marta Coronado.

Marta Coronado.

Oliver Koch, Nathalie Douxfils, Veerle Francke, Iris Bouche, Alix Eynaudi, Anne Teresa De Keersmaeker, Guy Gypens, Anne Van Aerschot and Luc Galle, Cairo (1999). Photo Fumiyo Ikeda.

Ursula Robb, Fumiyo Ikeda, Nathalie Douxfils,
Taka Shamoto and Marta Coronado, Cairo (1999).
Photo Taka Shamoto.

Suman Hsu and Farooq Chaudry.
Photo Roberto Oliván de la Iglesia.

Frank Vercruyssen and Cynthia Loemij,
performance of *Quartett* (1999). Photo HS.

Martin Kilvády, Marta Coronado, Jean-Luc Plouvier,
Oliver Koch, Alix Eynaudi, rehearsal *I said I* (1999).
Photo HS.

Anne Teresa De Keersmaeker and Jolente
De Keersmaeker (1997). Photo HS.

Osman Kassen Khelili, Brice Leroux, Mark Lorimer,
Sarah Ludi, Samantha Van Wissen and Oliver Koch,
Bogota (1996). Photo HS.

Fumiyo Ikeda, Nadine Ganase, Iris Bouche, Cynthia Loemij, Nathalie
Million, Samantha Van Wissen, Sarah Ludi, Marion Levy, Michèle Anne
De Mey, Anne Mousselet, Adriana Boriello and Anne Teresa
De Keersmaeker, filming *Rosas danst Rosas*, Leuven (1996). Photo HS.

Cynthia Loemij, Sarah Ludi, Samantha Van Wissen
and Anne Mousselet, filming *Rosas danst Rosas*,
Leuven (1996). Photo HS.

Anne Teresa De Keersmaeker, Adriana Boriello,
Fumiyo Ikeda and Michèle Anne De Mey, filming
Rosas danst Rosas, Leuven (1996). Photo HS.

Students P.A.R.T.S. with Elizabeth Corbett (2001).
Photo Nathalie Willems.

Students P.A.R.T.S. with John Wisman (1996).
Photo HS.

T[illegible] Mey and Fernand Schirren,
gradua[illegible] P.A.R.T.S. (1999). Photo HS.

Students P.A.R.T.S. with Meg Stuart and Damaged Goods (1999). Photo HS.

Marion Dijkstra, kitchen P.A.R.T.S. Photo HS.

Wieger Klooster and Mieke Vervecken, kitchen P.A.R.T.S. Photo HS.

Jan Ritsema opening P.A.R.T.S. (1998). Photo HS.

Graduation party P.A.R.T.S. (1998). Photo Yves Gervais.

Diploma P.A.R.T.S. (1998). Photo Yves Gervais.

Anne Teresa De Keersmaeker, Theo Van Rompay and Fernand Schirren, opening P.A.R.T.S. (1995). Photo HS.

Bernard Foccroulle and Pina Bausch, opening P.A.R.T.S. (1995). Photo HS.

Anne Teresa De Keersmaeker and Fernand Schirren, P.A.R.T.S. (1996). Photo HS.

Offices Rosas (1995). Photo Hans Roels.

Offices and janitorial residence Rosas (1995). Photo Hans Roels.

Rosas Performance Space. Photo Frédérique Debras.

Rehearsal studio Rosas.
Photo Frédérique Debras.

Rehearsal studio Rosas.
Photo Frédérique Debras.

Rosas Performance Space and P.A.R.T.S. studios.
Photo Frédérique Debras.

Luc Galle, Kees Eijrond, Herman Sorgeloos,
Guy Peeters and Guy Gypens, São Paulo (1995).
Photo Nathalie Douxfils.

Nathalie Douxfils, Marion Ballester,
Cynthia Loemij and Guy Peeters, São Paulo (1995).
Photo HS.

Anne Mousselet, Rio de Janeiro (1995).
Photo Guy Gypens.

Anne Teresa De Keersmaeker and Bernard Foccroulle
with King Albert II and Queen Paola, Théâtre Royal
de la Monnaie, Brussels (1995).

Kosi Hidama and Misha Downey, Rio de Janeiro (1995).
Photo Nathalie Douxfils.

Johanne Saunier, Anne Mousselet, Cynthia Loemij
and Marion Levy, Pinnacles Desert, Australia (1994).
Photo Guy Gypens.

Kees Eijrond, Alfarim (1994).
Photo Guy Gypens.

Philipp Egli, Frank Chartier, Thomas Hauert,
Christian Spuck and Misha Downey, rehearsal *Kinok*
(1994). Photo HS.

D. Keersmaeker and Irvine Arditti,
Brussel (1993). Photo HS.

Anne Teresa De Keersmaeker, Marion Ballester, Christian Spuck and Frank Chartier, rehearsals *Kinok* (1994). Photo HS.

Rolf Hind, Bruce Campbell, Ann Weckx, Frank Vandezande and Luc Galle, Rome (1993). Photo Frank Vandezande.

Janet Williams and Phillippe Herreweghe, rehearsals *Mozart/Concert Arias*, Avignon (1992). Photo HS.

Anne Teresa De Keersmaeker and Mark Bruce, Avignon (1992). Photo HS.

Thomas Hauert, Mark Bruce, Anne Teresa De Keersmaeker, Nordine Benchorf and Vincent Dunoyer, Avignon (1992). Photo HS.

Anne Mousselet, Muriel Hérault and Anne Teresa De Keersmaeker, Avignon (1992). Photo HS.

Vincent Dunoyer, Anne Teresa De Keersmaeker, Nordine Benchorf, Johanne Saunier, Muriel Hérault, Thomas Hauert, Eduardo Torroja, Anne Van Aerschot and Anne Mousselet, Avignon (1992). Photo HS.

Chris Buckley, Avignon (1992). Photo HS.

Anne Teresa De Keersmaeker and Janet Williams, Avignon (1992). Photo HS.

Janet Williams and Bernard Foccroulle, Avignon (1992). Photo HS.

Thomas Hauert, Joanne Fong, Philipp Egli and Anne Teresa De Keersmaeker, rehearsal *Erts* (1992). Photo HS.

The Arditti Quartet, Jean-Luc Ducourt, Anne Teresa de Keersmaeker, Vincent Dunoyer, Thomas Hauert Oliver Koch, Eduardo Torroja, Bruce Campbell, rehearsal *Erts* (1992). Photo HS.

Anne Teresa De Keersmaeker, Nathalie Million, Johanne Saunier and Roxane Huilmand, rehearsal restaging *Rosas danst Rosas* (1992).

Anne Teresa De Keersmaeker and Cynthia Loemij, Seattle (1991). Photo HS.

Anne Teresa De Keersmaeker and Cynthia Loemij, Seattle (1991). Photo HS.

Frank Vandezande, Nathalie Million, Herman Sorgeloos, Johanne Saunier and Fumiyo Ikeda, USA (1991). Photo Guy Gypens.

Nathalie Million, Seattle (1991). Photo HS.

Johanne Saunier, Seattle (1991). Photo HS.

Carlotta Sagna, Seattle (1991). Photo HS.

Cynthia Loemij, Muriel Hérault and Anne Teresa De Keersmaeker, rehearsal *Rosas danst Rosas*, Miami (1991). Photo Guy Gypens.

Alex Fostier and Frank Vandezande, Montréal (1991). Photo HS.

Anne Teresa De Keersmaeker and Herman Sorgeloos, Vienna (1991). Photo Guy Gypens.

Jean-Luc Ducourt, Marion Levy, Frank Vandezande, Anne Teresa De Keersmaeker and Johanne Saunier, Moscow (1990). Photo Fumiyo Ikeda.

Johan Leysen and Johanne Saunier, Haarlem (1990). Photo HS.

Marion Levy, rehearsal *Achterland* (1990). Photo HS.

Nathalie Million, Johanne Saunier, Fumiyo Ikeda, Vincent Dunoyer, Marion Levy and Carlotta Sagna, rehearsal *Achterland* (1990). Photo HS.

Bruce Campbell, Nordine Benchorf and Vincent Dunoyer, rehearsal *Achterland* (1990). Photo HS.

Carlotta Sagna and Johanne Saunier, rehearsal *Stella* (1989). Photo HS.

Herman Sorgeloos, Celesta Rottiers, Anne Teresa De Keersmaeker, Walter Hus and Stefan Poelmans, Yokohama (1989). Photo Fumiyo Ikeda.

Jordi Cassanovas Sempere, Fumiyo Ikeda and Nicole Balm, Lisbon (1989). Photo Fumiyo Ikeda.

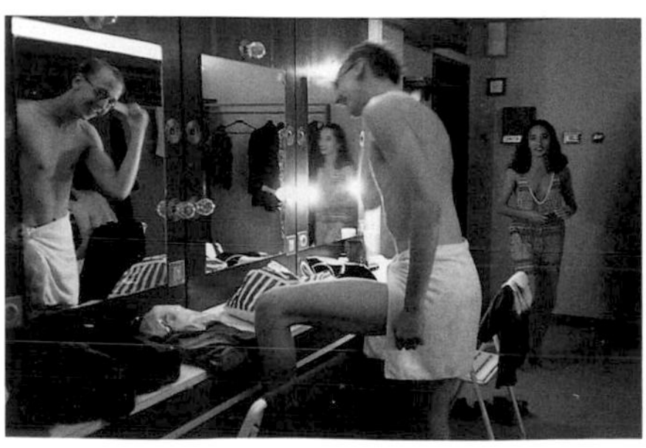
John Jasperse and Nadine Ganase, Lisbon (1989). Photo Fumiyo Ikeda.

Pere Pladeval Vallcorba, Lisbon (1989). Photo Fumiyo Ikeda.

Fatou Traore, Lisbon (1989). Photo Fumiyo Ikeda.

Laure Bonicel and Fumiyo Ikeda, Lisbon (1989). Photo Fumiyo Ikeda.

Jean-Luc Ducourt, Oscar Dasi y Perez, Pierre Droulers and Fumiyo Ikeda, Rotterdam (1988). Photo Fumiyo Ikeda.

Natalia Espinet Valles, Rotterdam (1988). Photo Fumiyo Ikeda.

Johanne Saunier (1988). Photo HS.

Fumiyo Ikeda and Roxane Huilmand (1988).
Photo HS.

Natalia Espinet Valles and Vincente Saez,
Milaan (1988). Photo Fumiyo Ikeda.

Michèle Anne De Mey, Mark Willems, Wouter Steenbergen, Fumiyo Ikeda, Johanne Saunier, Jean-Luc Ducourt, Oscar Dasi y Perez, Nicole Balm, John Jasperse, Natalia Espinet Valles, Nathalie Million and Nordine Benchorf, rehearsal *Ottone Ottone* (1988). Photo HS.

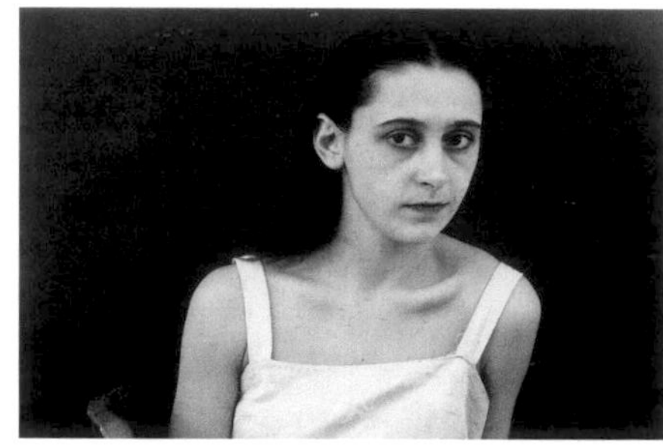

Anne Teresa De Keersmaeker, *Elena's aria*
in New York (1987). Photo Peggy Kaplan.

Nadine Ganase, *Elena's aria* in New York (1987).
Photo Peggy Kaplan.

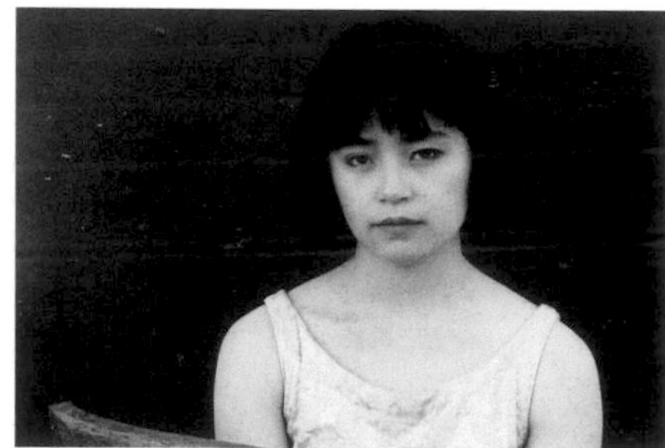

Fumiyo Ikeda, *Elena's aria* in New York (1987).
Photo Peggy Kaplan.

Roxane Huilmand, *Elena's aria* in New York (1987).
Photo Peggy Kaplan.

Michèle Anne De Mey, *Elena's aria* in New York (1987).
Photo Peggy Kaplan.

Anne Teresa De Keersmaeker, Nadine Ganase, Johanne
Saunier and Fumiyo Ikeda, Yugoslavia (1987).

Roxane Huilmand, Johanne Saunier and Nadine
Ganase, Stuttgart (1987). Photo Fumiyo Ikeda.

André Verbist, performance of *Medeamaterial*
(1987) video still Walter Verdin.

114. Kitty Kortes Lynch, performance of *Medeamaterial* (1987) video still Walter Verdin.

115. Hugo De Greef and Gudrun Schotsaert. Photo Fumiyo Ikeda.

116. Adriana Boriello, Michèle Anne De Mey, Anne Teresa De Keersmaeker and Bert De Raeymaeker (1983). Photo Fumiyo Ikeda.

Walter Hus, Peter Vermeersch, Eric Sleichim, Thierry De Mey (1983). Photo M.F. Plissart.

Anne Teresa De Keersmaeker, Nadine Ganase, Adriana Boriello and Fumiyo Ikeda (1983). Photo Michiel Hendryckx.

Anne Teresa De Keersmaeker and Jean Luc Breuer, performance of *Asch* (1980). Photo Alun de H.

'Compliance is not my Style'

Anna Luyten

I've always liked to do everything; always had an incredible number of desires. The mountain of work that goes with that just has to be done. I cannot change up my greedy nature.'

'There was once a woman who killed a man while he was sitting in his bath,' my uncle told me. I was still a child when I used to listen to his stories. 'It really happened,' he said. 'My mother told me and she heard it from her mother who had heard the story through the grapevine.'
In the evenings I used to sit on the farm cart like a princess together with my three sisters and my brother. We rode home from the fields with the harvest. I've never forgotten the dead man in the bath. Later I discovered that that was the story of Charlotte Corday and Jean-Paul Marat.
In my youth I was surrounded by people whose lives kept pace with the rhythm of the large farm in Brabant, on the edge of a big city. We lived under the eagle eyes of spinster aunts and a robust grandmother who was born at the end of the nineteenth century. My father also worked on the farm of his father who had died at a young age. The atmosphere was that of a Cyril Buysse novel. My mother was a teacher of Dutch and history. Always up and about. I grew cacti. I rode on a farm horse called Bella. I was given a dog. We had to make sure that the harvest was gathered before it began to rain. We played in the street. My uncle taught me to drive a tractor. When the harvest was gathered, I was allowed to cross the fresh stubble-field in the van.

My father was intelligent, but also very fearful. He was always restless. He possessed a kind of irrationality yet at the same time he also had a quite exceptional strength. He could do some foolish things. One day, he made a wooden board on which he wrote *House For Sale* and put it up in front of our house. We couldn't stop laughing.
I remember that he once called for me and then put a dead mole in my hands. He laid the mole in a little box and covered it in gift-wrapping paper. 'Give it to your teacher,' he said. I ran happily to school with the little packet in my hand.
My mother was a very lively woman. She was very enterprising. She taught for many years. In the evenings and on Sundays she was often away giving lectures to the Country Women's Institute.
I cannot say that I come from an artistic background. However, whenever we went to Spain, we always visited some castle or other or a church building on the way. My mother could sometimes be quite insistent. After the tenth Roman church building, my father thought that 'enough was enough.' All that fuss about a bad *Guide Bleu*. Why did we have to go via Bourg-Madame when the route was badly signposted. My mother got out at the traffic lights and walked along the street. The five children starting to cry in the back of the car. My mother was being called back by her weeping offspring: 'We don't want to go to Spain at all. We want to go back home!'
My family was like that. It was a family where emotions were not suppressed. Our love was intense, deep, but sometimes rather clumsy. I had a box of coloured *Chicklets* ready specially for arguments. Whenever I heard any squabbling, I took my little box and went and sat down under the old, wooden desk. I covered my ears and began to chew very hard.
Years later, my father came in his wheelchair to see my dance performances. Mother, who had always been the stronger, pushed him.
And years later, I sat at my mother's sickbed to keep watch, my newly born son on my breast. She died before father. I also lost my father some months after the birth of my daughter.

I was the daughter of *Maurice of Frans of Keske*. That was what people in the village called us: the *Keske* family. The three eldest girls were sent to boarding school. We went together to the 'Heilig Hart' in Heverlee. I do not know why. Perhaps our parents were anxious to keep us off the streets, for the village politics of Wemmel have always played a major part for the family: my father's brother and my great uncle were both CVP Mayors (Flander's political Catholic party).
Boarding school has a strange impact on a child of twelve. You learn what it is to be alone. I became a *freak*. What I did was (in my view) not normal for a child of twelve. In the Greek lessons we read Xenophon. Our teacher had said that it would be useful to analyse some difficult texts. I took the *Anabasis* and began to analyse all the words one by one: genitive, indicative, third person plural. I had an exercise book in which I analysed every word in full. If I made a few mistakes, then I would erase those words with a 'tint killer'. Then I found that my exercise book looked rather dirty so I wrote out the entire exercise book again. And then I learnt the entire book by heart. I can still recite all my Greek principal parts. I wanted to master everything. I confess that I have always been very ambitious. Whatever must be done and however much work it takes, it just has to be done. I also have this attitude to my work as a choreographer.

As a little girl, I had what was perhaps a very normal longing for a tutu. I wanted to dance. My mother was tired of bringing us to Strombeek-Bever every week. Travelling ten kilometres just to dance for a few hours. She purchased a wooden floor, huge mirrors, and wooden *bars* and looked for a good dance teacher. She founded a little school in Wemmel. Lieve Curias, a girl of nineteen who had just finished her studies, became the teacher. She gave us lessons in classical and modern ballet, and also lessons in improvisation. She was inspiring. It was the heyday of Béjart, but Lieve Curias also went with us to watch more adventurous dances performances.

After three years at boarding school, I was allowed to move into lodgings alone in Brussels. I was sixteen and I drew up a strict working schedule. Mudra, the dance training given by Maurice Béjart, was what I wanted. If I had not been admitted to Mudra, I might have tried the Herman Teirlinck theatre training. In the evenings I took dance class at a private school: the 'Ecole de la danse, de la musique et des arts du spectacle Lilian Lambert'. Classical, modern, song, improvisation, theatre, I did everything. I wore myself out. I remember how tired I was as I sat in class. In time, I even went to the dance academy during the midday break. I loved it so much. I enjoyed doing Latin and Greek very much, but dance was my language.

The final French examination. Miss Delmez, the little plump teacher asked (in French): 'And, Miss De Keersmaeker, what do you want to do next year?' I replied: 'Me, I am going to be a dancer, Miss.'
On a morning of that same week, I ran to an audition with terror in my heart. I was so frail and slender. I had even been on a diet. I have never done that again. Forty-six kilos. Someone put a number on my ribs. I danced. I knew, I had a feeling that dance was the only way for me to express myself. A jury was watching. I will never forget the horror; the realisation that your future depended on someone else's judgement. I realised soon enough that I would never be a top class ballerina.
After my training at Mudra, I went to New York to study at the New York University's School of The Arts. I also did an audition in America: for adverts for a brand of jeans. I did not get the job. You only had to dance with your bottom. There was little future in that. I looked for another career. I sold clothes in a boutique in Soho. The clothes were of poor quality and ugly yet I still told several women that they looked gorgeous, and they were happy. And now, after all these years, if I feel down, I sill tend to go out buy clothes, nice ones.
In New York I met people who later proved to be very important for my work. Musicians who worked with Steve Reich. The performance of *Fase, four movements to the music of Steve Reich* followed a little later. One year after that, I formed my own ensemble.
In the first decade, I built everything up together with Hugo De Greef. He, with the people from Radeis, offered me the opportunity to show my work. I have had lots of reasons to be grateful to men during my career. Kees Eijrond, whom I met in a restaurant and who became general director. Guy Gypens, who became manager of Rosas. Without Theo Van Rompay, the P.A.R.T.S. school would never have happened.
And I am also very grateful to Bernard Foccroulle from La Monnaie. Working together with an artist on a large project, organising it together, has been very instructive. It has given me a lot of energy. Those men have ensured that over the years my work has reached a wider public. I think that is important. I do not want to stay entrenched in a little world. They have put my work into a border context. They have helped me to take the great 'desire' which I have always had, into wider territories. They have helped to plan my career.

At Mudra, I met Michèle Anne De Mey and her brother Thierry. He helped me to write my French thesis. It was about Antonin Artaud. I worked together with Michèle Anne on my first productions. Afterwards, she began a solo career. I still work together with Thierry, a spiritual companion from the very beginning. Dancers such as Fumiyo Ikeda and Cynthia Loemij have been there for almost twenty years.
The comings and goings of dancers. That has always been important to me. Painful, too. In my work, my relationship with the dancers is so strong that I always have to find a fresh balance in the group when someone leaves. I have never had any pleasure in seeing someone leave.

I'm emotional. I'm a romantic. I look for an area of intensity by working with structures and rigidity. There is always chaos around. Whatever quicksand is and whatever wind is, I want to combine them with pure, self-evident order. In order to have a firm basis, there has to be something to offer resistance. Dance is also something physical. I want to give it an abstract beauty. I am involved with dancers, but also with the abstract organisation of time and space. I am looking for an ideal formula to put everything together. Sometimes this becomes an obsession. I think that the dancers are sometimes driven crazy by it.
In time, I have discovered that everything crystalises into a very simple duality. Opening and closing; horizontal and vertical; man and woman; day and night. There is one, two, and three and then a whole eternity. If things become simple, then all problems with structures disappear. If I look back at all the pieces that I've made, I see how everything is interwoven. All those productions. Each piece was both a sequel to, and a destruction of, the previous piece. When I began working with spoken texts, my sister, Jolente, a maker of theatre, came on board. With her, I have the feeling that we are a real duo. We complement each other perfectly. I think in a more structured way than she does. Jolente has brought a lot of warmth into the performances. I have a certain strictness about me. An uncertainty. A fear. Jolente can work together with a group splendidly. She has a dramaturgically sharp insight. She has made everything easier, she has brought more joy into it.

There are so many superfluous things. Shops where you can have your nails treated. The market determines things everywhere, people just have to consume. We are being dragged along in a downward spiral which is based upon the supposition that material welfare is the absolute standard of happiness. It is so difficult to oppose this current. Perhaps the only solution is to stop consuming altogether, or sta[illegible] consuming less. It is a distressing feeling that as a citiz[illegible]n in a democr[illegible] you can no longer offer any resistance with your vote
I have always been interested in politics i[illegible]e that I also regard politics as a system which organises relationships and affairs between people. However, I understand the increasing disinterest in politics which now reigns. In the la[illegible]t twenty years, political leaders have handed over all power to the market economy. I have the feeling these days that there are no longer any real leaders. And most people prefer to vote for Betty from the TV show Big Brother than for a politician.

Everything has to be so simple and monotonous. Everywhere. Everything has to be swallowed quickly. In the media. In art as well. As an artist, I have a responsibility. I also have to fight against the competition from television which wants to ensure that nothing is too difficult. But I want to take up my responsibility. It is a challenge for me to practise maintaining a balance in my performances and to find a middle way between something intellectually challenging which refuses to take the easy option and something which is not lacking in thrill and enjoyment.
I still want to give people the 'desire' not just to accept indiscriminately what is immediately visible, but to ask questions. I also want to help them dream.

Seeing wild dreams come to nothing. Loving and losing. Saying goodbye. Letting go. I know all about that. I myself gave up dancing for a while. I think that I made a mistake there. By dancing, I can give most of what I have to offer. The dancing stage is the place where I feel free. In dancing, you build your own ratio of time and space, and that creates openness. I can say things better in dance. I have the feeling that I still have a lot to learn. I have the feeling that I am on the point of making a fresh start. I think that as you get older, your head thinks more clearly.
Stand by Your Man, that song by Tammy Wynette, why do I like listening to it now? *I Will Always Love You*. What have those songs got to offer? I am not afraid of oversimplification. Life is sometimes as it is in songs. Sometimes, at least. I would like to think so. Love. It's still something which preoccupies me. Men and women. The relationship. The contrast. The duality. It is the basis of energy. It is a search for complementary essence. I hope that as the years go by I might be more at peace about it. That it might become more spiritual.
I will probably always have that eternal longing to be lost in something or someone. Even if I know it is impossible. I have been completely absorbed in my work for such a long time. The first twelve years of my career consisted of nothing else. Then I became a mother. That brought another reality apart from dance. There was a lot of happiness. There were also practical problems. Combining all the roles which you play in life is sometimes difficult. But I cannot give up the greed. A *pigsty* on Sundays, that is what I sometimes miss now. A bed in which mum and dad lie together, where the children crawl under the sheets in the morning and go wild. I don't have a pigsty, but the father of my children is there. Together and yet separate. In two houses.
Love. Perhaps I have expected too much of it. Or perhaps I could not handle it. I have loved men and made mistakes in love affairs. I have suffered setbacks. Maybe the life that I lead is not compatible with the life of another. Those questions are now poignant. What do I need now in order to be happy? Does love mean being totally absorbed in another? Is that sharing? Can distance and depth be combined? Maybe I shouldn't think so passionately about all these things. Maybe real power comes from admitting that a little less is okay. But I do not want to become lethargic. It is so exciting when you are not at peace, unrest stirs up mischief. I play around too much with limits. The heart is also a muscle. You can wrench it, tear it out, sprain it, it can be split and it grows together again, but there are always things which you can no longer do afterwards. A pain which always recurs with a certain movement. And at the same time, every injury is a challenge to examine things afresh.

If I have experienced a turnaround in recent years, it is that I have a new faith in the balance between wanting things and letting them happen. In the past, I just *wanted* everything. Now I know that I cannot have everything. Children, school, love, dance, choreography, and film. It is by no means easy to combine the entire list harmoniously. I have to learn to be less greedy. But I am happy that I have so much.
I have people around me who want to give so much. I have slowly understood that the more you give, the more you receive. I have become somewhat milder in recent years. That does not mean that I accept everything. Compliance is not my style. I am practising my flexibility.

The above text is an adaptation of an interview previously published in De Standaard Magazine

Dossier Rosas

Productions

Asch

Choreography
Anne Teresa De Keersmaeker.

Danced by and created with
Jean Luc Breuer and Anne Teresa De Keersmaeker.

Music
Serge Biran and Christian Coppin.

Lighting design
Remon Fromont.

Costume design
Anne Teresa De Keersmaeker.

Produced by: Avila.
Co-produced by: Europalia 1980 (Belgium) and De Nieuwe Workshop.

Premiere
21 October 1980, Nieuwe Workshop, Brussel, Belgium.

Number of performances: 5.

Tour
Brussel.

Poster
Jean-Claude Wouters.

Fase, four movements to the music of Steve Reich

Anne Teresa De Keersmaeker created *Violin Phase and Come Out* during her time at New York University. *Violin Phase* premiered during the Festival of Early Modern Dance in Purchase, NY (April 1981). *Come Out* was created with Jennifer Everhard and premiered in October 1981 at the Tisch School of the Arts, NYU.

Choreography
Anne Teresa De Keersmaeker.

Danced by and created with
Anne Teresa De Keersmaeker and Michèle Anne De Mey.

Music
Steve Reich *(Violin Phase, Piano Phase, Clapping Music, and Come Out)*.

Lighting design
Remon Fromont and Mark Schwentner.

Costume design
Martine André and Anne Teresa De Keersmaeker.

Produced by: Schaamte (Creation) and Rosas & De Munt/La Monnaie (Restaging).

Premiere
18 March 1982, Beursschouwburg, Brussel, Belgium.

Awards
Bessie Award, New York, (1999).

Number of performances: 149.

Tour
Adelaide, Amsterdam, Annecy, Antwerpen, Arnhem, Avignon, Berlin, Bourges, Bristol, Brussel, Caen, Den Bosch, Den Haag, Dilbeek, Edinburgh, Eindhoven, Enschede, Frankfurt, Genève, Gent, Groningen, Haarlem, Hasselt, IJmuiden, Istres, Leiden, Leuven, Liège, Lille, London, Macon, Meylan, Milano, Modena, Montpellier, Neerpelt, New York, Paris, Purmerend, Rotterdam, Rouen, Saitama, Salzburg, Sittard, Strombeek-Bever, Tilburg, Turnhout, Utrecht, Valladolid, Waregem, Wemmel, Wevelgem, Wien, Wuppertal, Zürich.

Poster
Jacques Jauniaux.

Rosas danst Rosas

Choreography
Anne Teresa De Keersmaeker.

Danced by and created with
Adriana Borriello, Anne Teresa De Keersmaeker, Michèle Anne De Mey, Fumiyo Ikeda.
Restaging
Joanne Fong, Nadine Ganase, Muriel Hérault, Roxane Huilmand, Cynthia Loemij, Nathalie Million, Anne Mousselet, Johanne Saunier, Samantha Van Wissen.

Music
Thierry De Mey and Peter Vermeersch.
Musicians
Thierry De Mey, Walter Hus, Eric Sleichim, Peter Vermeersch.

Set design
Anne Teresa De Keersmaeker.

Lighting design
Remon Fromont.

Costume design
Rosas.

Produced by: Rosas & Kaaitheater (Creation) and Rosas & De Munt/La Monnaie (Restaging).
Co-produced by: Klapstuk.

Premiere
6 May 1983, Théâtre de la Balsamine, Brussel, Belgium (Presentation: Kaaitheaterfestival).

Awards
Bessie Award, New York (1988).
Eve du Spectacle, awarded by l'Association des Journalistes du Spectacle (1989).

Number of performances: 199.

Tour
Aalst, Amsterdam, Antwerpen, Arnhem, Avignon, Barcelona, Bari, Belfort, Bogota, Boston, Brussel, Budapest, Châtillon, San José, Den Bosch, Dieppe, Douai, Eindhoven, Fiesole, Frankfurt, Gent, Granada, Groningen, Guanajuato, Haarlem, Hamburg, Hasselt, Hong Kong, Jerusalem, Kopenhagen, Kopenhagen, Leipzig, Leuven, Liège, Lisboa, Ljubljana, London, Los Angeles, Mexico City, Montpellier, Montreal, München, Namur, Neerpelt, New York, Ottawa, Paris, Perth, Praha, Rennes, Roma, Rotterdam, Rouen, Santarcangelo, Seattle, Strasbourg, Tilburg, Tokyo, Torino, Toulouse, Turnhout, Udine, Utrecht, Waregem, Warsaw, Weert, Wellington, Wien, Zürich.

Poster
Gorik Lindemans.

Elena's aria

Choreography
Anne Teresa De Keersmaeker.

Danced by and created with
Anne Teresa De Keersmaeker, Michèle Anne De Mey, Nadine Ganase, Roxane Huilmand, Fumiyo Ikeda.

Music
Di Capua *(Vieni sul mar, O sole mio, and Santa Lucia)*, Bizet *(Pêcheurs de perles)*, Donizetti (Lucia di Lammermoor), Mozart *(Sonata c-dur KV 545 facile/andante)*.

Text
Fragments from Leo Tolstoy *(War and Peace)*, Bertold Brecht *(Surabaya Johnny, warum bin ich nicht froh)*, Wolfgang Kolb, Fidel Castro, Dostojevski *(The Idiot)*.

Lighting design
Anne Teresa De Keersmaeker.

Costume design
Rosas/Annette De Wilde.

Produced by: Rosas & Schaamte
In collaboration with Festival van Vlaanderen.

Premiere
18 October 1984, Koninklijke Vlaamse Schouwburg, Brussel, Belgium.

Number of performances: 56.

Tour
Alkmaar, Amsterdam, Antwerpen, Arnhem, Bari, Breda, Brugge, Brussel, Den Bosch, Eindhoven, Frankfurt, Gent, Grenoble, Groningen, Hasselt, La Louvière, Leuven, Liège, Middelburg, Milano, Namur, New York, Nijmegen, Paris, Rotterdam, Rouen, Strombeek-Bever, Tilburg, Utrecht, Waregem, Zug.

Poster
Gorik Lindemans.

Bartók/aantekeningen

Choreography
Anne Teresa De Keersmaeker.

Danced by and created with
Anne Teresa De Keersmaeker, Nadine Ganase, Roxane Huilmand, Fumiyo Ikeda, Johanne Saunier.

Music
Béla Bartók *(Quatuor N°4)*, Bulgarian folk music, Russian Partisan songs.

Text
Fragments from Peter Weiss *(Die Verfolgung und Ermordung Jean Paul Marats...)*, Georg Büchner *(Lenz)*.

Set design
Gisbert Jäkel.

Lighting design
Gisbert Jäkel and Herman Sorgeloos.

Costume design
Rosas.

Dramaturgy
Marianne Van Kerkhoven.

Musical adviser
Walter Hus.

Produced by: Rosas & Schaamte
Co-produced by: Holland Festival and Festival dEté de Seine-Maritime.
In collaboration with Zürcher Theater Spektakel, De Munt/La Monnaie.

Premiere
16 May 1986, C.B.A. Theatre, Brussel, Belgium (Presentation: Kaaitheaterfestival).

Number of performances: 84.

Tour
Alkmaar, Amsterdam, Antwerpen, Brugge, Brussel, Den Bosch, Dilbeek, Genève, Granada, Grenoble, Groningen, Haarlem, Hamburg, Hasselt, Ivry, Kortrijk, Leuven, Liège, Ljubljana, London, Milano, Namur, Ottawa, Paris, Poitiers, Rotterdam, Rouen, Rovereto, Salzburg, Stuttgart, Subotica, Tilburg, Turnhout, Utrecht, Zagreb, Zürich.

Poster
Gorik Lindemans.

Verkommenes Ufer / Medeamaterial / Landschaft mit Argonau n

Director/Choreograph
Anne Teresa De Keersmae

Danced and acted by, creat
Kitty Kortes Lynch, Johan Ley

Text
Heiner Mülle

Music
Pointer Siste Ludwi
(Grosse Fuge), I fror

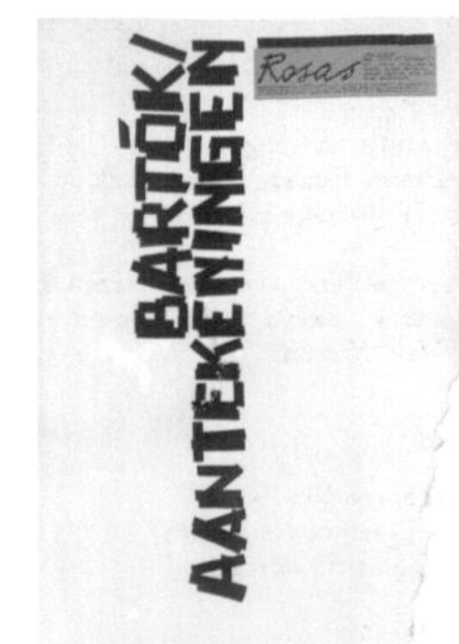

Set design
Herman Sorgeloos.

Lighting design
Anne Teresa De Keersmaeker and Herman Sorgeloos.

Costume design
Anne Teresa De Keersmaeker.

Produced by: Rosas & Schaamte.

Co-produced by: Springdance Festival.

Premiere
4 April 1987, Springdance Festival, Utrecht, the Netherlands.

Number of performances: 30.

Tour
Berlin, Brussel, Haarlem, Leuven, London, Milano, Stuttgart, Utrecht.

Mikrokosmos

Choreography
Anne Teresa De Keersmaeker.

Set design
Herman Sorgeloos.

Lighting design
Herman Sorgeloos.

Costume design
Rosas

I. Mikrokósmos, seven pieces for two pianos
Danced by and created with
Jean-Luc Ducourt and Johanne Saunier (Creation)
Restaging
Marion Ballester, Mark Bruce, Philipp Egli, Martin Kilvády, Oliver Koch, Marion Levy, Mark Lorimer, Samantha Van Wissen.

Music
Béla Bartók.

Music performed live by
Walter Hus and Stefan Poelmans (Creation), Laurence Cornez, Jean-Luc Fafchamps, Michael Frohnmeyer, Stefan Ginsburgh, Jean Luc Plouvier, Sachiko Yoshida (Restaging)

II. Monument / Selbstporträt mit Reich und Riley (und Chopin ist auch dabei) / im zart fliessender Bewegung
Music
György Ligeti.

Music performed live by
Walter Hus and Stefan Poelmans (Creation), Laurence Cornez, Jean-Luc Fafchamps, Michael Frohnmeyer, Stefan Ginsburgh, Jean-Luc Plouvier, Sachiko Yoshida (Restaging).

III. Quatuor N° 4
Danced by and created with
Nadine Ganase, Roxane Huilmand, Fumiyo Ikeda, Johanne Saunier.
Restaging
Anne Teresa De Keersmaeker, Joanne Fong, Cynthia Loemij, Sarah Ludi, Anne Mousselet, Samantha Van Wissen.

Music
Béla [illegible]k.

Mus[illegible]ormed live by
Mon[illegible] Quartet (Creation).
The[illegible]uartet (Restaging).

Pro[illegible]
Ros[illegible]itheater.

Prem[illegible]
1 Oct[illegible]987, Halles de Schaerbeek, Brusse[illegible]
Belgiu[illegible]resentation: Kaaitheater).

Awards
Japan D[illegible]nce Award for the best [illegible]reign prod[illegible]tion, awarded by the 21st Dance Society of J[illegible] (1989).

Number of performances: 60.

Tour
Antwerpen, Brighton, Brussel, Caen, Douai, Düsseldorf, Glasgow, Grenoble, Hasselt, Köln, Leuven, London, Lyon, Marne-la-Vallée, Palermo, Paris, Rennes, Rotterdam, Rouen, Salzburg, Utrecht, Yokohama.

Poster
Jan-Kees Schelvis.

Ottone Ottone

Choreography
Anne Teresa De Keersmaeker.

Artistic Assistant
Jean-Luc Ducourt.

Danced by and created with
Nicole Balm, Nordine Benchorf, Michèle Anne De Mey, Pierre Droulers, Jean-Luc Ducourt, Natalia Espinet Valles, Nadine Ganase, Fumiyo Ikeda, John Jasperse, Kitty Kortes Lynch, Nathalie Million, Oscar Dasi y Perez, Vincente Saez, Johanne Saunier, Wouter Steenbergen, Marc Willems.
Restaging
Laure Bonicel, Bruce Campbell, Anne Teresa De Keersmaeker, Kees Eijrond, Pere Pladevall Vallcorba, Carlotta Sagna, Jordi Cassanovas Sempere, Fatou Traore.

Music
Claudio Monteverdi (*L'Incoronazione di Poppea*).

Set design
Herman Sorgeloos.

Lighting design
Herman Sorgeloos.

Costume design
Rosas and Herman Sorgeloos.

Dramaturgy
Marianne Van Kerkhoven.

Produced by: Rosas & Kaaitheater
Co-produced by: Théâtre de la Ville, Rotterdam 88, Danse à Aix, De Munt/La Monnaie.

Premiere
22 September 1988, Halles de Schaerbeek, Brussel, Belgium (Presentation: Kaaitheater, De Munt/La Monnaie).

Number of performances: 52.

Tour
Aix-en-Provence, Amsterdam, Antwerpen, Barcelona, Brussel, Gent, Kassel, Lisboa, Luxembourg, Milano, München, Paris, Rotterdam, Rouen, Salzburg, Tilburg, Utrecht, Wien.

Poster
Gorik Lindemans.

Stella

Choreography
Anne Teresa De Keersmaeker.

Artistic Assistant
Jean-Luc Ducourt.

Danced by and created with
Fumiyo Ikeda, Marion Levy, Nathalie Million, Carlotta Sagna, Johanne Saunier.

[illegible]usic
[illegible]yörg[illegible] (*Eight studies for piano*).

[illegible]s from Tennessee Williams (*A Streetcar* [illegible]), Johann Wolfgang von Goethe (*Stella*), [illegible]sawa (*Rashomon*).

[illegible]rgeloos

[illegible]esign
[illegible]uco[illegible]

Costume design
Rosas.

Produced by: Rosas.
Co-produced by: Théâtre de la Ville, Hebbeltheater, Festival dEté de Seine-Maritime, deSingel.
In collaboration with Kaaitheater and Toneelschuur.

Premiere
9 March 1990, Toneelschuur, Haarlem, the Netherlands.

Awards
London Dance and Performance Award (1991).

Number of performances: 81.

Tour
Aalst, Amsterdam, Antwerpen, Bergen, Brussel, Caen, Frankfurt, Glasgow, Granada, Haarlem, Hamburg, Helsinki, London, Miami, Minneapolis, Montreal, Moscow, New York, Paris, Rotterdam, Rouen, Seattle, Toronto, Utrecht, Wien, Zagreb, Zürich.

Poster
Herman Sorgeloos.

Achterland

Choreography
Anne Teresa De Keersmaeker.

Director
Jean-Luc Ducourt.

Danced by and created with
Nordine Benchorf, Bruce Campbell, Vincent Dunoyer, Fumiyo Ikeda, Marion Levy, Nathalie Million, Carlotta Sagna, Johanne Saunier.
Restaging
Iris Bouche, Marta Coronado, Alix Eynaudi, Muriel Hérault, Martin Kilvády, Oliver Koch, Cynthia Loemij, Anne Mousselet, Roberto Oliván de la Iglesia, Ursula Robb, Taka Shamoto, Rosalba Torres, Samantha Van Wissen.

Music
György Ligeti (*Eight studies for piano*) and Eugène Ysaÿe (*Three sonatas for solo violin*).

Music performed live by
Irvine Arditti and Rolf Hind (Creation). Laurent Korcia, George Van Dam, Jan Michiels (Restaging).

Set design
Herman Sorgeloos.

Lighting design
Jean-Luc Ducourt.

Costume design
Ann Weckx.

Musical adviser
Walter Hus.

Produced by: Rosas.
Co-produced by: Stichting Van Gogh 1990, Rotterdamse Schouwburg, Théâtre de la Ville.
In collaboration with Kaaitheater, De Munt.

Premiere
27 November 1990, De Munt/La Monnaie, Brussel (Presentation: Kaaitheater, De Munt/La Monnaie).

Number of performances: 92.

Tour
Amsterdam, Antwerpen, Barcelona, Brussel, Budapest, Creil, Frankfurt, Grenoble, Hamburg, Hasselt, Hong Kong, Le Havre, Leuven, Lisboa, Ljubljana, London, Metz, Montpellier, Montreal, New York, Nîmes, Ottawa, Paris, Perth, Rennes, Roma, Rotterdam, Rouen, Salzburg, St. Etienne, Stockholm, Tarbes, Tokyo, Toulouse, Utrecht, Wellington, Zürich.

Poster
Paul Gees. Jan-Kees Schelvis.

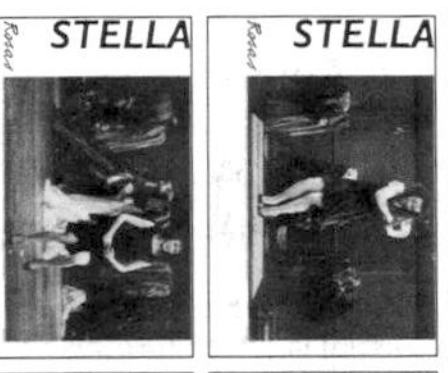

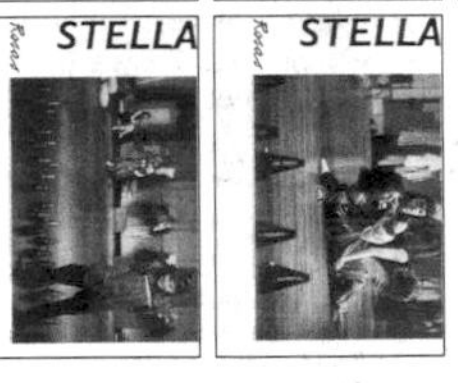

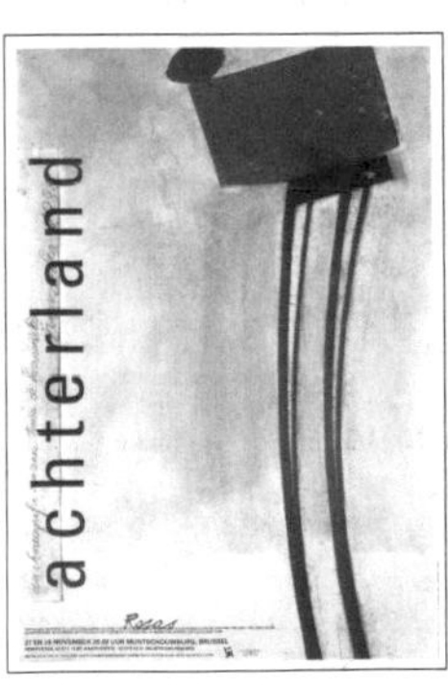

Erts

Choreography
Anne Teresa De Keersmaeker.

Director
Jean-Luc Ducourt.

Concept
Anne Teresa De Keersmaeker and Jean-Luc Ducourt.

Danced by and created with
Nordine Benchorf, Bruce Campbell, Vincent Dunoyer, Thomas Hauert, Muriel Hérault, Oliver Koch, Marion Levy, Cynthia Loemij, Nathalie Million, Anne Mousselet, Johanne Saunier, Eduardo Torroja, Samantha Van Wissen.
Restaging
Mark Bruce, Joanne Fong, Philipp Egli.

Music
Ludwig Van Beethoven *(Op.133 Grosse Fuge)*, Anton Webern *(Op.5 Fünf Sätze für Streichquartett)*, Alfred Schnittke *(String Quartet N°2)*, Luciano Berio *(Sequenza V for trombone, Sequenza III for voice)*, The Velvet Underground *(Sunday Morning, Waiting for my Man, All Tomorrows Parties)*.

Text
Fragments from Tennessee Williams *(A Streetcar Named Desire)*.

Music performed in part live by
Arditti String Quartet (Creation).
Mondriaan String Quartet and The Duke Quartet (Restaging).
Johanne Saunier (Voice).

Video
Walter Verdin, Anne Teresa De Keersmaeker, Jean-Luc Ducourt.
Video Assistant
Anne Van Aerschot.

Set design
Herman Sorgeloos.

Lighting design
Jean-Luc Ducourt (Creation).
Jim Clayburgh (Restaging).

Costume design
Ann Weckx.

Musical adviser
Georges-Elie Octors.

Produced by: Rosas & De Munt/La Monnaie.
Co-produced by: Théâtre de la Ville and octobre en normandie.

Premiere
2 February 1992, Halles de Schaerbeek, Brussel (Presentation: De Munt/La Monnaie).

Number of performances: 33.

Tour
Amsterdam, Antwerpen, Brussel, Gent, Leicester, Paris, Rotterdam, Rouen, Stockholm.

Poster
Jan-Kees Schelvis.

Mozart/Concert Arias, un moto di gioia

Choreography
Anne Teresa De Keersmaeker.

Director
Jean-Luc Ducourt.

Concept
Anne Teresa De Keersmaeker and Jean-Luc Ducourt.

Danced by and created with
Nordine Benchorf, Mark Bruce, Bruce Campbell, Vincent Dunoyer, Thomas Hauert, Muriel Hérault, Marion Levy, Cynthia Loemij, Nathalie Million, Anne Mousselet, Johanne Saunier, Eduardo Torroja, Samantha Van Wissen.
Restaging
Marion Ballester, Philipp Egli, Joanne Fong, Kosi Hidama, Suman Hsu, Oliver Koch, Mark Lorimer, Sarah Ludi.

Music
Wolfgang Amadeus Mozart *(Un moto di gioia mi sento K 579, Cassation in B dur K 99/63 - menuet 2, Vado ma dove? Oh, Dei K 583, Cassation in B dur K 99/63 - allegro 1, Serenade in c moll K 388 — andante, Cassation in B dur K 99/63 - menuet 1, Chi sà, chi sà, qual sia K 582, Serenade in c moll K 388 — menuet, Cassation in B dur K 99/63 - allegro 2, Per pietà, bellidol mio K 78/73, Cassation in B dur K 99/63 - andante 2, Alma grande e nobil core K 578, Rondo für Klavier in a moll K 511, Bella mia fiamma, addio - resta, oh cara K 528, Gigue für Klavier in G dur K 574, Vorei spiegarvi, oh Dio! K 418, Chio mi scordi di te? - non temer, amato bene K 505, Serenade in c moll K 388, allegro final, Nehmt meinen Dank, ihr holden Gönner! K 383)*.

Music performed live by
Orchestre des Champs Elysées, conductor: Philippe Herreweghe (Creation).
De Munt/La Monnaie Symphony Orchestra, conductor: Philippe Herreweghe (Restaging).
Anima Eterna, conductor: Jos Van Immerseel (Restaging).
Soloists.
Charlotte Margiono, Isolde Siebert, and Janet Williams (Creation).
Henriette Bonde-Hansen, Patricia Biccire, Ursula Hesse, Lena Lootens, Sandrine Piau, Elzbieta Smytka (Restaging).

Set design
Herman Sorgeloos.

Lighting design
Jean-Luc Ducourt.

Costume design
Rudy Sabounghi.

Musical adviser
Georges-Elie Octors.

Produced by: Rosas & De Munt/La Monnaie.
Co-produced by: Sevilla Expo 92, Festival van Vlaanderen, octobre en normandie.

Premiere
30 July 1992, Cour d'Honneur du Palais des Papes, Festival d'Avignon, France.

Number of performances: 43.

Tour
Amsterdam, Antwerpen, Avignon, Brussel, Dresden, Copenhagen, Le Havre, London, Paris, Rotterdam, Sevilla.

Poster
Jan-Kees Schelvis.

Toccata

Choreography
Anne Teresa De Keersmaeker.

Danced by and created with
Marion Ballester, Anne Teresa De Keersmaeker, Vincent Dunoyer, Fumiyo Ikeda, Marion Levy, Johanne Saunier.
Restaging
Misha Downey, Suman Hsu, Brice Leroux.

Music
Johann Sebastian Bach *(Toccata in e-moll BWV914, Fantasie und Fuge a-moll BWV904, Französiche Suite V in e-moll BWV816, Sonate in d-moll nach der Violinsonate a-moll BWV964, Nun komm der Heiden Heiland)*.

Music performed live by
Jos Van Immerseel (Creation)
Martine Chappuis, Yoko Kaneko, Leo Van Doesselaar (Restaging).

Set design
Herman Sorgeloos.

Lighting design
Remon Fromont.

Costume design
Carine Lauwers.

Musical adviser
Georges-Elie Octors.

Produced by: Rosas & De Munt/La Monnaie.
Commissioned by: Holland Festival.
Co-produced by: octobre en normandie and Theater am Turm.

Premiere
27 June 1993, Beurs van Berlaghe, Amsterdam, the Netherlands (Presentation: Holland Festival).

Number of performances: 78.

Tour
Amsterdam, Antwerpen, Bangkok, Brussel, Burlington, Columbus, Douai, Frankfurt, Gent, Grenoble, Kortrijk, Le Havre, Leuven, London, Lyon, Malmö, Minneapolis, Namur, Ottawa, Paris, Praha, Roma, Rotterdam, Rouen, Stockholm, Toronto, Turnhout, Utrecht, Wien.

Poster
Gert Dooreman.

Kinok

Choreography
Anne Teresa De Keersmaeker.

Set design
Herman Sorgeloos.

Lighting design
Remon Fromont.

Costume design
Nathalie Douxfils.

I. Rosa
Dancers
Suman Hsu and Osman Kassen Khelili.
(created by Fumiyo Ikeda and Nordine Benchorf for the film Rosa by Peter Greenaway).

Music
Béla Bartók *(Sonata for violin, Melodia and Presto)*.
Music performed live by
George Van Dam (Creation) and Louise Fuller.

II. Kinok
Danced by and created with
Marion Ballester, Franck Chartier, Misha Downey, Philipp Egli, Thomas Hauert, Suman Hsu, Osman Kassen Khelili, Brice Leroux, Sarah Ludi, Christian Spuck.
Restaging
Kosi Hidama, Mark Lorimer.

Music
Thierry De Mey *(Kinok)*.
Assistant
François Deppe.
Music performed live by
Ictus Ensemble.

III. Grosse Fuge
Dancers
Marion Ballester, Franck Chartier, Misha Downey, Philipp Egli, Thomas Hauert, Suman Hsu, Osman Kassen Khelili, Sarah Ludi, Christian Spuck (Creation).
Kosi Hidama, Oliver Koch, Cynthia Loemij, Mark Lorimer, Samantha Van Wissen (Restaging).

Music
Ludwig van Beethoven *(Op.133 G[illegible]e Fuge)*.
Music performed live by
The Duke Quartet.

Produced by: Rosas & De Munt/La Monnaie.
Co-produced by: KunstenFESTIVALdesArts.

Premiere
18 May 1994, Lunatheater, Brussel, Belgium (Presentation: KunstenFESTIVALdesAr[illegible]

Number of performances: 4[illegible]

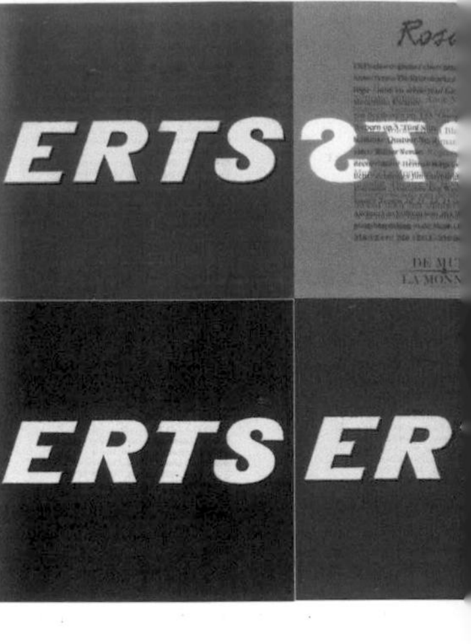

Tour
Antwerpen, Bogota, Brussel, Frankfurt, Gent, München, Nantes, Nîmes, Rio de Janeiro, Roubaix, Rouen, São Paulo, Sevilla, Turnhout, Utrecht, Zürich.

Poster
Jan-Kees Schelvis.

Amor constante, más allá de la muerte

Choreography
Anne Teresa De Keersmaeker.

Directors
Anne Teresa De Keersmaeker and Thierry De Mey.

Danced by and created with
Marion Ballester, Misha Downey, Philipp Egli, Kosi Hidama, Suman Hsu, Osman Kassen Khelili, Brice Leroux, Marion Levy, Cynthia Loemij, Mark Lorimer, Sarah Ludi, Anne Mousselet, Johanne Saunier, Samantha Van Wissen.

Music
Thierry De Mey *(Kinok, Unknowness, Violin Concerto, Amor Constante)*.

Musical assistant
François Deppe.

Music performed live by
Ictus Ensemble.

Set design
Herman Sorgeloos.

Lighting design
Jan Versweyveld.

Costume design
Rosas and Rudy Sabounghi.

Assistant to the choreographer
Anne Van Aerschot.

Produced by: Rosas & De Munt/La Monnaie
Co-produced by: Lisboa 94 Cultural Capital, Théâtre de la Ville, Het Muziektheater.

Premiere
30 November 1994, Cirque Royal, Brussel, Belgium (Presentation: De Munt/La Monnaie).

Number of performances: 39.

Tour
Amsterdam, Antwerpen, Brussel, Lisboa, Montpellier, Montréal, Mulhouse, Paris, Rotterdam, Yokohama.

Poster
Gorik Lindemans.

Erwartung/Verklärte Nacht

Verklärte Nacht was part of an opera and dance evening set to the music of Arnold Schönberg in the De Munt/La Monnaie. The first part of the evening consisted of *Erwartung*, a short opera by Schönberg, directed by Klaus Michael Grüber.

Choreography
Anne Teresa De Keersmaeker.

Danced by and created with
Marion Ballester, Misha Downey, Kosi Hidama, Suman Hsu, Osman Kassen Khelili, Oliver Koch, Brice [illegible]ux, Marion Levy, Cynthia Loemij, Ma[illegible]er, Sarah Ludi, Anne Mousselet, Joh[illegible]nier, [illegible]antha Van [illegible]sen.

M[illegible]
[illegible]e[illegible]rklär[illegible]

Set design
Gilles Aillaud.

Lighting design
Vinicio Cheli.

Costume design
Rudy Sabounghi.

Produced by: Rosas & De Munt/La Monnaie.

Premiere
4 November 1995, De Munt/La Monnaie, Brussel, Belgium.

Number of performances: 19.

Tour
Brussel, Paris, Wien.

Poster
Gilles Aillaud.

Woud, three movements to the music of Berg, Schönberg and Wagner

Choreography
Anne Teresa De Keersmaeker.

Danced by and created with
Marion Ballester, Iris Bouche, Farooq Chaudry, Kosi Hidama, Suman Hsu, Oliver Koch, Sarah Ludi, Cynthia Loemij, Mark Lorimer, Samantha Van Wissen.
Restaging
Bruce Campbell, Alix Eynaudi, Fumiyo Ikeda, Martin Kilvády, Roberto Oliván de la Iglesia, Ursula Robb, Taka Shamoto, Rosalba Torres.

Music
Alban Berg *(Lyrische Suite)*, Arnold Schönberg *(Op.4 Verklärte Nacht)*, Richard Wagner *(Wesendonck Lied nr.3 Im Treibhaus)*.

Music performed live by
The Duke Quartet, Helen Kamminga, Sophie Harris (Creation)
Singer
Kerstin Witt (Composition).
Martina Borst, Martina Dike, Ursula Hesse (Restaging).

Set design
Gilles Aillaud and Anne Teresa De Keersmaeker.

Lighting design
Vinicio Cheli *(Verklärte Nacht)*, Anne Teresa De Keersmaeker, Guy Peeters.

Costume design
Rudy Sabounghi and Nathalie Douxfils.

Musical analysis
Georges-Elie Octors.

Assistant to the choreographer
Anne Van Aerschot.

Produced by: Rosas & De Munt/La Monnaie.
Co-produced by: Théâtre de la Ville.
In collaboration with Teatro Central, Seville.

Premiere
19 December 1996, Teatro Central, Seville, Spain.

Number of performances: 72.

Tour
Alès, Amiens, Amsterdam, Antwerpen, Brussel, Caen, Ferrara, Gent, Grenoble, Hasselt, Helsinki, Irvine, Liège, Lille, Ludwigsburg, München, New York, Paris, Rennes, Rotterdam, Rouen, San Francisco, Sevilla, Stockholm, Turnhout, Vestfold.

Poster
Jan-Kees Schelvis.

Three solos for Vincent Dunoyer

Concept and Dance
Vincent Dunoyer.

Set design and lighting design
Herman Sorgeloos and Frank Vandezande.

Costume design
Elizabeth Jenyon.

I. Dances with TV and Mic.
Choreography
The Wooster Group.

Music
J. Brahms, E. Grieg, M. Mussorgsky, W. Horvitz, and J. Lurie.

II. Solo for Vincent.
Choreography
Anne Teresa De Keersmaeker.

Music
Heinz Holliger *(Studie über Mehrklange)*, Robert Schumann *(Werke für Oboe und Klavier)*.

III. Carbon.
Choreography
Steve Paxton.

Sound Tape
Vincent Dunoyer and Alexandre Fostier.

Produced by
Rosas & De Munt/La Monnaie
In collaboration with
Springdance Festival and Klapstuk Festival.

Premiere
20 April 1997, Paardenkathedraal, Utrecht, the Netherlands (Presentation: Springdance Festival).

Number of performances: 75.

Tour
Aalst, Antwerpen, Belo Horizonte, Berlin, Brugge, Brussel, Cherbourg, Frankfurt, Genève, Gent, Grenoble, Haarlem, Leuven, Lisboa, Nyon, Ottawa, Paris, Rouen, Tongeren, Toronto, Toulouse, Utrecht, Wien, Yokohama, Zürich.

Poster
Herman Sorgeloos.

Just before

Director/Choreography
Anne Teresa De Keersmaeker.

In collaboration with
Jolente De Keersmaeker.

Danced by and created with
Iris Bouche, Bruce Campbell, Farooq Chaudry, Alix Eynaudi, Fumiyo Ikeda, Martin Kilvády, Oliver Koch, Cynthia Loemij, Roberto Oliván de la Iglesia, Ursula Robb, Taka Shamoto, Rosalba Torres.

Music
Pierre Bartolomée *(Mezza Voce)*, Johannes Brahms, John Cage *(The Perilous Night, A Room for Piano, Seven Haiku)*, Claude Debussy *(Prélude pour piano n°6 du premier livre – des pas dans le neige)*, Thierry De Mey *(Unknowness)*, Magnus Lindberg *(Related Rocks)*, Steve Reich *(Drumming and Nagoya Marimbas)*, Yannis Xenakis *(Rebonds)*.

Text
Created with the dancers.

Music performed live by
Ictus Ensemble.

Musical analysis
Georges-Elie Octors.

Set design and lighting design
Jan Versweyveld.
Assistant
Geert Peymen.

Costume design
Dries Van Noten.
Assistants
Nathalie Douxfils and Veerle van den Wouwer.

Dramaturgy
Sigrid Bousset.

Assistant to the choreographer
Anne Van Aerschot.

Produced by: Rosas & De Munt/La Monnaie
Co-produced by: Théâtre de la Ville.

Premiere
12 November 1997, De Munt/La Monnaie, Brussel, Belgium.

Number of performances: 45.

Tour
Amsterdam, Antwerpen, Brussel, Caen, Dresden, Frankfurt, Gent, Hasselt, Leuven, Manchester, Paris, Roeselare, Rotterdam, Stockholm, Wien.

Poster
Herman Sorgeloos.

Mikrokosmos / Quatuor N°4 / Duke Bluebeards Castle

Duke Bluebeard's Castle was the first opera that Anne Teresa De Keersmaeker directed. The evening began with two choreogrphies that she had previously made to Bartók's *Mikrokósmos* and *Quatuor N°4*.

Choreography/Director
Anne Teresa De Keersmaeker.

Set design
Gisbert Jäkel.

Lighting design
Konrad Lindenberg.

Costume design
Rudy Sabounghi.
Assistant
Nathalie Douxfils.

Dramaturgy
Marianne Van Kerkhoven.

Assistant to the choreographer
Johanne Saunier and Dagmar Pischel.

I. Mikrokósmos, Seven Pieces for Two Pianos.
Dancers
Oliver Koch/Martin Kilvády and Johanne Saunier.

Music
Béla Bartók.

Music performed live by
Jean-Luc Fafchamps and Jean-Luc Plouvier.

II. Quatuor N°4.
Dancers
Cynthia Loemij, Sarah Ludi, Anne Mousselet, Samantha Van Wissen.

Music
Béla Bartók.

Music performed live by
The Duke Quartet.

III. Duke Bluebeard's Castle.
Music
Béla Bartók.
Libretto
Béla Balázs.

Music performed live by
De Munt/La Monnaie Symphony Orchestra, conductor: Lothar Zagrosek.
Soloists.
Bluebeard: Victor Braun and Ronnie Johansen.
Judith: Svetelina Vassileva and Anne Schwanewilms.
Minstrel: Annie Henderyckx-Szikora.

Dancers
Cynthia Loemij, Sarah Ludi, Anne Mousselet, Johanne Saunier, Samantha Van Wissen.

Musical Analysis
Georges-Elie Octors.

Filming
Thierry De Mey.
Dancers in the film
Iris Bouche, Bruce Campbell, Alix Eynaudi, Fumiyo Ikeda, Martin Kilvády, Oliver Koch, Cynthia Loemij, Sarah Ludi, Anne Mousselet, Roberto Oliván de la Iglesia, Ursula Robb, Johanne Saunier, Taka Shamoto, Rosalba Torres, Samantha Van Wissen.

Produced by: De Munt/La Monnaie
In collaboration with: Rosas.

Premiere
22 February 1998, De Munt/La Monnaie, Brussel, Belgium.

Number of performances: 16.

Tour
Brussel, Rotterdam.

Poster
Herman Sorgeloos.

Drumming

Choreography
Anne Teresa De Keersmaeker.

Danced by and created with
Iris Bouche, Bruce Campbell, Marta Coronado, Alix Eynaudi, Fumiyo Ikeda, Martin Kilvády, Oliver Koch, Cynthia Loemij, Roberto Oliván de la Iglesia, Ursula Robb, Taka Shamoto, Rosalba Torres.
Restaging
Benjamin Boar, Jordi Galí, Igor Shyshko, Clinton Stringer, Julia Sugranyes, Jakub Truszkowski.

Music
Steve Reich *(Drumming)*.

Set design and lighting design
Jan Versweyveld.
Assistant
Geert Peymen.

Costume design
Dries Van Noten.
Assistants
Nathalie Douxfils and Veerle van den Wouwer.

Assistant to the choreographer
Anne Van Aerschot.

Produced by: Rosas & De Munt/La Monnaie.
Co-produced by: La Bâtie – Festival de Genève.
In collaboration with Impuls Tanz Wien.

Premiere
7 August 1998, Sofiënsäle, Wien, Austria (Presentation: Impuls Tanz Wien).

Awards
Golden Laurel Wreath for the best choreography in Sarajevo (October 1998).

Number of performances up to December 2002: 148.

Tour
Adelaide, Amiens, Annecy, Antwerpen, Bergen, Berlin, Biwako, Bordeaux, Brighton, Brugge, Brussel, Buenos Aires, Burlington, Cairo, Caracas, Cergy-Pontoise, Châlons-en-Champagne, Chicago, Columbus, Créteil, Dresden, Düsseldorf, Evry, Genève, Glasgow, Hannover, Hasselt, Johannesburg, Köln, Kortrijk, La Rochelle, Le Havre, Le-Blanc-Mesnil, Leuven, Lisboa, London, Ludwigsburg, Lyon, Maubeuge, Metz, Minneapolis, Montpellier, Montreal, Nanterre, Nantes, New York, Newcastle, Oita, Oldenburg, Ottawa, Paris, Pittsburgh, Porto, Praha, Rennes, Roeselare, Rotterdam, Rouen, Rovereto, Saitama, Sarajevo, Seattle, Sevilla, Stockholm, Toronto, Toulouse, Utrecht, Valence, Warwick, Wien.

Poster
Herman Sorgeloos.

The Lisbon Piece

The Lisbon Piece was the first choreography that Anne Teresa De Keersmaeker created outside her own company. She created *The Lisbon Piece for the* Companhia Nacional de Bailado in Lisbon at the invitation of director Jorge Salavisa.

Choreography
Anne Teresa De Keersmaeker.

Assistant to the choreographer
Elizabeth Corbett.

Danced by and created with
Companhia Nacional de Bailado: Xavier Carmo, Filipa Castro, David Fielding, Isabel Galriça, Filipe Portugal.
Restaging
Paulina Santos, Leonor Távora.

Music
Thierry De Mey *(Frisking, Aire)*, Eric Sleichim *(Hymne, Vista)*.

Set design and lighting design
Jan Versweyveld.

Costume design
Nathalie Douxfils.

Rehearsal director
Isabel Fernandes.

Produced by
Companhia Nacional de Bailado.
In collaboration with Rosas.

Premiere
26 November 1998, Teatro Sao Carlos, Lisboa, Portugal (Presentation: Companhia Nacional de Bailado).

Quartett

A performance by
Jolente De Keersmaeker, Frank Vercruyssen, Anne Teresa De Keersmaeker, Cynthia Loemij.

Text
Heiner Müller.

Set design and lighting design
Herman Sorgeloos and Thomas Walgrave.

Costume design
Ann D´Huys.

Produced by: Tg Stan & Rosas
Co-produced by: Kaaitheater.

Premiere
4 March 1999, Kaaitheater, Brussel, Belgium.

Number of performances up to December 2002: 47.

Tour
Århus, Amsterdam, Antwerpen, Bergen, Brussel, Frankfurt, Gent, Groningen, Haarlem, Hamburg, Leuven, London, Münster, Paris, Porto, Rotterdam, Salzburg, Stockholm, Tongeren.

Poster
Thomas Walgrave.

For

For was a part of
together by dar
choreographie
Miller, Leine
by Michael S
were also pre

Choreograpl
Anne Teresa

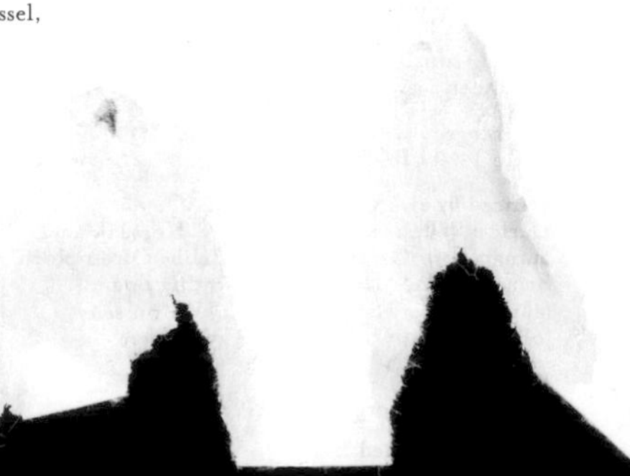

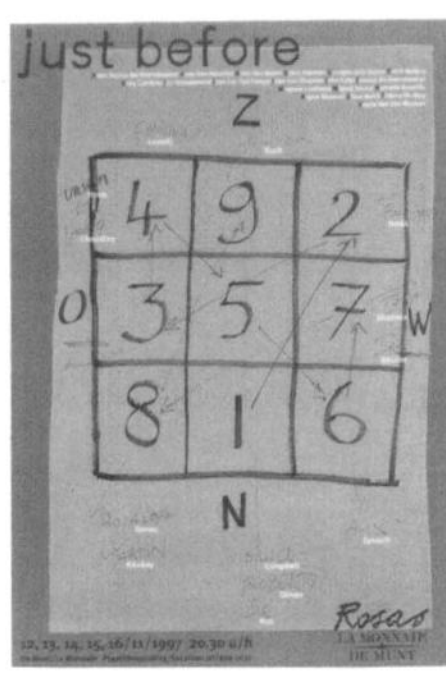

Dancers
Anne Teresa De Keersmaeker and Elizabeth Corbett.

Music
Blindman Quartet/Eric Sleichim *(Poortenbos Suite: Tongues, Lié/Délié Suite: Tied & Untied)*.

Set and lighting design
Luc Galle, Frank Vandezande, Herman Sorgeloos.

Costume design
Nathalie Douxfils.

Produced by
Springdance & Rosas.
Co-produced by
Kaaitheater and Wiener Tanzwochen.

Premiere
25 April 1999, Springdance Festival, Utrecht, the Netherlands.

Number of performances: 11.

Tour
Brussel, Gent, Paris, Utrecht, Wien.

I said I

Director/Choreography
Anne Teresa De Keersmaeker.

In collaboration with
Jolente De Keersmaeker.

Danced by and created with
Iris Bouche, Marta Coronado, Alix Eynaudi, Fumiyo Ikeda, Martin Kilvády, Oliver Koch, Roberto Oliván de la Iglesia, Ursula Robb, Taka Shamoto, Rosalba Torres.

Music
Bernd Aloïs Zimmerman *(Vier kürze Stücke)*, Luciano Berio *(Les mots sont allés)*, Anton Webern *(Opus 11: I-II-III and Opus 7: I-II-II-IV)*, Johannes Brahms *(Intermezzo opus 119, Symphony N°3 in F majort, opus 90 – allegro, 4th movement, and Opus 8-Adagio con Brio)*, Kaija Saariaho *(Petals)*, d.j. Grazzhoppa *(Turntable Battle)*, Fabrizio Cassol *(Newspapers Improvisation)*, AKA Moon *(I said I)*, Jean-Luc Plouvier *(Selfaccusation)*, George Van Dam *(Rosalba 505)*.

Music performed live by
Ictus Ensemble, Fabrizio Cassol, d.j. Grazzhoppa.

Text
Peter Handke *(Self-Accusation)*.

Set design and lighting design
Jan Joris Lamers.

Costume design
Dries Van Noten.
Assistants
Nathalie Douxfils and Veerle van den Wouwer.

Assistant to the choreographer
Anne Van Aerschot.

Produced by: Rosas & De Munt/La Monnaie
Co-produced by: Théâtre de la Ville.

Premiere
6 May ... unatheater, Brussel, Belgium
(Pres... De Munt/La Monnaie &
Kaai...

Nu... rmances: 44.

To...
... am, Antwerp
... nover, Lisb...
... real, Paris,

... Lero...
k Lorim...
... ianne Sau... Wi...

...usic
...rnold Schönb... te Nacht).

Music perforr...
De Munt/La M... ...cte... ...ony Orchestr...
conductor: Ant... Mo... ...).

Choreography
Anne Teresa De Keersmaeker.

Text
Gerardjan Rijnders, tg Stan, fragments from: Anton Tsjechov *(Three Sisters)*, Multatuli *(Minnebrieven)*, Daniil Kharms *(Incidences, I sat on the roof)*, Shuntaro Tanikawa *(Evening)*, Don Delillo *(Underworld)*, Jack Gilbert *(The Forgotten Dialect of the Heart)*.

Actors Tg. Stan
Jolente De Keersmaeker, Sara De Roo, Damiaan De Schrijver, Frank Vercruyssen.

Dancers Rosas
Iris Bouche, Marta Coronado, Anne Teresa De Keersmaeker, Alix Eynaudi, Fumiyo Ikeda, Martin Kilvády, Oliver Koch, Cynthia Loemij, Roberto Oliván de la Iglesia, Ursula Robb, Taka Shamoto, Clinton Stringer, Rosalba Torres, Jakub Truszkowski.

Music
Fabrizio Cassol & AKA Moon.

Music performed live by
AKA Moon (Fabrizio Cassol, Michel Hatzigeorgiou, Stéphane Galland, Fabian Fiorini).

Set design
Thomas Walgrave, Tg. Stan & Rosas.

Lighting design
Thomas Walgrave.
Assistants
Guy Peeters and Koen Raes.

Costume design
Anke Loh.
Assistants
Nathalie Douxfils and Inge Büscher.

Assistant to the choreographer
Anne Van Aerschot.

Rehearsal director
Mark Lorimer.

Produced by: Tg Stan, Rosas, De Munt/La Monnaie.
Co-produced by: Théâtre de la Ville, Tanztheater International/Expo 2000 Hannover.

Premiere
18 May 2000, Rosas Performance Space, Brussel, Belgium (Presentation: De Munt/La Monnaie, KunstenFESTIVALdesArts, in collaboration with Brussel 2000, Cultural Capital of Europe).

Number of performances: 51.

Tour
Aix-en-Provence, Amsterdam, Antwerpen, Berlin, Brussel, Frankfurt, Gent, Hamburg, Hannover, Leuven, Lisboa, Paris, Salzburg, Wien.

Poster
Jurgen Persijn.

Rain

Choreography
Anne Teresa De Keersmaeker.

Danced by and created with
Marta Coronado, Igor Shyshko, Alix Eynaudi, Fumiyo Ikeda, Cynthia Loemij, Ursula Robb, Taka Shamoto, Clinton Stringer, Rosalba Torres, Jaku... Tru...kowski.
Re... ...in...
Ju... ...u... ... Samantha Van Wissen.

... usicians).

... esign

Assistants
Veerle Van den Wouwer and Anne-Catherine Kunz.

Musical analysis
Georges-Elie Octors.

Assistant to the choreographer
Anne Van Aerschot.

Rehearsal director
Mark Lorimer.

Produced by: Rosas & De Munt/La Monnaie.
Co-produced by: Théâtre de la Ville.

Premiere
10 January 2001, De Munt/La Monnaie, Brussel, Belgium.

Number of performances up to December 2002: 81.

Tour
Amsterdam, Antwerpen, Bourges, Brasilia, Brest, Brugge, Brussel, Chalon sur Saône, Clermont-Ferrand, Douai, Drachten, Forbach, Hasselt, Leipzig, Leverkusen, London, Ludwigsburg, Marseille, Martigues, Namur, Nantes, Nice, Nürnberg, Ottawa, Paris, Porto, Porto Alegre, Reims, Rennes, Rio De Janeiro, Roeselare, Rotterdam, Rouen, São Paulo, Toronto, Toulouse, Venezia, Wien.

Poster
Jan Joris Lamers.

Small hands (out of the lie of no)

Choreography
Anne Teresa De Keersmaeker.

Danced by and created with
Anne Teresa De Keersmaeker and Cynthia Loemij.

Music
Henry Purcell *(Hail! Bright Cecilia!, Welcome to all the Pleasures, Music for a While – from Oedipus – Z583, Songs from Orpheus Britannicus)*.

Set design and lighting design
Jan Versweyveld.
Assistant
Geert Peymen.

Costume design
Anne-Catherine Kunz.

Produced by: Rosas & De Munt/La Monnaie.

Premiere
27 June 2001, Rosas Performance Space, Brussel, Belgium (Presentation: De Munt/La Monnaie & Kaaitheater).

Number of performances up to December 2002: 38.

Tour
Antwerpen, Brussel, Gent, Hasselt, Kortrijk, Leuven, Lisboa, Paris, Rotterdam, Salzburg, Wien.

Poster
Jan Joris Lamers.

(but if a look should) April me

Choreography
Anne Teresa De Keersmaeker.

Danced by and created with
Beniamin Boar, Marta Coronado, Alix Eynaudi, Jordi Galí, Fumiyo Ikeda, Cynthia Loemij, Ursula Robb, Taka Shamoto, Igor Shyshko, Clinton Stringer, Julia Sugranyes, Rosalba Torres, Jakub Truszkowski.

Music
Thierry De Mey *(Les Fiançailles Silence must be!)*, Igor Stravinsky *(Les Noces)*, Yannis Xenakis *(Peau – Pleïades)*, Gérard Grisey *(Stèle)*, W.A. Mozart *(Le Nozze di Figaro, Act 4, scene 8 Susanna)*, Morton Feldman *(King of Denmark)*, Parveen Sultana *(Rosiya Moke Bulaye "Thumri")*, L. Subramanyam *(Raga Alapana)*, traditional Indian and Italian music.

Music in part performed live by
Ictus Ensemble (Miquel Bernat, Kuniko Kato, Gerrit Nulens, Georges-Elie Octors, Jessica Ryckewaert, Michael Weilacher, Alexandre Fostier).

Set design and lighting design
Jan Versweyveld.
Assistant
Geert Peymen.

Costume design
Inge Büscher.
Assistant
Anne-Catherine Kunz.

Musical analysis
Georges-Elie Octors.

Assistant to the choreographer
Anne Van Aerschot.

Rehearsal director
Pascale Gigon.

Produced by: Rosas & De Munt/La Monnaie.
Co-produced by: Théâtre de la Ville.

Premiere
3 April 2002, De Munt/La Monnaie, Brussel, Belgium.

Number of performances up to December 2002: 20.

Tour
Antwerpen, Brugge, Brussel, Forbach, Leverkusen, Paris, Rouen, Wien.

Poster
Paul Boudens.

Repertory Evening

The Repertory Evening was composed for the celebration of the twentieth anniversary of Rosas in De Munt/La Monnaie in Brussels.

Choreography
Anne Teresa De Keersmaeker.

Set design and lighting design
Jan Versweyveld.
Assistant
Geert Peymen.

Costume design (adjustments for the *Repertory Evening*)
Anne-Catherine Kunz and Els Mommaerts.

Assistant to the choreographer
Anne Van Aerschot.

I. Violin Phase.
Danced and created by
Anne Teresa De Keersmaeker.
Music
Steve Reich *(Violin Phase)*.
Costume design
Anne Teresa De Keersmaeker.

II. French Suite.
Dancers
Fumiyo Ikeda, Vincent Dunoyer, Marion Levy.
Music
J.S.Bach *(Französische Suite V, BWV 816)*.
Music performed live by
Jos Van Immerseel (Creation).
Claire Chevallier (Restaging).
Costume design
Carine Lauwers.

III. Quatuor N°4.
Dancers
Samantha Van Wissen, Sarah Ludi, Johanne Saunier, Cynthia Loemij (Creation).
Anne Teresa De Keersmaeker (Restaging).
Music
Béla Bartók *(Quatuor N°4)*.
Music performed live by The Duke Quartet.
Costume design
Anne Teresa De Keersmaeker/Rosas.

IV. The Lisbon Piece.
Assistant to the choreographer
Elizabeth Corbett.
Dancers
Companhia Nacional de Bailado: Xavier Carmo, David Fielding, Isabel Galriça, Filipe Portugal, Paulina Santos (Creation)
Leonor Távora (Restaging).
Music
Thierry De Mey (*Frisking, Aire*), Eric Sleichim (*Vista*).
Costume design
Nathalie Douxfils.
Rehearsal director
Isabel Fernandes.

V. Grosse Fuge.
Dancers
Nordine Benchorf, Beniamin Boar, Jordi Galí, Thomas Hauert, Mark Lorimer, Igor Shyshko, Clinton Stringer, Jakub Truszkowski.
Director
Jean-Luc Ducourt.
Music
Ludwig Van Beethoven *(Grosse Fuge Op. 133)*.
Music performed live by
The Duke Quartet.
Costume design
Nathalie Douxfils.
Rehearsal directors
Nordine Benchorf and Pascale Gigon.

VI. Ch'io mi scordi di te?
Dancers
Nordine Benchorf and Anne Mousselet.
Music
Wofgang Amadeus Mozart (KV 505).
Costume design
Rudy Sabounghi.

Produced by: Rosas & De Munt/La Monnaie.

Premiere
11 April 2002, De Munt/La Monnaie, Brussel, Belgium.

Number of performances: 12.

Tour
Brussel, Paris, Rouen, Wien.

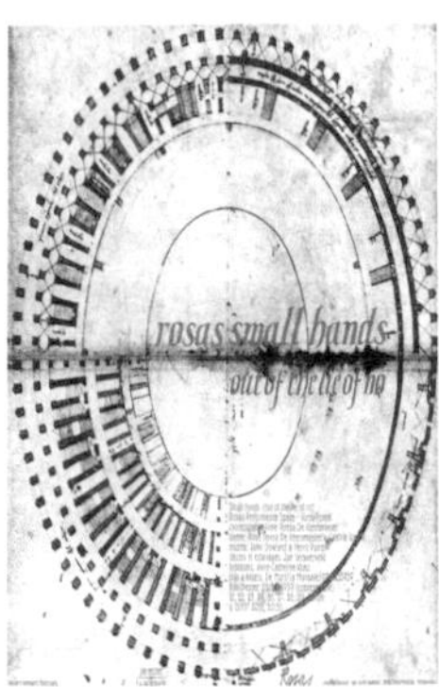

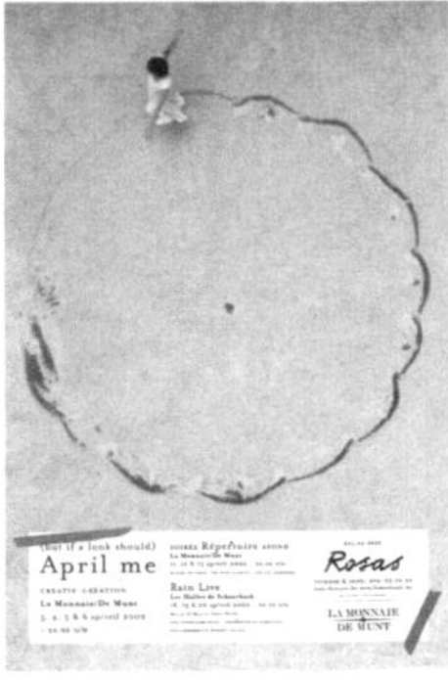

Films

Répétitions

1984, 45', colour.

Répétitions is a documentary about the rehearsal process of *Elena's aria* (1984).

Director
Marie André.

Choreography
Anne Teresa De Keersmaeker.

Dancers
Anne Teresa De Keersmaeker, Michèle Anne De Mey, Nadine Ganase, Roxane Huilmand.

Camera and Editing
Marie André.

Directors of photography
Yves Kremer, Luc Bériot.

Sound
Paul Delnoye.

Produced by: Image Vidéo, Brussels Audio Visual Centre, Schaamte, Polygone.

Hoppla!

1989, 16mm, 52', colour.

Hoppla! is the film version of two of De Keersmaeker's choreographies to the music of Béla Bartók *(Quatuor N°4, 1986 and Mikrokosmos, 1987).* The film was shot in the Ghent University Library (architect: Henry Van de Velde).

Director
Wolfgang Kolb.

Choreography
Anne Teresa De Keersmaeker.

Dancers
Anne Teresa De Keersmaeker, Jean-Luc Ducourt, Nadine Ganase, Roxane Huilmand, Fumiyo Ikeda, Johanne Saunier.

Music
Béla Bartók *(Mikrokósmos, Seven Pieces for Two Pianos, Quartet N°4).*
Music performed by
Walter Hus, Stefan Poelmans
Mondriaan Kwartet.

Director of photography
Philippe Maendly.

Editing
Rudi Maerten.

Camera
Remon Fromont, Philippe Guilbert, Philippe Maendly.

Sound
Ricardo Castrc

Produced b \.O.productions.
Co-produ by: Kaaitheater, Rosas, La Sept, and Arcan & Zed Ltd
In collaboration with Channel 4, NDR, NOS, Théâtre de la Ville, and RTBF.
Supported by the Ministry of the Flemish Community, Le Cargo Grenoble, BRTN.

Awards
Solo d'Oro, 1st prize at the 5th International Video and Television Festival of Riccione TTVV (1989).
Grand Prix Dance Video, Festival of Sète (1989).

Monoloog van Fumiyo Ikeda op het einde van Ottone Ottone

1990, Betacam, 6', black and white.

A video by
Walter Verdin, Anne Teresa De Keersmaeker, Jean-Luc Ducourt.

Choreography
Anne Teresa De Keersmaeker.

In collaboration with Jean-Luc Ducourt.

Dancer
Fumiyo Ikeda.

Camera
Mathias Vanbuel.

Produced by:
Rosas, Audio Visual Service of the Catholic University of Louvain, Walter Verdin, Flemish Theatre Institute.

Ottonc Ottone 1991

1991, Betacam, colour, 52' (part I) + 50' (part II).

Ottone Ottone is a video adaptation of a stage production of the same name from 1988. The video was shot in the Théâtre Varia in Brussels.

A video by
Walter Verdin and Anne Teresa De Keersmaeker.

Choreography
Anne Teresa De Keersmaeker.

Artistic Assistant
Jean-Luc Ducourt.

Dancers
Nicole Balm, Laure Bonicel, Pierre Droulers, Jean-Luc Ducourt, Kees Eijrond, Nadine Ganase, Fumiyo Ikeda, John Jasperse, Nathalie Million, Oscar Dasi y Perez, Carlotta Sagna, Johanne Saunier, Jordi Cassanovas Sempere, Wouter Steenbergen, Fatou Traore, Pere Pladevall Vallcorba.

Music
Claudio Monteverdi *(L'Incoronazione di Poppea).*

Camera
Marc Renard, Mathias Vanbuel, Danny Elsen, Walter Verdin.

Editing
Walter Verdin.

Assistant to the director
Anne Van Aerschot.

Produced by: Rosas
Co-produced by: BRT – Artistic Affairs Service, Audio Visual Service of the Catholic University of Louvain.

Rosa

1992, 35mm, 16', black and white
Rosa was shot in the foyer of the Ghent Opera House.

Director
Peter Greenaway.

Choreography
Anne Teresa De Keersmaeker.

In collaboration with
Jean-Luc ' ucourt.

Dancers
Nordine Benchorf, Fumiyo Ikeda.

Music
Béla Bartók *(Sonata for Violin, Melodia and Presto).*

Music performed live b
Irvine Arditti.

Director of photography
Sacha Vierny.

Camera
Chris Renson.

Editing
Chris Wyatt.

Costume design
Ann Weckx.

Produced by: Entropie.
Co-produced by: Rosas, De Munt/La Monnaie, octobre en normandie, Festival International de Nouvelle Danse Montréal, Centre Georges Pompidou/Ircam.

Awards
Dance Screen Award, Frankfurt Dance Screen Festival (June 1992).
Award for the best adaptation, Frankfurt Dance Screen Festival (June 1992).
Selection for the 49th Mostra Internazionale d'Arte Cinematografica in Venice (1992).
Selection for the Rotterdam Film Festival (1992).
Special Jury Commendation in the 'Black and White Short Film Competition' at the Film Festival in Cork.

Mozart/Materiaal

1993, Betacam SP, 52', colour

Mozart/Materiaal is a documentary about the rehearsal process of *Mozart/Concert Arias, un moto di gioia* including footage of the premiere at the Festival d'Avignon.

Directors
Jurgen Persijn and Anna Torfs.

Editing
Peter Missotten.

Sound
Benoit Bruwier.

Produced by: Rosas.
Co-produced by: De Munt/La Monnaie, Audio Visual Service of the Catholic University of Louvain.
In collaboration with: BRTN Cultural Service.

Achterland

1994, 35mm, 84', black and white.

Achterland is the film adaptation of a stage production of the same name from 1990. The film was shot in the set of the stage production in the Rosas rehearsal studio.

Director
Anne Teresa De Keersmaeker.

In collaboration with
Herman Van Eyken.

Dancers
Nordine Benchorf, Bruce Campbell, Vincent Dunoyer, Fumiyo Ikeda, Marion Levy, Cynthia Loemij, Nathalie Million, Johanne Saunier.

Music
György Ligeti *(Eight studies for piano)*, Eugène Ysaÿe *(Three sonatas for solo violin).*

Music performed live by
Irvine Arditti and Rolf Hind.

Director of photography
Louis Philippe Capelle
(based on the lighting design for the performance by Jean-Luc Ducourt).

Camera
Chris Renson, Renaat Lambeets.

Sound
Dirk Bombey.

Costume design
Ann Weckx.

Set design
Herman Sorgeloos.

Editing
Ludo Troch.

Assistants to the director
Annemie Vandeputte and Anne Van Aerschot.

Produced by: Avila.
Executive production: Alice in Wonderland.
Co-produced by: Rosas, BRTN, NOS.
Supported by the Ministry of the Flemish Community, the European Union 16:9 action plan.
In collaboration with Amaya, ZDF/arte, SVT1, De Munt/La Monnaie.

Awards
IMZ Dance Screen Award, Lyon (1994).
Award for the Best Adaptation at the Festival du Film sur l'art, Montreal (1995).

Tippeke

1996, 16mm, 18', colour.

Tippeke is based on a nursery rhyme and was made in 1996, as part of the stage production *Woud, three movements to the music of Schönberg, Berg and Wagner.*

Director
Thierry De Mey.

Choreography and Dance
Anne Teresa De Keersmaeker.

Music
Thierry De Mey.
In collaboration with
François Deppe, Serge Lemouton, IRCAM/Centre Georges Pompidou.

Director of photography
Aliocha Van der Avoort.

Camera
Aliocha Van der Avoort, Thierry De Mey.

Editing
Boris Van der Avoort, Isabelle Boyer.

Sound
Peter Pernt.

Assistants to the director
Peter Pernt, Pascal Gigon.

Produced by: **Rosas**
In collaboration with Inscape, Thierry De Mey, Jan Roekens.

Awards
Grand Prix Carina Ari of the Festival International Media Dance in Boulogne-Billancourt (2000).

Rosas danst Rosas

1997, 35mm, 57', colour

Rosas danst Rosas is the film adaptation of a stage production of the same name from 1983. The film was shot in the RITO school in Leuven, Belgium (architect: Henry Van de Velde).

Director
Thierry De Mey.

Choreography
Anne Teresa De Keersmaeker.

Dancers
Cynthia Loemij, Sarah Ludi, Anne Mousselet, Samantha Van Wissen.

Music
Thierry De Mey and Peter Vermeersch.

Director of photography
Michel Houssiau.

Camera
Philippe Guilbert, Jorge Leon.

Editing
Rudi Maerten.

Sound
Ricardo Castro.

Mixage
Thomas Gauder.

Assistant to the director
Anne Van Aerschot.

Produced by: Avila & Sophimages.
Co-produced by: NPS, BRTN TV2, ZDF/Arte, Le Fresnoy, Rosas.
Supported by: Fonds Film in Vlaanderen (Flanders Film Fund), Direction de l'Audiovisuel de la Communauté Française de Belgique, National Lottery, P.A.R.T.S.

Awards
Award for the best production at the International Widescreen Festival, Amsterdam (September 1997).
Grand Prix International Video Dance, Stockholm (1997).
Nomination at the Film and Architecture Film Festival, Graz (November 1997).
Special Jury Award at the International Festival for Film and New Media on Art, Athens (December 1998).

Fase

2002, 35mm, 58', colour

Fase is the film adaptation of the stage production *Fase, four movements to the music of Steve Reich* (1982). The four movements were shot in four different locations: *Piano Phase* in the Rosas Performance Space in Vorst; *Come Out* in the new Coca Cola building in Anderlecht; *Violin Phase* in a forest in Tervuren; *Clapping Music* in the Felix Pakhuis in Antwerp.

Director
Thierry De Mey.

Choreography
Anne Teresa De Keersmaeker.

Dancers
Anne Teresa De Keersmaeker and Michèle Anne De Mey.

Music
Steve Reich *(Violin Phase, Piano Phase, Clapping Music, Come Out)*.

Directors of photography
Walther Vanden Ende *(Piano Phase*, based on the lighting design for the performance by Remon Fromont).
Michel Houssiau *(Come Out & Violin Phase)*.
Remon Fromont *(Clapping Music)*.

Editing
Rudi Maerten.

Camera
Chris Renson, Pierre Gordower, Jean-Jacques Mathy, Aliocha Van der Avoort, Renaat Lambeets.

Mixage
Thomas Gauder.

Assistant to the director
Anne Van Aerschot.

Produced by: Avila & Sophimages.
Co-produced by: Rosas, ARTE France, NPS TV, RTBF Brussels, Bruges 2002.
Supported by: Fonds Film in Vlaanderen, National Lottery.
In collaboration with: C-sales, VRT.

Small hands

2001, DV CAM, 42 min., colour.

Small hands is a video adaptation of the stage production *Small hands (out of the lie of no...)* (2001). The video was shot during rehearsals and performances in the Rosas Performance Space in June 2001.

Directors
Aliocha Van der Avoort and Boris Van der Avoort.

Choreography
Anne Teresa De Keersmaeker.

Dancers
Anne Teresa De Keersmaeker and Cynthia Loemij.

Music
Henry Purcell.

Camera
Aliocha Van der Avoort.

Editing
Boris Van der Avoort.

Produced by: Rosas, Boris Van der Avoort, Aliocha Van der Avoort.

Corps Accords

2002, Betacam SP, colour.

Corps Accords is a documentary about the rehearsal process of *April me*. The shooting took place from May 2001 up until the first performances in April 2002 in De Munt/La Monnaie in Brussels.

Director
Michel Follin.

Choreography
Anne Teresa De Keersmaeker.

Dancers
Beniamin Boar, Marta Coronado, Alix Eynaudi, Jordi Galí, Fumiyo Ikeda, Cynthia Loemij, Ursula Robb, Taka Shamoto, Igor Shyshko, Clinton Stringer, Julia Sugranyes, Rosalba Torres, Jakub Truszkowski.

Music
Thierry De Mey *(Les Fiançailles, Silence must be!)*, Igor Stravinsky *(Les Noces)*, Yannis Xenakis *(Peau – Pleïades)*, Gérard Grisey *(Stèle)*, W.A. Mozart *(Le Nozze di Figaro, Act 4, scene 8 Susanna)*, Morton Feldman *(King of Denmark)*, Parveen Sultana *(Rosiya Moke Bulaye Thumri)*, L. Subramanyam *(Raga Alapana)*, traditional Indian and Italian music.

Musicians
Ictus Ensemble (Miquel Bernat, Kuniko Kato, Gerrit Nulens, Jessica Ryckewaert, Michael Weilacher, Georges-Elie Octors).

Set and lighting design
Jan Versweyveld.
Assistant
Geert Peymen.

Costume design
Inge Büscher.
Assistant
Anne-Catherine Kunz.

Musical Analysis
Georges-Elie Octors.

Singing Instructor
Lucie Graumann.

Technical Management
Luc Galle.

Director of Pl[illegible]ap[illegible]
Michel Baudo[illegible]

Sound
Alain Sironv[illegible]

Editing
Christine Carrière.

Assistant to the director
Micha Wald.

Production Assistant
Anne Van Aerschot.

Rehearsal director
Pascale Gigon.

Produced by: Idéale Audience and Versus production.
Co-produced by: ARTE France, RTBF Brussels, Rosas.
In collaboration with: NPS, SFDRS, ORF.
Supported by: Centre National de la Cinématographie, PROCIREP, MEDIA programme of the European Commission.

Rosas 2002/2003

Kees Eijrond, general director; Anne Teresa De Keersmaeker, artistic director; Guy Gypens, general manager; Anne Van Aerschot, assistant to the artistic director; Pascale Gigon, rehearsal director; Beniamin Boar, Marta Coronado, Alix Eynaudi, Fumiyo Ikeda, Jordi Galí Melendez, Cynthia Loemij, Elizaveta Penkova, Ursula Robb, Taka Shamoto, Igor Shyshko, Clinton Stringer, Julia Sugranyes, Johan Thelander, Rosalba Torres, Jakub Truszkowski, dancers; Luk Van den bosch, administrator; Hanne Van Waeyenberge, assistant to the administrator; Bob Van Langendonck, financial administrator, Lena Dierckx, tour management; Koen Van Muylem, press and promotion; Chris Maes, secretary to the director; Johanna Buys, reception; Luc Galle, technical director; Patrick Martens, technical administration and production management; Frank Vandezande, Kristof Van Dijck, Marianne Kiekens, technicians; Anne-Catherine Kunz, costume; Evelyne Sax, physiotherapist; Hassan El Boutzakhti, janitor; Ahmed Musa Osman, Czeslaw Wnorowski, technical maintenance; Maria Leandro, Maria Vega Sanchez del Sol, maintenance.

P.A.R.T.S. 2002/2003

Anne Teresa De Keersmaeker, director; Theo Van Rompay, deputy director; Kees Eijrond, general manager; Elizabeth Corbett, dance development co-ordinator; Cecilia De Moor, administrator; Lieve Demin, programme co-ordinator; Lief Bigaré, planning and communication; Peter Fol, technician; Rabia Aghrib, maintenance; Mieke Vervecken-Pieters, Sara De Groote, Lud Hoskens, Cuong Van Long, kitchen.

Rosas is Company in Residence at De Munt/La Monnaie
Bernard Foccroulle, director; Bernard Coutant, finance director; Josep Marie Folch, technical director

Rosas is subsidised by the Ministry of the Flemish Community-Administration for Culture and supported by the National Lottery.

PARTS is an initiative of Rosas and De Munt/La Monnaie and is subsidised by the Ministry of Education of the Flemish Community and receives additional financial support from the Ministry of Culture of the Flemish Community, the Flemish Community Commission of the Brussels-Capital Region and the DÉPARTS network. DÉPARTS is supported by the European Commission (programme "Culture 2000").

Rosas/P.A.R.T.S.
Van Volxemlaan 164, B-1190 Brussels
Tel: +32 2 344 55 98
Fax: + 32 2 343 53 52
http://www.rosas.be mail@rosas.be
http://www.parts.be mail@parts.be

Exhibition Rosas XX

The publication of the book *Rosas/Anne Teresa De Keersmaeker, if and only if wonder* coincided with the opening of the exhibition *Rosas XX* in the Palais des Beaux Arts (Brussels, 19/10/02-05/01/03).

Rosas XX was co-produced by Rosas and The Palais des Beaux Arts.

Rosas
Michel Uytterhoeven, curator; Sara Jansen, assistant-curator; Guy Gypens, producer; Hanne Van Waeyenberge, project co-ordinator; Koen Van Muylem, communication; Anne Teresa De Keersmaeker, historic advise.

Palais des Beaux Arts
Paul Dujardin, director-general; Thomas Simon, COO; Anne Mommens, director of exhibitions; Sophie Lauwers, project co-ordinator; Ludo Willems, technical director; Roger Vander Meulen, technical co-ordinator; Philippe Braem, Inge Roskams, Claude Lorent, press en communication.

Rosas XX was supported by:
Ministry of the Flemish Community, Department of Visual Arts and Museums; Ministry of the Flemish Community, Co-ordination Brussels; European Commision (programme "Culture 2000"); Flemish Community Commission of the Brussels-Capital Region; National Lottery; Rosas; Palais des Beaux Arts; De Munt/La Monnaie; Théâtre de la Ville, Paris; Holland Festival, Amsterdam; Impuls Tanz, Vienna; Flemish Theatre Institute; Contredanse.

TENTOONSTE
LLING/EXPO
SITION ROSA
SXX/ANNE T
ERESA DE K
EERSMAEKE
R/20/10/2002
-05/01/2003/
PSK/PBA/BXL

Tentoonstelling/Exposition
RosasXX/Anne Teresa De Keersmaeker
Paleis voor Schone Kunsten/Palais des Beaux-Arts
20/10/2002-05/01/2003

10-18 u/h, op woensdag tot 21 u./le mercredi jusqu'à 21 h.
Gesloten op maandag, 25 december en 1 januari/
Fermé le lundi, le 25 décembre et le 1er janvier.
7 euro, 5 euro (reductiehouders/avec réduction)

Info: 02-507.84.84 infoexpo@pskpba www.rosas.be

Een productie van Rosas en het Paleis voor Schone Kunsten/
Une production de Rosas et du Palais des Beaux-Arts

Met de steun van/avec le soutien de: TV Brussel, La Libre Essentielle, De Standaard
VU/ER: Guy Gypens, Van Volxemlaan 164, 1190 BXL. Grafisch ontwerp/Graphisme: Paul Boudens

Rosas

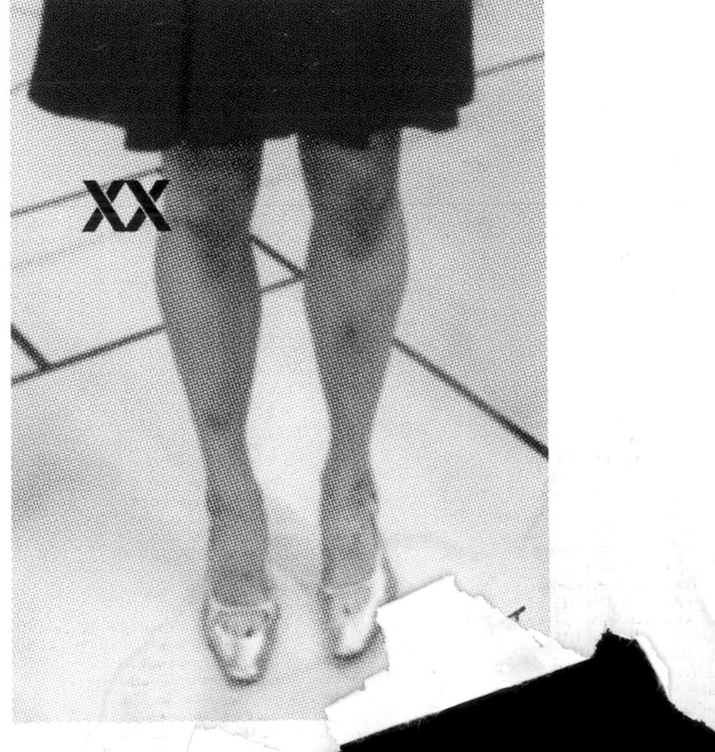

Credits ouverture

P. 4: Photos Clive Mitchell
P. 5: Spiral in hair Anne Teresa De Keersmaeker. Photo Herman Sorgeloos
P. 6: Photo Pierre Lefèbre
P. 7: Photo André Vigneau
P. 8: Ernst Peter Fischer, *Das schöne und das Biest: Ästhetische Momente in der Wissenschaft*, Piper Verlag, 1997, p. 96-97; I Ching table ; Cover CD *A Love Supreme*, John Coltrane (Universal Music Group)
P. 9: R.A. Feuillet, *Chorégraphie ou l'art de décrire la danse*, Arnaldo Forni Editore, 1983, p. 78-79 *(Table des Contre-temps)*; Maurice Buyens (red.), *Gebarenwoordenboek*, Fevlado and Garant Uitgeverij, 1995, p. 214, p. 555
P. 10 – 11: Photo Editions Baudouin, Paris
P. 12: Anne Teresa De Keersmaeker (photo archive Anne Teresa De Keersmaeker)
P. 13: Marie-Jeanne Lindemans (photo archive Anne Teresa De Keersmaeker) Children playing (photo archive Anne Teresa De Keersmaeker)
P. 14: Maurits De Keersmaeker and Albion II (photo archive Anne Teresa De Keersmaeker) Lauterbrunental, Stechelberg (Breithorn, Tschingelhorn) (archive Anne Teresa De Keersmaeker)
P. 15: Mongolia (archive Anne Teresa De Keersmaeker) Nilgiri Mountain, the Himalayas, Nepal. Photo Anne Teresa De Keersmaeker
P. 16: Paul Grillo, *Form, Function and Design*, Dover Publications, NY, 1960, p. 182
P. 17: Video still *Violin Phase*, Thierry De Mey
P. 18: Matila C. Ghyka, *Le nombre d'or*, Gallimard, 1997, pl. XVIII, pl. XIX, pl. XXII, pl. XXIII
P. 19: Matila C. Ghyka, *Le nombre d'or*, Gallimard, 1997, pl. I *Pentagramme dans la grande rose d'Amiens (Photo Régnaut), Pentacles magiques, d'après un manuscrit allemand du cycle Faustien, Quintefeuilles de la Saint-Chapelle, portail sud (photo L.-P.)*; pl. XVII *L'homme -microcosme d'après Agrippa de Nettesheim, L'icosaèdre directeur dans l'enseignement chorégraphique de R. von Laban (Extrait de la Chorégraphie de R. von Laban, E. Diedrichs, éd.)*
P. 20: postcards personal archive Anne Teresa De Keersmaeker
P. 21: Gotthard Schuh, Java 1938, Nouvelles Images
P. 22: Agnes Propeck, 2002, *Sans titre (glaçons 1) pour Christian Lacroix, XCLX*
P. 23: Anton and Anna Franziska Jäger. Photo Anne Teresa De Keersmaeker
P. 24: De Standaard, March 12th 2002. Photos Belga
P. 25: X-Ray photo of refugees discovered in a container in Calais, 1999 (photo AP)
P. 26: Fernand Khnopff (1885 – 1921). Musées Royaux des Beaux-Arts de Belgique, Brussels
P. 27: Marie-France Boyer, *La langage des arbres*, Thames & Hudson, 1996, p. 75 *(en Thaïlande, on invoque Bouddha, dont la tête apparaît dans un tronc d'arbre)*

Fotocredits

P.42 : Anne Teresa De Keersmaeker, Jean Luc Breuer (AdH).
Anne Teresa De Keersmaeker (AdH).
Anne Teresa De Keersmaeker (AdH).
P.43 : Anne Teresa De Keersmaeker (AdH).
P.44 : Anne Teresa De Keersmaeker (WK).
P.45 : Jean-Luc Breuer (WK).
P.46 : Michèle Anne De Mey, Anne Teresa De Keersmaeker (CA).
Anne Teresa De Keersmaeker, Michèle Anne De Mey.
Anne Teresa De Keersmaeker, Michèle Anne De Mey (HS).
P.47 : Anne Teresa De Keersmaeker, Michèle Anne De Mey (HS).
P.48 : Michèle Anne De Mey, Anne Teresa De Keersmaeker (HS).
Michèle Anne De Mey, Anne Teresa De Keersmaeker (HS).
Michèle Anne De Mey, Anne Teresa De Keersmaeker (HS).
Michèle Anne De Mey, Anne Teresa De Keersmaeker (HS).
Anne Teresa De Keersmaeker (HS).
Michèle Anne De Mey, Anne Teresa De Keersmaeker, Thierry De Mey (HS).
P.49 : Kaisa Sandstrom, Frauke Mariën (HS).
P.50 : Anne Teresa De Keersmaeker, Michèle Anne De Mey.
Anne Teresa De Keersmaeker, Michèle Anne De Mey.
P.51 : Anne Teresa De Keersmaeker, Michèle Anne De Mey.
P.52 : Michèle Anne De Mey, Anne Teresa De Keersmaeker (HS).
Michèle Anne De Mey, Anne Teresa De Keersmaeker (HS).
P.53 : Anne Teresa De Keersmaeker, Michèle Anne De Mey (HS).
P.54 : Anne Teresa De Keersmaeker (HS).
Anne Teresa De Keersmaeker, Thierry De Mey (HS).
Anne Teresa De Keersmaeker (HS).
Anne Teresa De Keersmaeker (HS).
Anne Teresa De Keersmaeker, filmcrew Fase (HS).
(HS).
Anne Teresa De Keersmaeker, filmcrew Fase (HS).
Anne Teresa De Keersmaeker, filmcrew Fase (HS).
Anne Teresa De Keersmaeker, filmcrew Fase (Hs).
P.55 : Anne Teresa De Keersmaeker (HS).
p.56 : Anne Teresa De Keersmaeker, Michèle Anne De Mey (HS).
P.57 : Anne Teresa De Keersmaeker, Michèle Anne De Mey.
Anne Teresa De Keersmaeker (HS).
Michèle Anne De Mey (HS).
Anne Teresa De Keersmaeker, Michèle Anne De Mey (HS).
Anne Teresa De Keersmaeker, Michèle Anne De Mey (HS).
(HS).
P.58 : Fumiyo Ikeda (JLT).
Anne Teresa De Keersmaeker, Fumiyo Ikeda, Michèle Anne De Mey (JLT).
Michèle Anne De Mey(JLT).
Anne Teresa De Keersmaeker (JLT).
Anne Teresa De Keersmaeker, Michèle Anne De Mey (JLT).
Anne Teresa De Keersmaeker (JLT).
Michèle Anne De Mey (JLT).
P.59 : Fumiyo Ikeda (JLT).
P.60 : Adriana Boriello, Anne Teresa De Keersmaeker, Michèle Anne De Mey, Fumiyo Ikeda (JLT).
Fumiyo Ikeda, Adriana Boriello, Michèle Anne De Mey, Anne Teresa De Keersmaeker (JLT).
P.61 : (JLT).
Michèle Anne De Mey, Fumiyo Ikeda, Adriana Boriello, Anne Teresa De Keersmaeker (JLT).
P.62 : Roxane Huilmand, Fumiyo Ikeda, Nadine Ganase (HS).
P.63 : Cynthia Loemij, Nathalie Million, Samantha Van Wissen, Johanne Saunier (HS).
P.64 : Sarah Ludi (HS).
Nathalie Million, Johanne Saunier, Samantha Van Wissen (HS).
Sarah Ludi (HS).
Sarah Ludi (HS).
Cynthia Loemij, Nathalie Million, Samantha Van Wissen (HS).
Sarah Ludi (HS).
Nathalie Million, Samantha Van Wissen, Johanne Saunier (HS).
P.65 : Samantha Van Wissen, Anne Mousselet, Cynthia Loemij, Joanne Fong (HS).
Anne Teresa De Keersmaeker, Michèle Anne De Mey, Adriana Boriello, Fumiyo Ikeda (HS) :
Cynthia Loemij, Joanne Fong (HS).
Cynthia Loemij (HS).
P.66 : Anne Mousselet (HS).
Anne Mousselet (HS).
P.67 : Anne Mousselet (HS).
Anne Mousselet (HS).
P.68 : Samantha Van Wissen, Cynthia Loemij (HS).
P.69 : Samantha Van Wissen, Anne Mousselet, Cynthia Loemij, Sarah Ludi (HS).
P.70 : Anne Mousselet, Cynthia Loemij, Sarah Ludi, Samantha Van Wissen (AVA).
Walter Hus, Peter Vermeersch, Erik Sleichim, Thierry De Mey (MFP).
Samantha Van Wissen, filmcrew (HS).
Filmcrew (HS).
Anne Mousselet, Cynthia Loemij, Sarah Ludi, filmcrew (HS).
Filmcrew (HS).
P.71 : Cynthia Loemij, Sarah Ludi, Anne Mousselet, Samantha Van Wissen (HS).
P.72 : Nadine Ganase, Anne Teresa De Keersmaeker, Fumiyo Ikeda, Roxane Huilmand (HS).
Fumiyo Ikeda, Roxane Huilmand, Nadine Ganase (HS).
Fumiyo Ikeda, Michèle Anne De Mey, Anne Teresa De Keersmaeker (HS).
P.73 : Michèle Anne De Mey (HS).
P.75 : Fumiyo Ikeda (HS).
P.76 : Set (HS).
P.77 : Set (HS).
P.78 : Anne Teresa De Keersmaeker, Michèle Anne De Mey, Roxane Huilmand, Fumiyo Ikeda, Nadine Ganase (HS).
Anne Teresa De Keersmaeker, Michèle Anne De Mey, Roxane Huilmand, Fumiyo Ikeda, Nadine Ganase (HS).
Anne Teresa De Keersmaeker, Michèle Anne De Mey, Roxane Huilmand, Fumiyo Ikeda, Nadine Ganase (HS).
P.79 : Anne Teresa De Keersmaeker, Michèle Anne De Mey, Roxane Huilmand, Fumiyo Ikeda, Nadine Ganase (HS).
Anne Teresa De Keersmaeker, Michèle Anne De Mey, Roxane Huilmand, Fumiyo Ikeda, Nadine Ganase (HS).
Anne Teresa De Keersmaeker, Michèle Anne De Mey, Roxane Huilmand, Fumiyo Ikeda, Nadine Ganase (HS).
P.80 : Roxane Huilmand, Nadine Ganase, Fumiyo Ikeda, Michèle Anne De Mey, Anne Teresa De Keersmaeker (HS).
P.81 : Roxane Huilmand, Koen Bauwens, Michèle Anne De Mey, Hugo De Greef, Bert De Raeymaeker, Fumiyo Ikeda, Nadine Ganase (HS).
Roxane Huilmand, Anne Teresa De Keersmaeker, Michèle Anne De Mey, Nadine Ganase (HS).
P.82 : Anne Teresa De Keersmaeker (HS).
Anne Teresa De Keersmaeker, Johanne Saunier, Nadine Ganase (HS).
P.83 : Fumiyo Ikeda, Johanne Saunier (HS).
P.85 : Nadine Ganase, Johanne Saunier, Fumiyo Ikeda, Anne Teresa De Keersmaeker (HS).
Johanne Saunier, Fumiyo Ikeda, Nadine Ganase, Anne Teresa De Keersmaeker (HS).
P.86 : Fumiyo Ikeda (HS).
P.88 : Anne Teresa De Keersmaeker, Johanne Saunier, Nadine Ganase (HS).
P.89 : Anne Teresa De Keersmaeker, Fumiyo Ikeda, Johanne Saunier, Nadine Ganase (HS).
(HS).
(HS).
Anne Teresa De Keersmaeker, Roxane Huilmand (HS).
Anne Teresa De Keersmaeker (HS).
P.90 : Kitty Kortes Lynch (WV).
Kitty Kortes Lynch (WV).
Johan Leysen (WV).
Kitty Kortes Lynch, Johan Leysen (WV).
Johan Leysen, Kitty Kortes Lynch (WV).
Kitty Kortes Lynch (WV).
Johan Leysen (WV).
Kitty Kortes Lynch (WV).
Kitty Kortes Lynch, André Verbist (WV).
Kitty Kortes Lynch (WV).
André Verbist (WV).
Kitty Kortes Lynch, Johan Leysen (WV).
P.91 : Kitty Kortes Lynch (HS).
P.92 : Johan Leysen (HS).
P.93 : Kitty Kortes Lynch, Johan Leysen (HS).
André Verbist (HS).
Kitty Kortes Lynch, Johan Leysen (HS).
P.94 : Kitty Kortes Lynch, Johan Leysen (HS).
P.96 : Johanne Saunier, Jean-Luc Ducourt (HS).
Jean-Luc Ducourt (HS).
Jean-Luc Ducourt, Johanne Saunier (HS).
P.97 : Walter Hus, Stefan Poelmans, Johanne Saunier, Jean-Luc Ducourt (HS).
P.98 : Roxane Huilmand, Fumiyo Ikeda, Nadine Ganase, Anne Teresa De Keersmaeker (HS).
Mark Lorimer, Samantha Van Wissen (HS).
Jean-Luc Ducourt, Johanne Saunier, Walter Hus (HS).
Fumiyo Ikeda, Mondriaan Kwartet (HS).
Philipp Egli, Marion Levy (HS).
Anne Teresa De Keersmaeker, Mondriaan Kwartet (HS).
P.99 : Roxane Huilmand, Fumiyo Ikeda, Nadine Ganase, Anne Teresa De Keersmaeker (HS).
P.100 : Anne Teresa De Keersmaeker, Fumiyo Ikeda, Roxane Huilmand, Nadine Ganase (HS).
Cynthia Loemij, Duke Quartet (HS).
P.101 : Cynthia Loemij, Anne Mousselet, Joanne Fong, Samantha Van Wissen, The Duke Quartet (HS).
P.102 : Fumiyo Ikeda (WV).
Johanne Saunier, Nathalie Million, Laure Bonicel (WV).
Nathalie Million (WV).
Wouter Steenbergen, John Jasperse (WV).
Carlotta Sagna (WV).
Carlotta Sagna (WV).
Carlotta Sagna (WV).
Fatou Traore (WV).
Fatou Traore (WV).
Laure Bonicel (WV).
Fumiyo Ikeda (WV).
Fumiyo Ikeda (WV).
Johanne Saunier (WV).
Laure Bonicel (WV).
Oscar Dasi y Perez, Laure Bonicel (WV).
Laure Bonicel (WV).
P.103 : Laure Bonicel (WV).
Nathalie Million (HS).
P.104 : Wouter Steenbergen, John Jasperse, Nicole Balm, Michèle Anne De Mey, Johanne Saunier, Nadine Ganase, Pierre Droulers (HS).
Carlotta Sagna, John Jasperse, Jordi Cassanovas Sempere, Pierre Droulers, Johanne Saunier, Jean-Luc Ducourt, Nadine Ganase, Oscar Dasi y Perez, Nathalie Million, Nicole Balm, Wouter Steenbergen, Laure Bonicel (HS).
P.105 : Fumiyo Ikeda, Johanne Saunier, Nadine Ganase (HS).
P.106 : Fumiyo Ikeda (WV).
P.107 : Jean-Luc Ducourt (WV).
P.108 : Nordine Benchorf (HS).
Johanne Saunier (HS).
P.109 : Nathalie Million (HS).
P.110 : Fumiyo Ikeda (HS).
Fumiyo Ikeda (HS).
Fumiyo Ikeda (HS).
Johanne Saunier (HS).
Marion Levy, Carlotta Sagna (HS).
Nathalie Million (HS).
Carlotta Sagna, Johanne Saunier, Nathalie Million (HS).
P.111 : Nathalie Million (HS).
P.112 : Fumiyo Ikeda (HS).
P.113 : Fumiyo Ikeda (HS).
P.114 : Marion Levy (HS).
P.115 : Carlotta Sagna, Nathalie Million, Johanne Saunier (HS).
P.116 : Fumiyo Ikeda (HS).
Johanne Saunier, Carlotta Sagna (HS).
Fumiyo Ikeda (HS).
Nathalie Million (HS).
P.117 : Carlotta Sagna, Marion Levy (HS).
Nathalie Million, Johanne Saunier (HS).
Jean-Luc Ducourt, Anne Teresa De Keersmaeker (HS).
Véronique Verbruggen, Marianne Van Kerkhoven, Celesta Rottiers (HS).
P.119 : Nathalie Million (HS).
P.120 : Irvine Arditti, Vincent Dunoyer, Bruce Campbell (HS).
George Van Dam, Roberto Oliván de la Iglesia (HS).
Laurent Korcia, Vincent Dunoyer (HS).
Irvine Arditti, Vincent Dunoyer (HS).
P.121 : Cynthia Loemij (HS).
P.122 : Irvine Arditti, Vincent Dunoyer, Bruce Campbell, Nordine Benchorf (HS).
Nordine Benchorf, Rolf Hind (HS).
Irvine Arditti, Vincent Dunoyer, Nordine Benchorf, Cynthia Loemij (HS).
Nordine Benchorf (HS).
P.124 : Jan Michiels, Martin Kilvády (HS).
Jan Michiels, Martin Kilvády (HS).
P.125 : Vincent Dunoyer (HS).
Samantha Van Wissen, Cynthia Loemij, Rolf Hind, Marion Levy, Johanne Saunier, Anne Mousselet (HS).
Vincent Dunoyer (HS).
Samantha Van Wissen, Cynthia Loemij, Rolf Hind, Marion Levy, Johanne Saunier, Anne Mousselet (HS).
Vincent Dunoyer (HS).

Carlotta Sagna, Fumiyo Ikeda, Rolf Hind, Marion Levy (HS).
Fumiyo Ikeda, Anne Teresa De Keersmaeker, Johanne Saunier, Marion Levy, Carlotta Sagna, Nathalie Million (HS).
P.126 : Johanne Saunier, Cynthia Loemij, Marion Levy, Fumiyo Ikeda, Nathalie Million (HS).
Nordine Benchorf (HS).
Fumiyo Ikeda, Rolf Hind, Marion Levy, Cynthia Loemij (HS).
Roberto Oliván de Iglesia, Martin Kilvády (HS).
Vincent Dunoyer (HS).
P.127 : Johanne Saunier, Nordine Benchorf (HS).
P.128 : Nordine Benchorf, Fumiyo Ikeda (HS).
Peter Greenaway, Fumiyo Ikeda (HS).
P.129 : Fumiyo Ikeda (HS).
P.130 : Anne Mousselet, Samantha Van Wissen (HS).
Anne Mousselet, Samantha Van Wissen, Johanne Saunier (HS).
Anne Mousselet, Samantha Van Wissen, Cynthia Loemij, Mark Bruce, Joanne Fong, Vincent Dunoyer, Philipp Egli, Marion Levy (HS).
Vincent Dunoyer, Nathalie Million (HS).
Vincent Dunoyer, Nathalie Million (HS).
P.131 : Nordine Benchorf, Muriel Hérault (HS).
P.133 : Vincent Dunoyer, Nathalie Million (HS).
P.134 : Joanne Fong, Samantha Van Wissen, Anne Mousselet, Marion Levy, Vincent Dunoyer, Cynthia Loemij, Nathalie Million (HS).
Marion Levy, Nathalie Million (HS).
P.135 : Cynthia Loemij, Arditti String Quartet (HS).
P.137 : Cynthia Loemij, Thomas Hauert, Anne Mousselet, Vincent Dunoyer, Mark Bruce (HS).
P.138 : Muriel Hérault, Marion Levy (HS).
Muriel Hérault, Marion Levy (HS).
Samantha Van Wissen (HS).
Eduardo Torroja, Johanne Saunier (HS).
Nathalie Million (HS).
Marion Levy, Muriel Hérault (HS).
P.139 : Nordine Benchorf, Anne Mousselet (HS).
P.140 : Vincent Dunoyer, Janet Williams (HS).
Philippe Herreweghe, Vincent Dunoyer, Janet Williams (HS).
Vincent Dunoyer, Janet Williams (HS).
P.141 : Cynthia Loemij, Muriel Hérault, Johanne Saunier, Anne Mousselet, Samantha Van Wissen (HS).
P.142 : Vincent Dunoyer (HS).
P.144 : Bruce Campbell, Cynthia Loemij, Thomas Hauert, Anne Mousselet (HS).
P.145 : (HS).
P.146 : Brice Leroux, Marion Levy (HS).
Suman Hsu, Brice Leroux, Marion Levy (HS).
P.147 : Suman Hsu (HS).
P.148 : Brice Leroux, Suman Hsu, Marion Levy, Marion Ballester (HS).
Brice Leroux, Marion Levy, Suman Hsu (HS).
Brice Leroux, Suman Hsu (HS).
P.149 : Vincent Dunoyer, Fumiyo Ikeda, Johanne Saunier (HS).
Jos Van Immerseel (HS).
P.150 : Fumiyo Ikeda, Anne Teresa De Keersmaeker, Marion Levy, Johanne Saunier, Vincent Dunoyer (HS).
P.151 : Marion Ballester (HS).
P.153 : Jean-Luc Fafchamps, Marion Ballester (HS).
P.154 : Osman Kassen Khelili, Jean-Luc Fafchamps, Sarah Ludi, Marion Ballester, Frank Chartier (HS).
P.155 : Osman Kassen Khelili, Jean-Luc Fafchamps, Misha Downey, Philipp Egli, Suman Hsu (HS).
P.157 : Mark Lorimer, Sarah Ludi (HS).
P.158 : George Alexander Van Dam, Gery Cambier, Takashi Yamane, Igor Semenoff, Francois Deppe, Jean-Luc Fafchamps, Georges-Elie Octors, Piet Van Bockstal, Jean-Luc Plouvier, Paul De Clerck, Dirk Descheemaeker (HS).
P.161 : Samantha Van Wissen, Suman Hsu, Marion Levy, Marion Ballester, Anne Mousselet, Sarah Ludi, Ictus ensemble (HS).
Anne Mousselet, Marion Levy, Suman Hsu, Marion Ballester, Samantha Van Wissen, Ictus ensemble (HS).
P.162 : Suman Hsu (HS).
Brice Leroux, Anne Mousselet (HS).
Cynthia Loemij, Brice Leroux, Anne Mousselet, Marion Levy, Osman Kassen Khelili, Johanne Saunier, Mark Lorimer, Suman Hsu, Philipp Egli (HS).
P.163 : Brice Leroux, Anne Mousselet, Mark Lorimer (HS).
P.164 : Anne Teresa De Keersmaeker, Samantha Van Wissen (HS).
Anne Teresa De Keersmaeker, Cynthia Loemij (HS).
Anne Teresa De Keersmaeker, Samantha Van Wissen (HS).
P.165 : Anne Teresa De Keersmaeker, Samantha Van Wissen (HS).
P.166 : Oliver Koch, Iris Bouche, Marion Ballester, Kosi Hidama (HS).
P.167 : Oliver Koch, Iris Bouche (HS).
P.168 : Oliver Koch, Cynthia Loemij, Kosi Hidama (HS).
Oliver Koch, Johanne Saunier, Samantha Van Wissen, Cynthia Loemij, Kosi Hidama (HS).
P.169 : Oliver Koch, Marion Ballester, Misha Downey, Suman Hsu, Kosi Hidama, Johanne Saunier (HS).
P.170 : Kosi Hidama, Osman Kassen Khelili, Samantha Van Wissen, Cynthia Loemij, Misha Downey (HS).
P.171 : Marion Ballester, Samantha Van Wissen, Mark Lorimer, Iris Bouche, Sarah Ludi (HS).
Cynthia Loemij (HS).
Cynthia Loemij (HS).
P.172 : Vincent Dunoyer (HS).
P.173 : Vincent Dunoyer (HS).
Vincent Dunoyer (HS).
P.175 : Rosalba Torres, Martin Kilvády, Alix Eynaudi (HS).
P.177 : Georges Elie Octors, Iris Bouche (HS).
P.178 : Alix Eynaudi, Cynthia Loemij, Gerrit Nulens, Georges Elie Octors, Miguel Bernat, Roberto Oliván de la Iglesia, Oliver Koch (HS).
Cynthia Loemij (HS).
P.179 : Taka Shamoto (HS).
Taka Shamoto (HS).
Bruce Campbell, Taka Shamoto (HS).
Bruce Campbell, Rosalba Torres, Taka Shamoto (HS).
Bruce Campbell, Rosalba Torres, Taka Shamoto (HS).
P.180 : Ursula Robb, Bruce Campbell, Miquel Bernat, Roberto Oliván de la Iglesia, Rosalba Torres, Martin Kilvády, Fumiyo Ikeda, Alix Eynaudi, Taka Shamoto (HS).
P.181 : Cynthia Loemij, Farooq Chaudry (HS).
Iris Bouche (HS).
P.182 : Ursula Robb, Fumiyo Ikeda, Alix Eynaudi, Iris Bouche, Taka Shamoto, Martin Kilvády, Rosalba Torres (HS).
P.183 : Martin Kilvády, Alix Eynaudi, Jean-Luc Fafchamps, Oliver Koch (HS).
Rosalba Torres, Martin Kilvády (HS).
P.184 : Samantha Van Wissen, Sarah Ludi, Cynthia Loemij, Anne Mousselet (HS).
P.185 : Taka Shamoto, Bruce Campbell (HS).
P.186 : Iris Bouche, Martin Kilvády (HS).
Svetelina Vassileva, Victor Braun (HS).
P.187 : Svetelina Vassileva, Victor Braun (HS).
P.189 : Marta Coronado, Cynthia Loemij, Alix Eynaudi (HS).
P.190 : (HS).
P.191 : Ursula Robb, Ictus ensemble (HS).
P.192 : Oliver Koch, Taka Shamoto, Cynthia Loemij, Roberto Oliván de la Iglesia (HS).
P.193 : Cynthia Loemij, Roberto Oliván de la Iglesia, Taka Shamoto, Fumiyo Ikeda, Martin Kilvády, Alix Eynaudi (HS).
P.194 : Jakub Truszkowski, Fumiyo Ikeda, Anne Teresa De Keersmaeker, Anne Van Aerschot (HS).
Audrey Ribaucourt, Miquel Bernat, Roberto Oliván de la Iglesia, Gerrit Nulens, Marta Coronado, Peter Van Tichelen, Jessica Ryckewaert (HS).
Shinsuke Ishihara, Julia Sugranyes, Georges-Elie Octors, Jakub Truszkowski, Fumiyo Ikeda (HS).
Jessica Ryckewaert, Kuniko Kato, Shinsuke Ishihara, Julia Sugranyes, Georges-Elie Octors, Martin Kilvády (HS).
P.195 : Martin Kilvády, Rosalba Torres, Oliver Koch, Marta Coronado, Ursula Robb, Cynthia Loemij, Fumiyo Ikeda (HS).
P.196 : Cynthia Loemij, Frank Vercruyssen (HS).
P.197 : Cynthia Loemij, Frank Vercruyssen (HS).
P.198 : Cynthia Loemij, Frank Vercruyssen (HS).
P.201 : Cynthia Loemij, Frank Vercruyssen, Jolente De Keersmaeker, Anne Teresa De Keersmaeker (HS).
P.202 : Anne Teresa De Keersmaeker, Elisabeth Corbett (HS).
P.203 : Anne Teresa De Keersmaeker, Elisabeth Corbett (HS).
P.205 : Roberto Oliván de la Iglesia, Iris Bouche, Taka Shamoto, Oliver Koch (HS).
P.206 : Marta Coronado, Taka Shamoto (HS).
P.207 : Fabrizio Cassol, dj Grazzhoppa (HS).
P.208 : Rosalba Torres (HS).
Marta Coronado, Iris Bouche, Fumiyo Ikeda, Martin Kilvády, Alix Eynaudi, Roberto Oliván de la Iglesia, Taka Shamoto (HS).
P.209 : Taka Shamoto (HS).
P.211 : (SL).
P.212 : Marta Coronado, Iris Bouche (BD).
Gerardjan Rijnders, Rosalba Torres (BD).
Damiaan De Schrijver, Gerardjan Rijnders (BD).
Alix Eynaudi, Clinton Stringer (BD).
P.213 : Taka Shamoto, Jakub Truszkowski, Clinton Stringer, Ursula Robb, Jolente De Keersmaeker, Martin Kilvády, Roberto Oliván de la Iglesia (HS).
Fabian Fiorini, Alix Eynaudi (BD).
Taka Shamoto, Alix Eynaudi (BD).
Fumiyo Ikeda, Martin Kilvády (BD).
Frank Vercruyssen, Jolente De Keersmaeker (BD).
P.214 : Stéphane Galland, Frank Vercruyssen, Taka Shamoto (HS).
P.215 : Damiaan De Schrijver, Fumiyo Ikeda (HS).
Jolente De Keersmaeker, Jakub Truszkowski (HS).
P.216 : Fabian Fiorini, Fabrizio Cassol, Frank Vercruyssen, Alix Eynaudi, Stéphane Galland (HS).
P.217 : Sara De Roo, Gerardjan Rijnders, Alix Eynaudi, Ursula Robb, Roberto Oliván de la Iglesia, Marta Coronado, Taka Shamoto, Oliver Koch, Iris Bouche, Anne Van Aerschot, Fabrizio Cassol, Fumiyo Ikeda, Anne Teresa De Keersmaeker, Jolente De Keersmaeker, Cynthia Loemij, Rosalba Torres (BD).
Ursula Robb, Damiaan de Schrijver, Martin Kilvády (HS).
Iris Bouche (HS).
P.218 : Michel Hatzigeorgiou, Marta Coronado, Rosalba Torres, Fumiyo Ikeda, Alix Eynaudi (HS).
P.219 : Ursula Robb, Frank Vercruyssen, Cynthia Loemij (HS).
P.220 : Michel Hatzigeorgiou, Fabrizio Cassol (HS).
Mark Lorimer, Oliver Koch, Ursula Robb, Cynthia Loemij (BD).
Ursula Robb, Roberto Oliván de la Iglesia (BD).
Clinton Stringer, Sara De Roo, Damiaan De Schrijver, Martin Kilvády (HS).
Anne Van Aerschot, Fabrizio Cassol (BD).
P.221 : Sara De Roo (HS).
Anne Teresa De Keersmaeker, Sara De Roo, Thomas Walgrave (BD).
Stéphane Galland, Damiaan De Schrijver (BD).
P.223 : Rosalba Torres, Alix Eynaudi, Fumiyo Ikeda (HS).
P.224 : Rosalba Torres, Cynthia Loemij, Jakub Truszkowski, Taka Shamoto, Fumiyo Ikeda, Marta Coronado, Igor Shyshko, Clinton Stringer, Ursula Robb, Alix Eynaudi (HS).
Ursula Robb, Igor Shyshko, Cynthia Loemij (HS).
Clinton Stringer, Jakub Truszkowski, Igor Shyshko (HS).
P.225 : Jakub Truszkowski, Clinton Stringer (HS).
P.226 : Jakub Truszkowski, Taka Shamoto, Fumiyo Ikeda, Cynthia Loemij, Marta Coronado, Igor Shyshko, Ursula Robb, Clinton Stringer, Alix Eynaudi (HS).
Jakub Truszkowski, Alix Eynaudi (HS).
P. 227 : Rosalba Torres, Jakub Truszkowski, Igor Shyshko, Cynthia Loemij (HS).
Cynthia Loemij, Igor Shyshko (HS).
P.230 : Jakub Truszkowski, Ictus ensemble (HS).
Kuniko Kato, Miquel Bernat (HS).
Kuniko Kato (HS).
P.231 : Ursula Robb, Cynthia Loemij, Clinton Stringer, Fumiyo Ikeda, Jakub Truszkowski, Rosalba Torres, Alix Eynaudi, Taka Shamoto (HS).
P.229 : Rosalba Torres, Clinton Stringer, Marta Coronado, Igor Shyshko, Jakub Truszkowski, Taka Shamoto, Cynthia Loemij, Ursula Robb, Fumiyo Ikeda, Alix Eynaudi (SL).
P.232 : Anne Teresa De Keersmaeker, Cynthia Loemij (HS).
P.233 : Anne Teresa De Keersmaeker, Cynthia Loemij (HS).
P.234 : Cynthia Loemij, Anne Teresa De Keersmaeker (HS).
P.235 : Cynthia Loemij, Anne Teresa De Keersmaeker (HS).
Cynthia Loemij (HS).
P.237 : Cynthia Loemij, Anne Teresa De Keersmaeker (HS).
P.238 : Cynthia Loemij, Anne Teresa De Keersmaeker (HS).
Anne Teresa De Keersmaeker, Cynthia Loemij (HS).
Cynthia Loemij (HS).
P.239 : Cynthia Loemij, Anne Teresa De Keersmaeker (HS).
P.241 : (HS).
P.242 : Igor Shyshko (HS).
P.243 : Cynthia Loemij, Ursula Robb, Beniamin Boar, Igor Shyshko, Taka Shamoto (HS).
Ursula Robb (HS).
P.244 : Igor Shyshko, Taka Shamoto (HS).
Marta Coronado, Jakub Truszkowski, Alix Eynaudi, Julia Sugranyes (HS).
P.245 : Rosalba Torres (HS).
Ursula Robb, Beniamin Boar, Alix Eynaudi, Marta Coronado, Igor Shyshko, Clinton Stringer (HS).
P.246 : Cynthia Loemij (HS).
P.248 : Igor Shyshko, Fumiyo Ikeda, Julia Sugranyes, Marta Coronado, Taka Shamoto, Jessica Ryckewaert, Kuniko Kato, Ursula Robb, Alix Eynaudi, Rosalba Torres (HS).
P.249 : Marta Coronado (HS).
Gerrit Nulens, Jessica Ryckewaert, Marta Coronado, Alix Eynaudi, Jakub Truszkowski, Fumiyo Ikeda, Rosalba Torres, Ursula Robb, Georges-Elie Octors, Miquel Bernat, Taka Shamoto, Cynthia Loemij, Michael Weilacher (HS).
P.250 : (HS).
(HS).
P.251 : Georges-Elie Octors (HS).
Alix Eynaudi, Michael Weilacher (HS).
Igor Shyshko (HS).
(HS).
P.252 : Marion Levy, Vincent Dunoyer (HS).
Jakub Truszkowski, Thomas Hauert, Mark Lorimer, Jordi Galí, Beniamin Boar, Igor Shyshko, The Duke Quartet (HS).
Samantha Van Wissen, Sarah Ludi, Cynthia Loemij, Johanne Saunier, The Duke Quartet (HS).
Igor Shyshko, Thomas Hauert, Nordine Benchorf, Mark Lorimer, The Duke Quartet (HS).
P.253 : Anne Teresa De Keersmaeker (HS).
P.254 : Isabel Galriça (HS).
P.257 : Nordine Benchorf, Anne Mousselet (HS).
P.258 : Jordi Galí, Beniamin Boar, Thomas Hauert, Vincent Dunoyer, Igor Shyshko, Mark Lorimer, Jakub Truszkowski, Sarah Ludi, Rick Koster, Johanne Saunier, Xavier Carmo, Clinton Stringer, Marion Levy, Isabel Galriça, Anne Teresa De Keersmaeker, Fumiyo Ikeda, Cynthia Loemij, Filipe Portugal, Paulina Santos, Samantha Van Wissen, David Fielding, John Metcalfe, Louisa Fuller, Sophie Harris, Jos Van Immerseel (HS).
P.259 : Sophie Harris, Louisa Fuller, John Metcalfe, Johanne Suanier, Cynthia Loemij, Anne Teresa De Keersmaeker, Samantha Van Wissen, Sarah Ludi, Filipe Portugal, Isabel Galriça, Xavier Carmo, Paulina Santos, David Fielding, Fumiyo Ikeda, Vincent Dunoyer, Marion Levy (HS).
Clinton Stringer, Beniamin Boar, Thomas Hauert, Jakub Truszkowski, Jordi Galí, Igor Shyshko, Mark Lorimer, Rick Koster, Sophie Harris, Louisa Fuller, John Metcalfe, Johanne Saunier, Cynthia Loemij, Anne Teresa De Keersmaeker, Samantha Van Wissen, Sarah Ludi, Filipe Portugal, Isabel Galriça, Xavier Carmo, Paulina Santos (HS)
P.316 : Anne Teresa De K
P. 317 : Anne Teresa De ... lew York, 1986 (PK).

Photographers

CA : Christian Altorfer.
AdH : Alun de H.
BD : Bernaded Dexters.
PK : Peggy Jarell Kaplan.
SL : Serge Leblon.
MFP : Marie-Françoise Plissart.
HS : Herman Sorgeloos.
JLT : Jean-Luc Tanghe.
AvA : Anne Van Aerschot.

Video stills

WK : Wolfgang Kolb.
WV : Walter Verdin.

Jean-Marc Adolphe (F)
Until 2002, Jean-Marc Adolphe was artistic consultant to the Paris Théâtre de la Bastille. He is the founder and editor of the art magazine *Mouvement*.

Georges Aperghis (G)
Georges Aperghis is a composer. He lives and works in Paris. In addition to chamber and orchestra music, his focus is mainly on opera. In 1976 he founded the Atelier Théâtre et Musique (ATEM).

Benjamin Barber (USA)
Benjamin Barber is professor at the University of Maryland and director of The Democracy Collaborative. He has written 14 books (including the bestseller *Jihad vs McWorld*, translated into fourteen languages), plays, musicals, poetry and a libretto.

Jérôme Bel (F)
Jérôme Bel is a dancer and choreographer. He danced with several companies until he began in 1994 as choreographer with *nom donné par l'auteur*. His work explores themes such as the body, language, identity and theatricality.

Paul Boudens (B)
Paul Boudens is a graphic designer. His clients include Dries Van Noten and Walter Van Beirendonck. He designed the graphics for MODE2001 LANDED-GELAND in Antwerp and subsequently became the graphic designer of the associated fashion magazine.

Laurent Busine
Laurent Busine is an art historian and archeologist. He was director of exhibitions at the Palais des beaux Arts in Charleroi (B). He is currently the curator of the new Musée des Arts Contemporains in Grand-Hornu near Mons (B).

Eric De Kuyper (B)
Eric De Kuyper worked for television and radio, wrote reviews of films, theatre, opera and ballet, and has directed five films. He founded *Versus*, a journal for film and the performing arts. In 1988, with *Aan zee*, he introduced a series of autobiographical novels for which he won several important literary awards

Josse De [illegible]
Josse De P[illegible] . theatre and film actor and theatre d[illegible] co-founder of the theatre compan[illegible] and of the artist collective Schaam[illegible]ntly he is artistic director of Bruge based t[illegible]npany Het Net.

Mark [illegible] (B)
Befo[illegible]ved to Portugal, Mark Deputter was artis[illegible]ctor of Kunstencentrum Stuc in Leuve[illegible]. Lisbon he programmed dance at the Centr[illegible]ultural de Belem. He is currently director of Danças na Cidade.

Tim Etchells (GB)
Tim Etchells is a writer and theatre director. He is director of the English theatre group Forced Entertainment. His written works include *The Dream Dictionary (for the Modern Dreamer)* and the collection of essays *Certain Fragments*.

Bernard Foccroulle (B)
Bernard Foccroulle is organist and director of La Monnaie/De Munt, the Belgian National Opera. When he became director of La Monnaie in 1990, he assembled a young artistic team that included conductor Antonio Pappano and choreographer Anne Teresa De Keersmaeker with Rosas as resident dance company.

Jonathan Harvey (GB)
Jonathan Harvey is a composer. He has been working closely with IRCAM in Paris since 1980. His compositions are performed throughout the world by the most important contemporary music ensembles. His opera *Inquest of Love* premiered in 1993 in London and one year later was performed at the Brussels Théâtre Royal de la Monnaie.

Sara Jansen (B)
Sara Jansen studied Japanese Studies and dance and theatre theory. She currently lives in New York where she teaches at New York University and is working on a doctorate on post-war Japanese dance. She did the research and archive work for Rosas XX and was assistant curator for the exhibition.

Helena Katz (BR)
Helena Katz studied philosophy, communication studies and semiotics. She lectures at the PUC in São Paulo where she also directs the Centre for Dance Studies. She writes on dance for all important newspapers and magazines in Brazil. Since 1986 she has been the regular dance critic for the newspaper O Estado de S. Paulo.

Christian Lacroix (F)
Christian Lacroix is a fashion designer. His baroque and exuberant designs created a furore in the 1980s. He designs haute couture, ready-to-wear, and has his own line of accessories and perfumes.

Rudi Laermans (B)
Rudi Laermans is professor at the Faculty of Social Sciences of the KU Leuven. In addition, he lectures at P.A.R.T.S., is an essayist and critic, and regularly writes on contemporary dance and the visual arts.

Gorik Lindemans (B)
Until 1998 Gorik Lindemans was active as visual artist. He designed several posters and programmes for Rosas. He lives and works in Brussels.

Laurence Louppe (F)
Laurence Louppe is a writer, critic and lecturer in aesthetics and history of dance. She studied dance and movement techniques, and works for theatre and dance companies. In addition to her articles on dance and the visual arts in various journals, she also has written three books on dance *(Danses Tracées, Galotta, H.Robbe/R.Deacon)*.

Anna Luyten (B)
Anna Luyten studied philosophy, applied literary theory and dramaturgy at the University of Ghent. She is journalist for the newspaper *De Standaard* and lectures in philosophy at the Dora Van der Groen theater institute.

Steve Paxton (USA)
Steve Paxton is a dancer and choreographer. He is chiefly known for his improvisational projects and is considered one of the most important innovators in dance in the second half of the twentieth century. He lives and works in Vermont, USA.

Alain Platel (B)
Alain Platel is a theatre director and choreographer. He is co-founder of the choreographer collective Les Ballets C de la B and in recent years he has also worked regularly with Victoria in Ghent.

Jean-Luc Plouvier (B)
Jean-Luc Plouvier is a musician and composer. After his studies in piano and chamber music in Mons, his focus has almost entirely been on contemporary music. He is co-founder and artistic coordinator of the Ictus Ensemble.

Steve Reich (USA)
The *Village Voice* in New York recently called Steve Reich "...the most important living American composer". His oeuvre extends from minimal and repetitive compositions from the 1960s and 1970s to the digital video operas *(The Cave, Three Tales)* he made in recent years with video artist Beryl Korot.

Arco Renz (D)
Arco Renz is a dancer, actor and choreographer. With the choreography *Elea: Sphingein* he completed his studies at P.A.R.T.S. in 1998. Since then, his choreographic work has been created within his company Kobalt Works. As actor and dancer he works regularly with Bob Wilson.

Jan Ritsema (NL)
Jan Ritsema is director of theatre and opera. He has worked for the largest Dutch theatre companies and he works frequenly with Kaaitheater in Brussels. In 1996 he surprised the dance and theatre world alike by creating a dance solo for himself. He then went on to make a dance duet with Jonathan Burrows. He teaches at P.A.R.T.S. and the Rijksacademie Amsterdam.

Paul Robbrecht (B)
Paul Robbrecht is an architect. The office of Robbrecht & Daem has been responsible for several much talked-about projects within and outside Belgium including the new Concert hall in Bruges.

Tiago Rodrigues (P)
Tiago Rodrigues is an actor, journalist and scenarist. He lives and works in Lisbon. In 1999 he acted in Platonov, a Tg Stan production.

Herman Sorgeloos (B)
Herman Sorgeloos is a photographer, set and light designer, graphic artist and theatre engineer. He has been engaged in all of these capacities for Rosas. Since 1984 he has been the house photographer for Rosas. Currently he is working freelance for several theatre companies and festivals.

Pieter T'Jonck (B)
Pieter T'Jonck is architect and research assistant at the University of Ghent. He regularly publishes works on dance, theatre, architecture and urban development in newspapers, magazines and books *(De Standaard, Financieel Ekonomische Tijd, Etcetera)*

Michel Uytterhoeven (B)
Michel Uytterhoeven studied pedagogy, dramaturgy and architecture. He was the first artistic director of Klapstuk, the Leuven dance festival, and later worked for the Flemish Opera and Antwerp 93. He is currently director of the Flemish Theatre Institute and was curator of the exhibition Rosas XX at the Palais des Beaux Arts.

Elke Van Campenhout (B)
Elke Van Campenhout studied philosophy and dramaturgy, and reviews dance and theatre for *De Standaard* and *Radio 3*. As freelance writer she contributed to several literary journals in Flanders.

Ivo van Hove (B)
Ivo van Hove is a director of theatre and opera. He was co founder of the theatre company De Tijd and was director of Zuidelijk Toneel for ten years. His productions are performed across Europe and he is regularly guest director for the New York Theater Workshop. Since 1998 he has been artistic director of the Holland Festival and since 2001 also of Toneelgroep Amsterdam.

Marianne Van Kerkhoven (B)
Marianne Van Kerkhoven is dramaturg for the Brussels Kaaitheater and in this capacity was involved with several Anne Teresa De Keersmaeker productions. Since 2001 she has also been affiliated with the Bruges theatre company Het Net. She regularly publishes articles on theatre and dance in, among others, *Etcetera*.

Peter Verhelst (B)
Peter Verhelst is a writer of short stories, poetry, novels and plays. In 2000 he won the Gouden Uil, one of the most important Dutch-language literature awards, for *Tongkat*.

Sigrid Vinks (B)
Sigrid Vinks is actress and dramatist. As dramatist she worked for professor Carlos Tindemans. Since 1984 she has been the travelling companion of Jan Decorte. She has acted in all of his theatre productions and translated several pieces for him.

Rosas/Anne Teresa De Keersmaeker

If and only if wonder

Authors
Jean-Marc Adolphe
Sara Jansen
Anna Luyten
Jean-Luc Plouvier
Pieter T'Jonck
Michel Uytterhoeven
Elke Van Campenhout
Marianne Van Kerkhoven

Testimonials
Georges Aperghis
Benjamin Barber
Jérôme Bel
Laurent Busine
Eric De Kuyper
Josse De Pauw
Mark De Putter
Tim Etchells
Bernard Foccroulle
Jonathan Harvey
Helena Katz
Christian Lacroix
Rudy Laermans
Gorik Lindemans
Laurence Louppe
Steve Paxton
Alain Platel
Steve Reich
Arco Renz
Jan Ritsema
Paul Robbrecht
Tiago Rodrigues
Ivo van Hove
Peter Verhelst
Sigrid Vinks

Photographers
Christian Altorfer
Frédérique Debras
Alun de H.
Bernaded Dexters
Yves Gervais
Michiel Hendryckx
Peggy Jarrell Kaplan
Serge Leblon
Elena Olivo
Marie-Françoise Plissart
Hans Roels
Herman Sorgeloos
Jean Luc Tanghe
Nathalie Willems
and video stills by Wolfgang Kolb
and Walter Verdin.

Editors
Guy Gypens
Sara Jansen
Theo Van Rompay

Translators
Oonagh Duckworth
Sara Jansen
Jan Sterckx

Editorial assistant
Chris Maes

Graphic Design
Paul Boudens

With thanks to
Anne Teresa De Keersmaeker Alain
Franco
Herman Sorgeloos
Koen Van Muylem

Published by La Renaissance du
Livre, Tournai, and Rosas, Brussels.

ISBN : 2-8046-0697-X
Registration of copyright: D/2002/8176/446

Printed in September 2002 by Lesaffre (CE).